15-3

THE PARLEMENT OF FOULYS

OLD & MIDDLE ENGLISH TEXTS
General Editor G. L. Brook

GEOFFREY CHAUCER

The Parlement of Foulys

Edited by
D. S. BREWER

MANCHESTER UNIVERSITY PRESS
*
BARNES & NOBLE, NEW YORK

First issued 1960
by Thomas Nelson & Sons Ltd

This edition 1972
© D. S. Brewer
issued by
MANCHESTER UNIVERSITY PRESS
316–324 Oxford Road
Manchester M13 9NR

ISBN 0 7190 0514 0

Published in the U.S.A. 1972 by
Harper & Row Publishers, Inc.
Barnes & Noble Import Division

Printed in Great Britain by Butler & Tanner Ltd
Frome and London

CONTENTS

ACKNOWLEDGMENT

Grateful acknowledgment is made to the Delegates to the Clarendon Press for permission to make the quotation from *The Allegory of Love* in Appendix V.

ABBREVIATIONS

(*a*) *The works of Chaucer*

Works—The Works of Geoffrey Chaucer, ed. F. N. Robinson, 2nd ed. (Cambridge, Mass., and London, 1957)

Anelida—Anelida and Arcite

BD—The Book of the Duchess

Boece—The Consolation of Philosophy by Boethius, translated by Chaucer

CT—The Canterbury Tales

HF—The House of Fame

Parlement—The Parlement of Foulys

Pity—The Complaint unto Pity

ProLGW—The Prologue to the Legend of Good Women

Romaunt—The Romaunt of the Rose

Troilus—Troilus and Criseyde

(*b*) *Other abbreviations*

EC—Essays in Criticism

EETS—Early English Text Society

EETS (E.S.)—Early English Text Society, Extra Series

MED—Middle English Dictionary, ed. H. Kurath and S. Kuhn (Ann Arbor, 1952–). Letters A, B, E, F so far published

Migne PL—Patrologia Latina, ed. J. P. Migne

MLR—Modern Language Review

MP—Modern Philology

OED—Oxford English Dictionary

PMLA—Publications of the Modern Language Association of America

Rot. Parl.—Rotuli Parliamentorum; ut et petitiones et placita in parliamento (1783)

SATF—*Société des Anciens Textes Français*

SP—Studies in Philology

INTRODUCTION

IN *The Parlement of Foulys* the variety of tone, the brightness of description, the vivid realism of the birds' debate, which are instantly attractive, are matched by the rich significances and subtle complexities of mood which lie beneath the surface of the poem. It appeals on several levels, and is the best of Chaucer's shorter pieces. Yet appreciation of it has varied. It was popular in the fifteenth and sixteenth centuries; among poets Shakespeare echoes it several times, and Spenser partly owes to it the greatness of the Mutabilitie Cantos. In the eighteenth century it was less regarded, and in the nineteenth and early twentieth centuries it has come to be treated more and more as a historical document, weighed down under a mass of speculation about the identity of the suitors. Only recently has interest in the whole poem, as poetry, revived. A new flexibility in our expectation of what poetry may be, a new assertion of the relevance of medieval poetry, have made it easier for the ' common reader ' to submit himself to the controlling power of Chaucer's imagination in a poem that is more unusual than it looks. More information about medieval life and literature has buttressed our new willingness to treat Chaucer as a great poet rather than a great joker. Readers are now in a better position to understand and appreciate Chaucer's artistic purposes than they have been for a couple of centuries.

Notwithstanding the now considerable amount of information available about the *Parlement*, and our freshened sense of its value, it has never been properly edited in its own right.[1] The aim of the present edition is to give a new text of the poem, together with such information about its circumstances, ideas, language, and modes of operation, as will make it easily accessible to the modern reader of poetry.

---

[1] It has only once even been edited on its own—a slight and derivative school edition of 1911.

ATTRIBUTION, AUTHOR, AND DATE

The *Parlement* is certainly by Chaucer, for he tells us so several times, of which the first is in *Prologue* F of *The Legend of Good Women*, which is reasonably to be dated about 1384–6.[1]

Of Chaucer himself little need be said here.[2] He was the son of a well-to-do wine-merchant; member of the King's personal household; courtier; diplomatic envoy to France and Italy; high customs official; later a member of Parliament. He lived much of his time in the City of London, and knew many of its most important men. He was a great reader of Latin, French, and Italian literature, and of science, philosophy, and religious works too. He touched contemporary life, and the international European culture of the fourteenth century, at many points. The richness of his knowledge of life and books, his power to illuminate the one with the other, and the sensibility, firmness, and charitable sympathy of his spirit, shine through the *Parlement*.

The *Parlement* is easy to date within a dozen or so years. It must have been written before it is mentioned in the *Prologue to the Legend*. It contains important Italian material, which Chaucer can hardly have acquired before what was probably his first visit to Italy, from which he returned in 1373. The poem is likely therefore to have been written between 1373 and 1385. According to the usual interpretation of the astronomical reference at ll. 117–18 (see note), the poem was probably begun in May in either 1374 or 1382. The later date is more likely. During the same period, 1373–85, Chaucer wrote many other works, including *The House of Fame*. Everything, metre, style, material, and a mistake in *The House of Fame* about ' King Cipioun ', who was not a king, points to the *House of Fame* being earlier than the *Parlement*, where ' Cipion ' is properly understood. Chaucer could hardly have written both poems, each of

---

[1] *The Complete Works of Geoffrey Chaucer*, ed. F. N. Robinson, 2nd ed. (1957), p. 839. All quotations except of the *Parlement* are taken from this edition, to be cited as *Works*.

[2] See Brewer, *Chaucer* (2nd ed., 1960), for a survey of his life and works.

which reveals extensive reading in Italian literature and in much else, in the year between his return from Italy and May 1374. He would have needed time to digest his Italian reading; and he was also at this time busy all day at the Customs House.[1] A very reasonable, if not certain, date for the *Parlement* is that it was begun in May 1382, and was ready for St Valentine's Day, 14 February 1383.

POETRY AND SOCIETY

To understand the nature of the *Parlement* as a St Valentine's Day poem, and to understand something of the reasons for its form and content, it is necessary to consider the social circumstances in which it was written.

The culture of the English court was part of an international court culture, common to the numerous royal and baronial courts of England, France, Italy, and other European countries. When the members of these courtly societies were at leisure their entertainments were largely conversation, stories, poems, and music, varied of course with dancing and other sports. The esquires of the English court, of whom Chaucer was one, were expected to help to ' occupy the court ' in talking of ' chronicles of kings and of others' policies, or in piping or harping, singing, or else martial acts '.[2] Froissart says that the chief subjects of conversation were those two ' eternal ' themes, Arms and Love.[3]

The theme of Arms merged into chronicles and king's policies, the serious matters of national politics. But when it was a question of sheer entertainment the chief subject matter was love, for even a story of chivalric adventure usually had love as its motive force. Conversation about love merged naturally into discussions, stories, poems, and songs about love. The relation between conversation, discussion, story, and song is very well illustrated in the works of Chaucer's older contemporary, Boccaccio. In *Il Filocolo*

[1] As he tells, *HF* 641–64. Cf. Brewer, *op. cit.*, pp. 48ff.
[2] Quoted by Brewer, *op. cit.*, p. 40.
[3] Cf. F. S. Shears, *Froissart* (1930), p. 16.

(which Chaucer drew on for the *Troilus*) Boccaccio describes how a group of courtly young people, both men and women, assemble in a beautiful garden to amuse themselves with discussing ' questions of love ', and with story, song, and music. There was a strong, though easy, formal element in such gatherings, and they were accustomed to elect one of their number as ' king ' or ' queen ' to rule the proceedings. Again, in the introduction to Boccaccio's poem *Il Filostrato* (which is the basis of Chaucer's *Troilus*) Boccaccio says that he has often been in the company of noble men and beautiful women, who have discussed the emotions of a young man in love. Boccaccio's poem is as it were a contribution to such discussion.

Poems and songs were a natural part of such entertainments. Poets were courtiers, and courtiers were poets. Poetry, whatever else it might be, was also social entertainment, and was highly valued as such. A whole elaborate institution, the *Cour Amoureuse*, was founded in the French court in honour of women; its chief aim was the presentation of love-poems to ladies in a kind of competition, with a prize for the best poem. The *Cour Amoureuse* first met in Paris on St Valentine's Day 1400. In theory there were over six hundred members, a membership extending to the minor clergy and the *petite bourgeoisie*, but the chief members were twenty-four Ministers, who were mostly great lords of the realm. The *Cour Amoureuse* had an elaborate charter (from which an extract is given in Appendix II) and was under the king's patronage. It was ruled by a ' Prince of Love ', who was a professional poet, and who kept with him ' musicians and gallants who could compose and sing all kinds of songs, *balades*, roundels, virelays, and other love-poems, and could play sweetly on instruments '. On St Valentine's Day 1400, after mass, the chief Ministers and others (probably not the whole six hundred) met in ' joyous recreation and conversation about love '. Love-poems were presented before ladies, who judged them, and awarded a golden crown and chaplet for the best poem.[1]

[1] For details of the *Cour Amoureuse* see A. Piaget, *Romania* 20 (1891), 417ff, and 31 (1902), 597ff.

Similar institutions, perhaps not quite so highly organised and well documented, certainly existed in the English court. For example, most of the court was divided into one of two amorous orders, the Flower or the Leaf, represented as in conflict with each other. Chaucer refers to the Flower and the Leaf in the *Prologue to the Legend of Good Women* (F, 71-2, G, 70-3), and shows that some debate existed between the two, about which love-poems were written. The same *Prologue* is also one of the many poems written, particularly by French poets, in honour of the cult of the *marguerite* or daisy. Yet again, the *Prologue to the Legend of Good Women* (F, 130ff) has an interesting reference to the birds singing about St Valentine's day.

It is clear enough, therefore, that in medieval courtly society, both in England and France, there were courtly institutions which as it were formalised the abounding and abiding interest in the discussion and description of love, and which gave rise to a number of love-poems by both French and English poets. There are a number of poems which seem to have been written especially for St Valentine's Day. The *Parlement* is the chief of these. Chaucer's *Complaint of Mars* is another important one, and there is also a shorter poem, *The Complaynt `d'Amours,* which is probably not by Chaucer. In French, Oton de Grandson wrote a number of Valentine poems, which do not seem to have influenced Chaucer, but of which *Le Songe Saint Valentin* portrays a somewhat similar general situation. (For a description of this poem see Appendix I.) There are also many references to St Valentine's Day in English literature up to the nineteenth century.

It seems also clear that in the late fourteenth-century English court there was some sort of festival on St Valentine's Day, for which Chaucer and other poets wrote poems. The festival may have been observed in France as well, for, apart from Grandson's poems, the *Cour Amoureuse* first met on St Valentine's Day, though after the first meeting it continued to meet regularly once a month for some years.

The nature and origin of the festival is obscure. There are no earlier references to it than those in the poems of

Chaucer and Grandson. Grandson is usually described as being the earlier, but there is no evidence for this, and he and Chaucer were exact contemporaries. Grandson spent many years in the English court, whose culture was largely dominated by France, and where French was as familiar a tongue as English. But the festival of St Valentine's Day may have been primarily English. Essentially, it consisted of some game, which persisted for centuries later in England, though not in France, in which men and women chose, or pretended to choose, their partners in love for the following year.[1] The ' lovers ' seem to have been often ' allegorised ', or represented, in poetry, according to a common medieval device, as birds.[2]

To celebrate and adorn this festival, poems were written that were usually the traditional ' complaints ', expressive of eternal and unrequited love. Thus in the introductory passage of Chaucer's *Complaint of Mars*, a bird calls to human lovers to choose their partners ' in humble wise ', and promises to sing of the ' complaint ' of Mars in honour of this high festival, ' for the worship of this highe feste ' (l. 22).

Again, the *Complaynt d'Amours* is an address by a lover to his lady, that contains in its last stanza all the typical elements of such poetry:

> This compleynte on seint Valentynes day,
> Whan every foughel chesen shal his make,
> To hir, whos I am hool, and shal alway,
> This woful song and this compleynte I make,
> That never yit wolde me to mercy take;
> And yit wol I evermore her serve
> And love hir best, although she do me sterve.
>
> (85–91)

---

[1] The old theory of its derivation from the pagan Roman festival of the Lupercalia is now held to be very unlikely ; see *Alban Butler's Lives of the Saints*, revised edition by H. Thurston and D. Attwater (1956), vol. i, p. 332. There are references to St Valentine by Gower, Charles d'Orléans, the Pastons, Chapman, Donne, Shakespeare, Pepys, etc. These references are all from courtly or at least upper-class writers. It seems not to have become a lower-class or ' folk ' festival until the eighteenth and nineteenth centuries.

[2] See below, p. 33, for details.

This stanza is closely similar to the beginning of the first
eagle's speech in the *Parlement* (416–20).

Whether poems such as this were ever in competition for
a prize, as in the *Cour Amoureuse*, is unknown. But at least
they must be imagined as poems for public occasions,
probably presented before, when not actually addressed to,
great ladies of the Court. Festivals such as these were the
occasion, as a reading of Froissart shows, of gorgeous and
stately pageantry. The chief persons present were the
highest in the land, and in the case of the *Parlement* they may
have included the young king Richard and his new bride
and queen, surrounded by their courtiers.[1] Since it was the
custom to choose partners, the choosing may have been
presided over by some great lady, corresponding to Nature
in the *Parlement*, or to the female eagle in Grandson's
Le Songe Saint Valentin.

THE LITERARY TRADITION

When poetry takes such a public, festival form, heard rather
than read, it must inevitably build on expected elements.
The bright ladies before whom poems were presented, the
bold knights and learned prelates who themselves ' writ with
ease ', required first that a poem be presented as entertain-
ment, immediately comprehensible in a familiar form; though
superficial novelties, fresh variations on customary con-
ventions, naturally sharpened the interest. The conventions
they knew were those of a particular kind of feeling, the
so-called ' courtly love'; and of particular forms in which
that feeling was described, the poetic ' love-vision ' and the
' *demande d'amour* '.

Much that is misleading has been written about ' courtly
love '. The term itself was invented in the late nineteenth
century and is less descriptive than the common medieval
term *fine amour*, ' refined love '. Chaucer translates the

[1] The famous frontispiece of the Corpus Christi College, Cambridge,
manuscript of the *Troilus* shows Chaucer reading to the king and queen
and an assembled company. The picture was, however, painted in the
early fifteenth century. It has been frequently reproduced.

term into English as ' fyn lovynge ',[1] which is unfortunately clumsy in modern English. It is important to note that Chaucer associates ' fyn lovyng ' in this passage in the *Prologue to the Legend* particularly with the nature of ' wife-hood ', and this association should dispose of the common error of supposing that *fine amour*, at any rate in England, was always adulterous. The concept of *fine amour* varies with poet, time, and country, and in Chaucer's poetry it is never adulterous.[2] The chief characteristics of *fine amour* may be perceived in the speech of the first eagle in the *Parlement* (416ff), and paralleled in a dozen places in Chaucer's other poetry. It is an exquisitely refined emotion, leading to the extremes of joy and sorrow. All the emphasis is upon the man's feelings. He feels that the lady is all perfection. To love her is to serve her. She is so superior that the least recognition of his ' service ' is more than he deserves, and all he can hope for is condescension, ' mercy ', ' pity ', ' grace '. He abases himself before her, though before no-one else, least of all before any possible rival. He is tormented by his love, but regards it as the most ennobling quality in him, and on it he bases his claim to the lady's ' pity '. His love is honourable in that it claims to be eternal, even if unrewarded; and in that (with the exception of the *Troilus*, which is arguably a special case) it leads to marriage.[3]

Apart from the implications of marriage, which are commoner in Chaucer's poetry than in French literature, where adultery is frequent, this set of feelings, these *grandeurs et misères* of love, are those of earlier French poetry. They are particularly the subject of the French love-visions which give the elements that Chaucer took over and adapted for the *Parlement*.[4]

---

[1] *ProLGW* F 544.

[2] On this point see further my articles, *MLR* **49** (1954), 461ff, and *EC* **5** (1955), 407ff.

[3] Father Gervase Matthew in a valuable essay has shown that in practically all English fourteenth-century poetry *fine amour* leads to marriage : *Essays Presented to Charles Williams* (1947), pp. 128ff.

[4] Summaries of some of the more significant poems in this tradition, with bibliographical details, will be found in Appendix I.

The form of these love-visions is simple. The love-sick poet describes how at first he could not sleep, but eventually fell asleep and dreamed. He usually dreams that it is May, and that he is in, or enters, a beautiful garden or park. He hears the birds singing, and then hears the birds debate about love. The hawk is always the first to speak, since, because he is used for falconry, ' the sport of kings ', he is regarded as the noblest bird. Then usually a guide conducts the poet to the god of love, or to Venus.

There is also a number of poems concerned with the question of who makes the best lover, a knight or a ' clerk ' (i.e. a learned man, who might also be in holy orders, and thus vowed to celibacy). These poems usually have a visit to the god of love, where there is a debate, and sometimes armed combat, between members of the god's council of birds.

Chaucer takes his central situation, a debate among birds, from these poems, or poems like them. He also adopts the convention of the sleepless poet, the dream, the garden or park, the guide, the summery description (somewhat oddly for a Valentine poem in wintry February), and the mythological figures. Each of these elements he changes, but they were all perfectly familiar.

In common with fourteenth-century French poets he also develops a stronger personal note in his poem. Machaut, in *Le Jugement dou Roy de Navarre*,[1] begins his poem with a long account, with some lively realism, of how he passed an uncomfortable, plague-stricken winter at Rheims. This makes a curious introduction to a conventional love problem, but is not altogether dissimilar in effect from Chaucer's account, early in the *Parlement*, of the Dream of Scipio. But unlike Machaut, and others, Chaucer penetrates the whole of his poem with this sense of personal concern. And whereas in developing the love-vision they abandoned the mythology and expanded the poem to inordinate length, Chaucer retained the old-fashioned machinery and the brevity.

---

[1] G. de Machaut, *Oeuvres*, ed. E. Hoepffner, SATF, t. i (1908).

Yet he made important changes. Instead of the poet who is in love, he presents the poet who is anxious *about* love. The dream follows the reading of the Dream of Scipio, which is part of Cicero's treatise *De re publica*, and which says nothing about love. Instead of the usual vague guide (often a lady) he presents the guide whom Cicero described in the Dream of Scipio. For the faded Ovidian mythology he substitutes the figures of Nature and Venus, rich in philosophical symbolism and poetic association.[1] (The substitution of Nature for the old god or goddess of love is indeed the key to the immensely wider implications of the *Parlement* as compared with the earlier love-visions.) The description of the garden takes on new force and significance. For the conventional bird-spokesmen of earlier poems he gives us vividly realised bird-characters such as are found nowhere else in literature save in the earlier English *Owl and Nightingale*. And in the debate of the birds, Chaucer used as apparent subject matter for the debate another medieval *genre*, the literary *demande d'amour*, ' question of love '.

The *demande d'amour* was one of the literary forms which arose naturally out of the courtly delight in discussing love. Indeed, it often did not clearly disentangle itself from the social forms which gave it birth. Some of the texts that survive almost suggest that they were notes for the playing of this courtly predecessor of the parlour game.

' Questions of love ' took many forms. Who is the best lover, a knight or a ' clerk '? Who suffers most, one whose lover is dead, or one whose lover is unfaithful? Would a lady prefer a loyal but indiscreet lover, or a lover who was certainly discreet but uncertainly faithful? Is a maid, a wife, or a widow best for a mistress? Deschamps has a whole poem consisting entirely of such questions, some of them rather indecent. The poem represents ladies as asking and answering the questions, and is perhaps close to such games of question and answer in real life at court. A typical question asks a lady which of two suitors she would accept, one handsome and richly dressed, the other ugly and badly

---

[1] See below, pp. 26ff.

dressed, but strong and bold? She answers, the second.[1]
There is a large collection of such questions, mostly in prose,
dating from the fourteenth and fifteenth centuries.[2] They
are in French, but no doubt correspond to similar discussions
in Richard's court.

The essence of a *demande d'amour* is a dilemma, in which
choice must be made between different but apparently equal
values. It is rarely serious. It is an amusing, flippant,
literary, and social game, where feelings are lightly engaged
and ingenious reasonings are valued; a sport of the mind,
very typical of the leisured, talkative, ratiocinative, youthful
courts of the period. The settings of Boccaccio's *Il Filocolo*
and *Il Decamerone*, with their young people in the beautiful
garden, and the plague a black shadow in the distance,
exactly reflect these courtly pastimes as practised in all the
courts of Europe.

Il Filocolo has in Book IV thirteen of these ' questions of
love '. The third is nearest the situation in the *Parlement*,
showing both the *Parlement*'s relation to, and difference from,
the usual tradition. A lady is to choose between three
suitors, one brave, one courteous and generous, one wise.
It is understood that no suitor has the virtues of the others.
Now this is very similar to the situation in the *Parlement*,
where the formel, the female hawk, also must choose between
three suitors. Here, however, the similarity ends, for
whereas in the typical form of the question the suitors are
equal but different, in the *Parlement* they are neither. Apart
from a little dramatic variety in manner of speech and
presentation of their claims, all three suitors make essentially
the *same kind* of appeal. Passion, loyalty, truth, humility,
these are the characteristics of all. But the first suitor is
obviously preferable. He is the most noble, eloquent,
dignified. Granted the premises of the whole concept of
love in the *demandes d'amour*, he is obviously and eminently

---

[1] E. Deschamps, *Oeuvres*, ed. G. Raynaud, SATF, t. viii (1893),
pp. 112ff.

[2] A. Klein, ' Die Altfranzösichen Minnefragen ', *Marburger Beiträge
zur Romanischen Philologie*, Heft i (Marburg, 1911).

preferable. In contrast with the usual *demande d'amour* (e.g. that in *Il Filocolo* just mentioned) no-one could be puzzled whom to choose. The terslet of the falcon states the obvious solution: no other bird so much as discusses it; and Nature, the deputy of God, agrees with it. The discussion among the lower birds is irrelevant to the ostensible problem.

There is a further difference from the usual type of the *demande d'amour*. The problem of the formel's choice is presented without the flippancy which was usually inherent in the question. Within the *question*, so to speak, love is taken quite seriously; it is *fine amour* at its best. Flippancy is however dramatically expressed by the cynical impatience of some of the lower birds with the whole concept of solemn devoted *fine amour*. By making such a division between the noble suitors and most of the lower birds Chaucer retains the generalised interest in the nature of love found in some of the thirteenth-century love-visions, and in *Le Roman de la Rose*.[1] The true, or rather, the more fundamental, question in the birds' debate is not who the formel should choose, but, what is the sense in *fine amour*? The lower birds discuss what shall happen to, or what ought to be the attitude of, *any* of the suitors who are rejected, whether all are rejected, or only two. The essence of *fine amour* was its disinterested loyalty; all the suitors have vowed eternal faithfulness as part of their claim of love. What is to happen to those who are unsuccessful? Are they to remain faithful, with the absolute certainty of no reward? Here is the question at the heart of the debate, developed with a rich sense of comedy and a subtle dramatic complexity by Chaucer.

What Chaucer has done is to graft a *demande d'amour* upon the form of the thirteenth-century love-vision. But he uses the ' question of love ' as a device to introduce a deeper, more general questioning of the whole nature of *fine amour*. Such questioning, and indeed, downright criticism, of *fine*

---

[1] For the influence of the *Roman*, which some have denied, but which is in fact considerable, see below, pp. 38ff.

amour existed in plenty in the Middle Ages, in sermons, satires, and, especially, in the second part of *Le Roman de la Rose*. The immediate criticism in the *Parlement* is nevertheless different from other medieval criticism, and very typical of Chaucer. Medieval criticism is so often based on rather remote theory; but the criticism spoken by most of the lower birds arises out of the familiar desires and necessities of ordinary life—one may say, out of the ordinary desire for marriage. For, noble as the suitors may be, it is clear that they are not going about their desire for a mate in a very practical way, since though they all promise everlasting devotion to the formel, two of them cannot possibly win her.

Of course the noble suitors would say, *do* say, that they are not seeking merely a mate; they seek their ' sovereign lady '. The issues are complex, and are not to be understood without reference to the whole poem. It is moreover a dramatic poem, and specific answers are not to be expected. And the premises, the ' natural ' thoughts and feelings which Chaucer and his audience took for granted, are not those of the modern world, any more than his language is. Some historical knowledge about the forms, ideas, images, and modes of operation of the poem needs to be acquired, just as the unfamiliar words need to be learnt. The use of Introduction, Notes, and Glossary is necessary for the modern reader. But these are necessary evils. Johnson's advice to the reader of Shakespeare holds good for the reader of Chaucer. ' When his fancy is on the wing, let it not stop at correction or explanation. . . . Let him read on through brightness and obscurity, through integrity and corruption; let him preserve his comprehension of the dialogue and his interest in the fable. . . . Parts are not to be examined until the whole is surveyed.'

THE POEM—AN APPROACH TO THE MEANING

The variety in the *Parlement* is characteristic of Chaucer and indeed of very much medieval poetry. But in this poem the variety is crucial. There is a brief account of The Dream of Scipio, which touches on heaven, earth, and hell; then the poet wanders in a timeless fertile park, sees gay Cupid, and lustful Venus in her beautiful temple where there is so much suffering; then he sees the surpassing beauty of benevolent, creative Nature, and hears the debate of diverse opinionated birds. All this is in some way concerned with the question of love, but from the conjunction of such various elements spring contradictions. This is the essence of the poem—the existence of a variety of apparently contradictory thoughts and attitudes about love (concretely or dramatically described for the most part), which puzzles the poet and yet brings him delight. At least a partial reconciliation is implicit in the figure of Nature, and the poem ends, if still questioningly, on a note of optimism.

The manner is as important as the matter, and varies accordingly. The style suits the immediate subject equally in the rather plain summary of The Dream of Scipio with its steady onward movement; in the fertile proliferation of names and the livelier metre of the description of the park; in the statelier movement and richer decoration of the descriptions of Cupid and Venus; in the courtly (though not stiff or stilted) diction of the noble birds; and in the livelier cackle of the vulgar birds. The contrasts in style are part of the piquancy of the poem.

For all the variety and the dramatic colouring of some of the speeches the manner is very personal to Chaucer. In this poem he finds for perhaps the first time his characteristic tone, his full range of meaning and richness of implication, combined with his own unique and apparently simple directness. Even after nearly six hundred years the speaking voice comes off the page with its own recognisable personal note. It has a calm assurance, an unforced certainty, a strength and ease and flexibility, which make it seem not only natural but even casual.

The ease and variety are part of the lightness of manner which is important in the poem. The lightness of manner is, like much else in the poem, the product of the sense of piquant contrasts in life.

> ʒit that thow canst not do, ʒit mayst thow se.
> For manye a man that may nat stonde a pulle,
> ʒit likyth hym at wrastelyng for to be,
> And demyn ʒit wher he do bet or he.
>
> (163–6)

This is a note struck at the very beginning of the poem:

> I dar nat seyn, ' his strokis been so sore ',
> But, ' God save swich a lord '—I sey na moore.
>
> (13–14)

We cannot dissociate manner from matter here, but the dexterity with which the mere tag ' I say no more ' is employed to suggest unspoken *nuances* of meaning is an excellent example of colloquial ease and delicacy of touch. This is not to say, however, that the poem is in any way frivolous or flippant in tone. Many passages, if not most, are perfectly serious.

The lightness of tone cannot be dissociated from the simplicity and freshness which everyone notices as one of Chaucer's most obvious characteristics. These qualities, dispersed throughout the poem, come out strikingly in the pure spontaneous joy of such a line as:

> But Lord, so I was glad & wel begoon!
>
> (171)

This is delightfully direct and unaffected, as easy to appreciate now as when it was first written. Some of Chaucer's marvellous freshness it is however more difficult for us to appreciate than it was for Chaucer's first audience. In vocabulary, for instance, it is clear that he often used words which were then fresh to the language, though they are not now. He probably did not actually introduce many new words, but he was never afraid of a neologism, and his early critics and followers all praised him for it. Again, his metre was entirely novel, though its novelty was softened for English ears by being based on a familiar feeling for stress (see p. 52 below). Such a combination of old and new is found everywhere in the poem. One may say, by a simplification which only partly distorts, that while the matter is old, the manner is new. But of course one must add that what is old is given a new twist, and what is new is carefully grafted on to the old. Chaucer was profoundly original and a great innovator; but he worked within the tradition, and was no revolutionary.

All this should suggest that however we may enjoy the freshness and simplicity of much of Chaucer's manner, it is not always as simple as it seems. The freshness, simplicity, and directness are truly there, but they spring from a mind which also shows itself subtle and sophisticated to a degree. It is at home with abstract ideas and is of rather a philosophical cast; and yet is also intensely sensitive to words, and trained to use them in a highly elaborate rhetorical tradition. In the first two stanzas of the *Parlement*, for example, the repetitions, ambiguities, and interjections, all of which have a personal tone and an easy colloquial force, are also figures of rhetoric, deliberately and artfully deployed (see p. 47 below). Fresh and simple Chaucer may be, at the appropriate time; but there was never a poet less simple-minded.

The mixture of subtlety and simplicity is yet another of the sets of contrasting elements which are at the heart of the poem, and which by their very presence set each other off, and also modify any tendency to extremes. Even the goddess Nature includes within herself something of this sense of opposites, though in her they are reconciled. She is both divine and homely, uniting in herself heaven and earth in easy harmony, yet not glossing over the contradictions inherent in earthly life. She is, in all her complexity and yet simplicity, the dominant image of the poem, and fit symbol indeed for Chaucer's whole poetic achievement.

The method Chaucer follows in the *Parlement* is to lay side by side, as it were, different attitudes to or aspects of love, in such a way as to arouse an implicit or explicit questioning. But the reader is left to draw his own conclusions. The connecting thread between the various sections is partly the poet's own questioning wonder. On first acquaintance the form has a certain dream-like arbitrariness;

but this soon resolves itself into the deeper, more suggestive symbolic coherence which can also be the property of dreams, and which is of the essence of the world of the poetic imagination. The poem is governed by what T. S. Eliot has called ' the logic of the imagination ', as contrasted with ' the logic of concepts '.[1]

The first two stanzas are a prologue, in which love is described as a lord of miracles indeed, but also of ' cruel ire '; the pains he gives are great, the joys anxious and transitory. This is a description of love that is hardly friendly; but the confession of Love's supreme power, and the poet's rueful allegiance to him—' God save swich a lord! '—shows him to be a follower of Love, while the tone is lightened with just a touch of half-comic regret. The poet's attitude is complex, with a hint of delicate ironic humour. A sense of opposites, and of tension between them, important throughout the poem, is established in these opening stanzas in both thought and style.

The third stanza changes the style to smoother narrative with the description of the poet's reading habits. He says he reads ' a certeyn thing to lerne '. What the certain thing is, we are never told in so many words. It may be rationalised as ' the nature of love ', but it is wrong to press the phrase too hard for its conceptual content. The phrase develops the note of bewilderment in the first two stanzas into a note of inquiry. The poem is to be as it were a quest, with the very subject of the quest precise yet inexplicable— or rather, the whole poem is the explanation. This fourth stanza merges into the first main section of the poem, the summary of the Dream of Scipio, which has as its chief function the suggestion of the ' philosophical ' penumbra within which the brighter, more obviously entertaining part of the poem will function. The Dream of Scipio in Chaucer's summary is a survey of heaven and earth in which the triviality, deceptiveness, and harshness of the world in comparison with heaven is emphasised. The poet says he read the book with eagerness, but finished it with disappointment.

---

[1] Introduction to the *Anabase* of St J. Perse, quoted by G. Williamson, *A Reader's Guide to T. S. Eliot* (1955), pp. 41-2.

The trouble with the Dream of Scipio is that it takes no account of the value of the world as God's creation, a creation which, according to medieval thought, sprang from, and was continuously maintained by, God's regulating love. To put it briefly, there is nothing about Nature or love in the Dream of Scipio. There is thus no feeling of release. The poet tells the story of the Dream of Scipio with interest and wonder, but also with a sense of frustration at the end. It is as if the poet can neither agree nor disagree with his authority. The account of the world given in the Dream of Scipio dissatisfies him; not because it is wrong but because it is incomplete.

It may perhaps be asked, what is the Dream of Scipio doing here at all, since it has nothing to say of the chief subject of the poem? The answer must be sought in ' the logic of the imagination '. The Dream of Scipio in brief compass surveys the wholé extent of heaven, earth, and indeed hell. It is concerned with the good life, in service of the ' common profit ' (73ff). It mentions the punishment of the lustful. It is, in brief, a total statement of a point of view that was often dominant in the medieval theory of life —the need to despise the world, and seek only heaven. Any general questioning of the nature of love in the Middle Ages was bound to take into account the ultimate human destiny of heaven or hell, and the total scheme of the universe. Chaucer, writing a poem that must first be entertainment, would not have wished, even if he had felt himself competent, to delve deep into theological matters. But the Dream of Scipio, itself in the form of a story, enabled him to suggest weighty ultimate considerations without overemphasising them, and·so capsizing his poem with their weight.[1] There was also another reason. The Dream of Scipio, as incorporated in Macrobius' Commentary (cf. Romaunt, 6–10), was part of a recognised authority on the truth of certain kinds of dreams. Chaucer uses this authority implicitly to introduce his own dream.

[1] See further below, under Nature, pp. 26ff. It did not matter in the fourteenth century that Cicero was a pagan author. He had long been accepted, with other veteres, as an ' authority '.

At the end of the Dream of Scipio, in making the transition to the next main section, the poet renews the note of doubt and seeking: he has what he does not want, and has not what he wants (89–91). He has Cicero's teaching in the Dream, but has no word of love.

The poet falls asleep and dreams. In his dream his guide is the same as the guide in Scipio's dream. So Chaucer in ' the logic of the imagination' connects the new material of experience with the old material of authority, and the old authority shelters the new experience—not that in the poet's dream there is no use of books, but that everything has a clear relation to experienced life. The poet's dream has a fresh immediacy, contrasting with the reported material of the Dream of Scipio. The development and the change of tempo are marked by the invocation to Cytherea, i.e. under a personification, to the planet Venus, which was thought in sober truth to control fertility, friendship, and love, and also to confer learning and eloquence. Venus is a very suitable planet to be invoked for such a poem as the *Parlement* (the planet is not to be confused with the ' mythological Venus' described a little later).[1]

In his dream the poet is immediately carried to the double gate, with its double message of hope and disaster. The ambivalence here echoes the ambivalence of love in the first two stanzas, and is also a foretaste of more ambivalence of love to come. With this passage the theme of love's ambivalence is repeated and the note of doubt and questioning is sounded again. As in the first two stanzas we are prevented from taking the doubt too sombrely; this time the lightening of tone is achieved by the guide's assurance that no part of the message applies to the poet, who is but a dull fellow. Then for the first time, selfish concern firmly and humorously abandoned, joy comes with the bright, positive description of the park and garden, which is the next main section of the poem—a refreshing contrast to the austerity of the Dream of Scipio. Here nothing is passive or flaccid. The very list of trees is given life and force by the attributes

---

[1] For details, see below, under Venus, pp. 30ff.

of human usefulness attached to each. And these attributes help also to keep the passage centred on human activity even in natural description. So the passage merges naturally into the description of Cupid and his followers, which itself leads us to the description of Venus and her temple.

The Cupid-and-Venus passage is the next section in the poem, and contrasts with the previous section, as that had contrasted with its predecessor. For though Cupid is surrounded by in the main pleasant qualities, and may be taken as representing fashionable love affairs, some of the qualities about him are evil and treacherous; through Cupid we are led to the miseries and calamities of the temple, with its gross phallic image of Priapus, and the titillating picture of the all-but-naked Venus. The temple is a hot-house of illicit sensuality; the walls tell stories of disastrous passion, ' withered stumps of time ', though there is beauty too. From this hot and spicy atmosphere the poet walks forth to comfort himself with the green freshness of the park (297). He does not comment on the feelings the place arouses. There is no need; it tells its own tale of love. But his need for comfort here renews the undertone of uneasy doubt and inquiry which had faded in his first contemplation of the park.

In immediate and contrasting juxtaposition the sunlike beauty of Nature eclipses the star of Venus, and all else. Here we enter the last and major section of the poem, the debate of the birds under Nature. Nature is the ' vicar ' (379), the deputy, of ' the almighty Lord '. She represents the created energies of the universe, especially those of reproduction, and she also represents, in herself, and through the birds under her care, the beauty, fulness, and orderliness of the creation.[1]

All the birds are met to carry out Nature's will: to choose their mates and to breed. The noble birds are to choose first, and the three noblest all make their claim for the same beautiful formel. The poet expresses his admiration of the speeches of these suitors (485–6), but in effect the questions

---

[1] For details, see below, under Nature, pp. 26ff.

in the poet's mind, felt earlier in his doubt and dissatisfaction and inquiry, are now dramatically expressed in the diverse attitudes of the various other birds to this question of love. At the same time, Nature herself, with her approval of the birds, or of some of them, is at least a partial answer to the earlier dilemma and bewilderment. The complex image of Nature, and the speeches of the birds, contrast with and implicitly correct the wrongful, selfish, and barren sensuality of the temple of Venus; Nature complements and crowns the full, positive image of the park; and she supplements the view of life represented by the Dream of Scipio. At the same time the debate of the birds continues to explore and portray the subtle complexities and conflicts within human love, especially in the relation of *fine amour* to the general necessities of life and of every-day existence.

The birds stand here as representatives of all living species, but especially of mankind. They compose a hierarchy of worth comparable to, though not exactly matching, that of fourteenth-century society, with the hawks and eagles highest, representing the highest, knightly class, and the other groups of birds lower in the scale. Nature, the vicar of God, whose word is law, endorses this hierarchy, and the most worthy birds have the right to choose their mates first (392). In the mating the initiative ' naturally ' rests with the male, but the female has an equal right to refuse his choice (409). Nature does not deny free will, nor does she constrain love.

Nature stimulates the birds to their duty of procreation by legitimate and natural pleasure (389). Such pleasure, and its aim, implanted by God's own design, are the elements left out of the Dream of Scipio and found distorted to selfish evil ends in the temple of Venus.

Within this generally satisfactory situation, however, there is still a problem. When the three suitors, vowing eternal fidelity, claim the same mate, they are doing more than merely claim a mate; they express love in the highest, most refined form known to the fourteenth century, *fine amour*. It is necessary to emphasise the noble quality of their love, because it is somewhat different from modern forms, and is therefore sometimes misunderstood. All that is necessary, however, is to take the statements of the suitors at their face value, as accepted by Nature, and as required by the context of the poem. There is no need to look for irony where no hint of it exists. The suitors, by Nature's own decree, are the most worthy of the birds. Each seeks the beloved entirely as his own. There is no indication that their love is against Nature's law, or that it is in any way guilty or immoral. Not even the lower birds, sharp enough critics, dream of its being so. The suitors are simply expressing *fine amour* as understood in dozens of fourteenth-century love poems, and there is no suggestion on any one's part that their love is not genuine and in accordance with Nature's law. The poet in all seriousness greatly admires their noble pleading (484–8). The lower birds, however, naturally become impatient. They are too coarse and ignorant to appreciate noble eloquence and fine feeling. To the poet their noise is ' lewedenesse ' (520). But though the poet has a somewhat Shakespearean contempt for the vulgar crowd, he has an equally Shakespearean capacity to present them with humorous toleration. Unrefined they may be, but they have their rights, among which is a right to Nature's ear, and our sympathy. The attitude towards them is not simple.

The superficial problem, as pointed out above (p. 12), has been presented in such a way as to make its solution obvious, granted that the formel is to choose any one at all. But the real interest of the debate is not in the immediate problem, which none of the lower birds discusses (no doubt their irrelevance has its point as a dramatic comment on their ignorance of *fine amour*). What they really discuss is a more fundamental problem, to do with the nature of *fine amour* itself when confronted with the actualities of life. It is clear that if three suitors love the same person, at least two of them must be rejected. Yet they have vowed everlasting love. What shall they do? All the possible solutions to this problem are offered by the lower birds. The solutions are presented dramatically, mostly in terms of impatient, cynical, selfish criticism, such as we should expect from the lower orders. Yet they also show all the reasonable, or at least possible, ways out of the dilemma. The goose says, let the rejected lover love another (as if our feelings were in our own control, and as if it were honourable to go back on one's word). The turtle-dove says, let the rejected lover remain for ever faithful. The duck jeers, and repeats in substance the goose's advice. The cuckoo says, let them *all* remain single.

Neither goose, duck, nor cuckoo are good spokesmen for sense, natural delicacy of feeling, nor honour. We are not expected to admire them. Yet one is bound to have sympathy for what they feel. In truth, doubt or even scepticism about hopeless loyalty in love carried to the length of a life-time's devotion are bound to have a place in every man's mind, ancient or modern, high or low. Pandarus expresses them in the *Troilus*,[1] and Malory makes Dinadan in the *Morte Darthur* express them again.[2] It is important that they should be expressed. Such lack of fine feeling may well be useful and necessary in certain men, perhaps in most.

But there is no certainty that Chaucer or Malory agreed that such unchivalrous attitudes were proper for their *noble* protagonists—for Troilus, or Launcelot, or for the suitors in the *Parlement*. Indeed, the probabilities are all the other way. To think that Chaucer approves wholeheartedly of the 'perfect reason of a goose' is as if we were to think that Shakespeare was in wholehearted agreement with Falstaff's view on honour. It is impossible to imagine such a thing. That does not deny some truth in what Falstaff says: in some cases a live dog is better than a dead lion. Nor need we deny truth and good sense to some of what the duck and goose have to say (the cuckoo is beyond the pale). It is perhaps natural for modern feelings, untrained in the refined exaltations and ardours of *fine amour*, to respond more easily

[1] iv, 400ff, though Chaucer interestingly and significantly suggests that Pandarus did not mean such 'unthrift' (431), such nonsense, and merely said such extraordinary things to save Troilus from death.

[2] *The Works of Sir Thomas Malory*, ed. E. Vinaver, 'The Book of Sir Tristram de Lyones', Section X (Oxford Standard Authors, 1954), pp. 511ff, especially pp. 515–16. But it is well understood that Sir Dinadan is a great joker, who loves all good knights, and is loved by all good knights, so that his railing against love is not to be taken seriously.

to the expression of the untutored reflexes of daily life than it was for Chaucer and for the courtly audience for whom the *Parlement* was first written. But certainly the piquancy in this final, rich section of the *Parlement* lies in the residuum of good sense expressed by the coarser birds. It is this residuum of good sense which helps to maintain the delicate ambivalence which is of the essence of the poem.

Nevertheless, it is also clear that the balance of sympathy in the poem is on the whole in favour of the noble birds against the vulgar; in favour also of the loyalty which was essential to *fine amour*, and of which the most explicit spokesman is one of the lower birds themselves, the modest and well-behaved turtle-dove. To remain chaste and faithful did not seem so impossible an ideal in the fourteenth century as it does to some critics who speak on the goose's side in the twentieth. In the ' scale of Nature ' in which the graded perfection of the created universe was held to exist, there was a place for chastity as well as for marriage. It was a higher place, a nobler state. Marriage was good, but chastity was better. Chaucer could assume that his audience would naturally believe this commonplace idea.[1] And so divine Nature encourages all three of the tercels, at the end of the inconclusive debate, to continue to ' serve ', that is, to love with *fine amour*, for yet another year. Who will actually win the formel is not, in fact, particularly important; the expected solution to the ostensible problem is offered, but it is postponed, and no-one has surely felt in any distress to know the outcome. It is the question about love which is of interest, not the fate of any individuals, for the poem is not about individuals.

For this latter reason we need not concern ourselves with the formel's feelings and motives. The lady's attitude to a lover was conventionally and properly remote. The formel's reluctance to be married is paralleled by that of Emily in *The Knight's Tale*, or by Criseyde's immediate response to Troilus's first advances. Like Virginia (in *The Physician's*

---

[1] Cf. Gower, *Works*, ed. G. C. Macaulay, i, 389–90, Langland, *Piers the Plowman*, ed. Skeat (Text, Passus XIX, 85–90), and below, under Nature, p. 29.

Tale), who is also a prime work of Nature, the formel is not yet ready for love. Her reluctance to choose a suitor is of course the necessary premise of the whole debate.

The debate is concluded with the joyous song of the little birds, so far unregarded, in honour of Nature. This delightful roundel creates a feeling of relief and happy enlargement, a feeling of new life warming old winter's bones, of the world stirring anew with perennial joy. The song corresponds rather to the feelings of joy and loving respect aroused by the contemplation of Nature than to any logical solution of the original problem. We feel ' the agreement of things bound together by the love that governs earth and sea and heaven ',[1] even if such love with difficulty binds the hearts of men.

The final stanza of the poem is an epilogue in which the poet, wakened by the joyful song of the birds, turns with refreshed spirit to renew his quest with hope. His implicit questions have not been finally answered. But in the ' logic of the imagination ', in the symbolic world of sleep and poetry, the joyous song of the departing birds, happy in the satisfaction of their own modest demands and in their delight in Nature, gives a feeling of release and reassurance, and the final words of the poem are themselves optimistic. Nothing has been resolved—ordinary logic is defeated or unimportant—but we are aware of a completed structure, of opposites balanced if not entirely reconciled. A complex whole of related thoughts, feelings, and experiences has been created, as in some small but elaborate medieval church, not quite symmetrical, but not meant to be, where arch meets springing arch, where a painted side-chapel leads off from the main chancel but is subsidiary and supporting to it, where there is a place for many things in an organised whole, and where are recognised the claims of both heaven and earth.

[1] *Boece*, II, m.8.

THE MYTHOLOGY

Medieval secular poetry was often adorned with figures drawn mainly from classical mythology, though the classical material was often moulded into shapes and significances very different from those of its origins. Mythological figures in medieval poetry were sometimes used playfully for sheer decoration, but more often were given allegorical significances, varying with the author's knowledge and interests, and not always consistent with each other even in the same work.[1]

(a) Nature

Chaucer refers us (316) to the De Planctu Naturae of Alanus de Insulis (Alan of Lille) for a picture of Nature.[2] This was the most elaborate and famous of all descriptions of Nature. It follows at length the normal pattern of beauty of the medieval feminine ideal,[3] but all is heightened and glorified: the diadem, for example, that fashionably encircles her head is composed of the seven planets, and her robe is adorned with living creatures. It is necessary for the scheme of the De Planctu that Nature should be represented as weeping for the sins of men, and with a rent in her garment that symbolises man's fall from grace; but this is not an essential part of the general concept underlying the personification, and

[1] Cf. J. Seznec, La Survivance des dieux antiques (1947, English translation 1953).

[2] For the history of the concept of Nature which culminated in the work of Alanus see J. A. W. Bennett, The Parlement of Foules : An Interpretation (1957), pp. 107ff, 194ff; E. R. Curtius, Europäische Literatur und lateinisches Mittelalter (Bern, 1948), English translation (to which all references are made), European Literature and the Latin Middle Ages (1953), pp. 106ff; C. S. Lewis, The Allegory of Love (1936), pp. 54–5, 77, 90ff. Chaucer knew a number of the earlier references to Nature (e.g. that in Metamorphoses, i, 21), and as we learn from HF, ii, 986, he knew the Anticlaudianus, another famous work of Alanus in which Nature is an important figure.

[3] Brewer, MLR 50 (1955), and C. Schaar, The Golden Mirror (Lund, 1955), pp. 269ff.

Chaucer disregards it. Much more to the point, for Chaucer, is the general rejoicing described in the *De Planctu* at the approach of Nature, and a part of this is quoted in C. S. Lewis's translation in Appendix V.

The full significance of Nature to Chaucer and his audience involves the general philosophy and the whole attitude to life of classical and medieval writers, of which obviously little can be said here. But it must be understood that the generally dominant attitude in the Middle Ages was the *contemptus mundi*, contempt for the world, which is quite strongly conveyed in the Dream of Scipio, and which is found at its most intense in the writings of Bernard of Clairvaux and in the *De Contemptu Mundi* of Pope Innocent III, which Chaucer himself translated, and which he used in *The Man of Law's Tale*. Such an attitude easily led to an extreme in which all value was denied to the natural world, to the self, and to all pleasure, especially sexual pleasure.[1]

However, this attitude was never exclusive nor uncontested. The Biblical emphasis on God as Creator, the influence of the ' School of Chartres ' and (in the thirteenth century) of Aristotle, and also, no doubt, normal human instincts, were opposed to it.[2] One of the fruits of this conflict was the medieval concept of Nature.

From the concept of God as creator, and from His perfection, was deduced the perfection of the world (even though man himself, in Adam's sin, had partially corrupted that perfection). The natural world itself might therefore appear, under certain conditions, as an object fit not for contempt but for study and delight. Such an attitude already appears in Macrobius' *Commentary*, where Macrobius says that the elements of the world are bound together by

---

[1] P. Rousselot, ' Pour l'histoire du problème de l'amour au moyen âge ', *Beiträge zur Geschichte der Philosophie des Mittelalters*, Band vi, Heft 6 (Münster, 1908), pp. 3ff; G. Paré, *Le Roman de la Rose et la scolastique courtoise* (Paris et Ottawa, 1941), p. 153, and *Les Idées et les Lettres au XIIIᵉ Siècle* (Paris et Ottawa, 1947), pp. 208ff.

[2] A. O. Lovejoy, in *The Great Chain of Being* (1936), traces the conflict back to self-contradictory tendencies in Plato.

the creator in an unbreakable chain—the famous ' golden chain ' which remained the regular figure, as late as Pope's *Essay on Man*, to express the graded perfection of the universe. Boethius expressed the same idea in a passage which is remembered by Chaucer when describing Nature in the *Parlement* (381), where in a hymn to God the Father and Creator he says, ' Thow byndest the elementis by nombres proporcionables.' [1] In this same passage Boethius says that God governs this world by ' everlasting reason ', and that the world is ' perfectly made '.

The ' golden chain ' corresponds in Boethius to the ' love that governs earth and sea, and also controls heaven '.[2]

These dual concepts of the contemptible worthlessness of the world, and of its love-guided perfection, were reconciled in the idea, adumbrated in Macrobius' *Commentary* and brought to its highest development in the work of Aquinas, of the ' scale of Nature '. Everything, or nearly everything, that existed was thought of as necessarily existing, but as graded in value. The farther away from God, the lower the value. Spiritual things were higher, material lower. The lower things might be despised in comparison with the higher, but even the lower things had some absolute value. Everything has a part to play in the divine plan of the fulness of nature. Thus virginity is a good; the sexual instincts, since they exist, and have been implanted by God the Creator, are also good, and therefore marriage, for the procreation of the species, is a good, though a lower good than virginity.[3] It was held to be a part of the perfection of the universe that it should be fully populated with the utmost diversity of existence—as Benedick says, ' the world must be peopled '. This is what Lovejoy has called ' the principle of plenitude '.[4] It is characteristic of this principle that the pleasures of the senses should be regarded as good in themselves, and part of the divine plan for the universe, even

---

[1] *Boece*, iii, m. 9.

[2] *Boece*, ii, m. 8, already referred to above, p. 25.

[3] Aquinas, *Contra Gentiles*, iii, cap. CXXXVI–CXXXVII, quoted by Paré, *Le Roman de la Rose*, p. 163.   [4] *Op. cit.*, pp. 50ff.

though sin had distorted men's attitude to and desire for such pleasures.[1]

The concept of Nature in the work of Alanus could not of course be influenced by the specific teachings of the later Aquinas, but in this respect Aquinas seems only to be making explicit within a vast system something that was well recognised before. Marriage, for example, had for a long time been a Christian sacrament.

The ' scale of Nature ' represents the graded perfection of the universe. The Nature of Alanus represents the general order of things. She also represents the creative energies of the universe. Although Nature cannot make a soul, Alanus calls her the deputy of God—His ' vicar ', a term taken over by both Jean de Meun and Chaucer.[2]

Symbol both of the Creator and of the holiness, orderliness, and beauty of His creation, Nature in Alanus, as in Chaucer, is especially concerned with procreation of the species. This special concern was emphasised in the second part of *Le Roman de la Rose*, where Jean de Meun takes over the Nature of Alanus.

Although Nature is thus concerned with procreation within the bounds of divine and human love and law, she is no enemy of chastity. In the *De Planctu* both Chastity and Hymen, god of marriage, are figures in Nature's retinue, and she makes much of both.[3] So, in Aquinas, both chastity

[1] Cf. *Parlement*, 388–9, which derives from *Le Roman de la Rose* (see note), which in turn derives from the *De Planctu Naturae* of Alanus, for which see below, p. 43. Cf. also Aquinas, *Summa Theologica*, i, q. 109, a.3 (quoted by Rousselot, *op. cit.*, pp. 16–17) and q. 98, a.2 (quoted by Paré, *op. cit.*, p. 153) and q. 151, a. 3 (quoted by Paré, *op. cit.*, p. 81). The most eloquent statement of the theme of marriage in connexion with the principle of plenitude is perhaps a sermon by Jeremy Taylor, *Works*, ed. R. Heber, v, 253–4.

[2] *Parlement*, l. 379, *Roman*, l. 16782, etc. The importance of the term ' vicar ' when it refers to the deputy of God is shown by Chaucer's application of it to the Virgin Mary in *An ABC* (l. 140) where it is not found in the source as printed by Skeat. It should equally be noted that the reference in the *Parlement* to Nature as ' full of grace ' (l. 319) is a phrase borrowed from the Angelic Salutation to Mary (Luke 1:28). Nature to Chaucer is holy.

[3] J. P. Migne, *Patrologia Latina*, 210, cols. 472–3.

and marriage are good, each equally a part of the divine order.

Nature, therefore, in the *Parlement* is a symbol of God's creative power working in the world by love and law. She is also a symbol of the order, stability, and beauty of that world, its graded perfection, its hierarchies of worth, its necessary desires. Nothing that she approves or decides can be bad. In this representation of Nature questions of man's sinfulness do not enter.

(b) *Venus*

Medieval writers found Venus a goddess and left her a personification. They also, like classical writers, knew her as a planet, which cast its influence upon the earth. There are therefore at least two chief ways of regarding Venus, rather different from each other.

The stamp on what we may here call the ' mythological Venus ' of the Middle Ages, whose origin was the goddess, was set by Fulgentius some time in the sixth century. He describes her as the daughter of Saturn, and says that this is an allegory of lust which rises out of excess (the allegory is based on the apparent connexion between *Saturn* and *saturitas*). He quotes the line from Terence, ' without Ceres (i.e. food) and Liber (another name for Bacchus, i.e. wine) Venus is cold ', which is quoted after him by unnumbered writers, and finds its way via the *Teseida* into the *Parlement* (275–6). Among her various associated properties are doves (*columbae*) because they are birds fervent in coition.[1] Fulgentius strongly disapproves of Venus and of what she signifies, and through him the ' mythological Venus ' in the Middle Ages usually signified carnal lust. In the *Roman de la Rose* Venus is the enemy of chastity (cf. the Middle English translation, the *Romaunt*, l. 3699). The description of Venus by Fulgentius was extremely well known, and is

---

[1] F. P. Fulgentii, *Opera*, ed. R. Helm (Lipsiae, 1898), pp. 39–40. It should be noted that the famous invocation to Venus by Lucretius at the beginning of the *De Rerum Natura* was not known in the Middle Ages until the fifteenth century.

reproduced by Chaucer either directly or at second-hand in *The House of Fame* (ll. 131–9).

In the *De Planctu*, however, Alanus treats this stock figure with some subtlety. He says Venus was originally good, and was originally appointed the assistant of Nature in her task of continually re-peopling the world, and to this end was married to Hymen, god of marriage, by whom she had a son, Cupid. Alanus thereby symbolises legitimate sexual desire directed to its proper ends, marriage and the begetting of legitimate offspring. Venus, however, rebelled and committed adultery with Antigamus (i.e. anti-marriage) by whom she had a bastard, Jocus. The present state of Venus, therefore, represents the misdirection and corruption of a desire originally natural and good.

Chaucer's placing of Venus within the park where Nature is supreme probably derives from his reading of the *De Planctu*. Venus is ' naturally ' a part of Nature's realm, but she represents corruption all the same, and lies apart.

For the details of his picture of Venus, however, Chaucer went to a passage in Boccaccio's *Teseida* (translated in Appendix IV). From the tone of this passage, from its association of Venus with stories of disastrous and illicit love, and from the general reputation of the ' mythological Venus ', it is clearly a representation of corrupted love. Chaucer's own additions to the list of lovers (cf. *Parlement*, 286ff and notes) clarify and enhance the impression made by Boccaccio's description. The Venus passage in the *Parlement* is clearly a moral allegory, signifying selfish, lustful, illicit, disastrous love.

Another ' Venus ', i.e. Cytherea, also appears in the *Parlement* (113–19). Cytherea is addressed as ' a blissful lady sweet ', and thus appears as a personification. The allegory has a scientific significance.[1] Cytherea signifies the planet

---

[1] A clear distinction must be made between the moral, scientific, and historical significances of the allegorical interpretations of the stories about the classical pagan gods. Each of these modes of understanding can be applied in turn to the same story, and may be independent and even inconsistent. The best example is the *Ovide Moralisé*,

Venus, who was always regarded, from classical times, as having a beneficent influence, and as controlling the fertility of plants, beasts, and men. She also bestowed learning and eloquence.[1] A knowledge of astrology was desirable in reading poetry, as the eagle points out in *The House of Fame* (ll. 970ff). The stars were thought of as controlling the world in accordance with God's plan, through the operation of scientific laws.

(c) Cupid

Cupid is sometimes represented in medieval literature, as in classical literature, as a child, son of Venus, often blind—for example, in the *House of Fame* (ll. 137–8). But the dominant image of Cupid in medieval literature is as the god of Love, a bold, active, imperious young man, arousing awe, by no means blind, but rather a hunter of men.[2] Thus he appears in the *Roman de la Rose*, the *Teseida*, the *Prologue to the Legend of Good Women*. Chaucer's account of him in the *Parlement* follows that in the *Teseida* closely, and there are no other influences present, save a few reminiscences, perhaps unconscious, of the *Roman*. In the *Teseida*, as in the *Parlement*, Cupid is represented as agreeable in himself, and surrounded by personifications of chiefly agreeable qualities, though some are treacherous.

[1] For a discussion of the various significations of Venus in the fourteenth century see Brewer, *op. cit.*, pp. 67–72, 75. Neckam writes of ' her ' concern with learning, *De Naturis Rerum*, ed. T. Wright (Rolls Series, 1863), p. 42; Vincent of Beauvais writes of ' her ' concern with eloquence, *Speculi Maioris*, t.i, lib. 15, cap. 45. Chaucer's knowledge of Vincent's well-known encyclopaedia is shown by his use of Vincent's classification of birds (*Parlement*, 323–9), by his mention of Vincent in *ProLGW*, G. 307, and by passages in *The Canterbury Tales*, for which see the articles of Pauline Aiken, listed in D. D. Griffith, *Bibliography of Chaucer, 1908–1953* (Seattle, 1955), p. 81.

[2] E. Panofsky, *Studies in Iconology* (1939).

ed. C. de Boer (Amsterdam, 5 vols., 1915–38), part of which Chaucer may have known (*Works*, p. 841).

THE BIRDS

(a) Birds as suitors

The association of love with spring, and spring with the song of birds, is characteristic of temperate climes. The literary treatment of this association between love, spring, and birds in the form of a debate was an integral part of the tradition of the love-vision.

There was also in the Middle Ages a strong tendency to portray lovers as birds. In Marie de France's *Yonec* a lover appears as a hawk. In the *De Amore* by Andreas Capellanus, a lover says, ' You should not call me by the dishonourable name of kite, but by the honourable one of tercel.' [1] Machaut in *Le Dit de l'Alerion* represents his four successive mistresses as eagles and falcons.[2] Grandson in two poems represents lovers and their ladies as birds,[3] as does Gower in the *Cinkante Balades*.[4] Chaucer himself follows the same convention in the *Squire's Tale*. Examples might easily be multiplied. The question arises, did Chaucer intend to represent particular individuals by his birds, or simply general types?

When existing persons are referred to allegorically, some clue must be provided. A general situation—especially so common a one as that existing between the formel and her suitors in the *Parlement*—is not sufficient guide. Chaucer occasionally used such personal allegories, and provided a clue, as in the *Book of the Duchess*.[5] Chaucer also made a veiled but clearly understandable reference to Anne of Bohemia, Queen of Richard II, in the *Troilus* (i, 171). No convincing case has ever been made for an allegorical application in his poems where there is no such specific reference. There is no specific reference in the *Parlement*,

[1] *De Arte Honeste Amandi*, second dialogue; noted by Bennett, *op. cit.*, p. 155.

[2] *Oeuvres*, ed. E. Hoepffner, SATF, t.ii, pp. 239ff.

[3] ' Le Songe Saint Valentin ' and ' Le Livre Messire Ode ', in *Oton de Grandson, Sa Vie et ses Poésies*, ed. A. Piaget (Lausanne, 1941).

[4] *Works*, vol. i, nos. 12, 19.

[5] *BD* 1318ff. Cf. also *The Monk's Tale, CT* VII, 2383ff.

and no need to assume a personal allegory to explain the poem.

In the past there has been much study of this pseudo-problem of who are represented by the formel and her suitors.[1] The favourite identifications have been Anne of Bohemia with the formel and Richard II with the first suitor, the second and third suitors being variously identified, and no identification generally accepted. Since the force of the identifications can depend only on the general situation, and scholars have not agreed on a general situation which fits the *Parlement*, the argument is weak. Moreover, Richard and Anne were betrothed in 1381, and it seems probable, if not certain, that the *Parlement* was begun in 1382 (see above, p. 2). In any case, the *Parlement* does not represent a betrothal—rather the reverse. Miss Rickert,[2] noticing this, proposed to identify the formel with Philippa, daughter of John of Gaunt, who of course did not marry Richard. But there is no evidence to show that he or Miss Rickert's other candidates were ever recognised as rival suitors for Philippa. In a word, all attempts to identify the formel and her suitors with particular persons have so far failed both on general grounds and in historical detail.

(b) Birds as representatives of social classes

In *Le Fablel* and associated poems (see below, pp. 129ff) the hawks represent the knightly class, and it is felt that no lover can be a *vilains*, or low-bred. The other birds do not, however, appear to represent specific classes of men. In the medieval bird-parliaments noted by Seelman,[3] most of which are political-ecclesiastical-moral satires in German dialects, advice is given to a king or (as in the *Pavo*) to the Pope, by birds some of which presumably represent special interests; but they do not seem to represent social classes. The English fourteenth-century political satire *On King Richard's Ministers* represents the ' ministers ' allegorically

---

[1] There is a useful summary by Robinson in Chaucer's *Works*, p. 791.
[2] *MP* 18 (1920), 1ff.
[3] *Jahrbuch des Vereins für niederdeutsche Sprachforschung*, 14 (1888), 101–47.

through puns on their names, and some of the ' ministers '
are birds. The parliament is composed of geese, but this
mocking reference is hardly an example of class feeling.[1]

In the *Parlement* it is clear that the suitors, being hawks,
and speaking and feeling in a courtly way, represent the
knightly class, as hawks always do. It is equally obvious
that the duck, the goose, and the cuckoo are coarse, or
foolish, or selfish, and Nature herself makes it clear that the
hawks are superior to them (393–400). The national parlia-
ment was composed of representatives of the knightly class
and representatives of what we would now call the middle
class—burghers, rich tradesmen, and so on. It is not unlikely
that the lower birds are in certain ways representative of
these classes, who were sometimes hostile to the court (the
peasants, who were in a state of revolt, hardly enter the
question). But it would be anachronistic to impose the
English nineteenth-century class concept on our reading of
the *Parlement*. The only class division known to medieval
theory was that into knights, clergy, and ploughmen. There
is no such division in the *Parlement*. The division of birds
into groups follows Vincent's classification of birds (323n).
Although we may be justified in feeling that some of the
lower birds have a flavour of the lower classes, the turtle-
dove (577ff) has not, and the other lower birds represent
attitudes which must be at some time present if not dominant
in the minds of all readers, even in those of the fourteenth-
century knightly class. That is part of the richness of
Chaucer's poem. Chaucer certainly reflects some traces of
class feeling in the *Parlement*, but one must not over-
emphasise what little there is.[2]

(c) Natural history

Chaucer's knowledge of birds was as much due to reading
as to observation, though there are more observed character-

[1] *Political Songs and Poems*, ed. T. Wright (Rolls Series, 1859, 2 vols.),
ii, 363.
[2] Cf. D. S. Brewer, ' Chaucer's Humour ', in *Proteus; Studies in
English Literature* (Tokyo, 1958), and M. Emslie, *EC* 5 (1955), 1ff.

istics in his list of birds than is usual. Chaucer is also unusual in omitting such fabulous birds as the chalaundre which is commonly mentioned in the Old French poems (cf. *Romaunt*, l. 663), and in including some birds that have disagreeable characteristics, such as the goose, cuckoo, and duck. The variety of the birds is significant. It symbolises the fulness of nature, and more particularly the structure and diversity of human society. At the same time the birds are closer to nature, have a stronger actuality, than those in the lists of other medieval poets.

In one way, however, they are not at all close to nature, for of course no writer on natural history, ancient or medieval, has ever suggested that birds actually meet on 14 February to choose their mates. A few ecclesiastical calendars note that birds begin to sing on 12 February,[1] and anyone may notice a considerable increase of activity among birds during this month; but why this particular fancy about the general meeting should have arisen in the courts of England and France in the late fourteenth century is completely unknown. The usual statement that courtiers took up a folk-festival is simply a guess based on late-nineteenth-century preconceptions about ' the folk '. All the evidence so far available points to high society as the originator of the idea. From the fourteenth to the seventeenth centuries all the references to St Valentine's Day are in literature written for the upper classes, or show the influence of that literature, and especially the influence of Chaucer himself.

It may have been that there was some tradition, or there arose some courtly game, towards the end of the fourteenth century, either in England or France (or even in Savoy, where Grandson came from), in which men and women chose partners on 14 February. This happens to be St Valentine's Day, but the custom has nothing to do with anything that is known of the various saints of that name. Once this game existed in court circles, the tendency to represent human lovers as birds, noted above (p. 33), encouraged by the new liveliness of the birds about the

---

[1] These are noted by K. H. Jackson, *Studies in Early Celtic Nature Poetry* (1935), 164–5.

middle of the month, may have given rise to the poetic fancy that birds mate on 14 February; for it is a well-established principle of modern anthropology that myths tend to be invented to explain rituals. Whatever its origin, the fancy has proved astonishingly long-lived in English life and literature, though not in French.[1] The curious may trace how this sophisticated courtly pastime spread down the centuries, reaching the lower classes by the nineteenth century (when Sam Weller sent his Valentine), and in the twentieth century, birds apparently forgotten, becoming widespread among the children of the United States.

(d) Birds and the national Parliament

In the Old French poems the debates among the birds often reflect the debates of the council that a king or nobleman maintained to advise him. In contrast, the birds in the *Parlement* are not in any sense in the retinue of Nature. They are different from the birds in other bird-parliaments. The quality of the debating and the composition of the members has more in common with the national Parliament, which in the latter part of the fourteenth century came to occupy an ever more important and vociferous part in the nation's affairs. On the other hand, there is no attempt to make the debate follow closely the form of a fourteenth-century Parliamentary debate, nor does there seem to be any evidence of an attempt to turn the work into a political satire by making the birds represent particular political personages or factions, any more than they represent real suitors or social classes.

At the opening of the national Parliament a speech was given by the Chancellor explaining why the Parliament had been called. This corresponds to Nature's opening speech (382ff).[2] Usually Lords and Commons then divided to deliberate separately. But they might sit together, as the

[1] Apart from Chaucer, the chief exponent of this fantasy in the fourteenth century is Grandson. See Appendix I.

[2] W. Pieper, ' Das Parlament in der m.e. Literatur ', *Herrig's Archiv*, **146** (1923), 187–212.

Commons requested in 1377, for the quicker dispatch of business.

A few words may have a Parliamentary flavour, as *statute* and *ordenaunce* (387n, 390), *delyuere* (491n), *presente* and *acceptyth* (531–2n), *remedie* (502), *common profit* (47, 75). Furthermore, *assentuz et accordez* (cf. 526, 608) are of very frequent occurrence in the Parliamentary jargon of the period.

There are constant indications of complaint, restiveness, and the desire for haste in the Parliaments of the 'seventies and 'eighties, as well as considerable hostility to the court. The tone of these may be lightly hinted at in the speeches of duck, cuckoo, and goose.

But of course no Parliaments discussed such matters as are found in Chaucer's *Parlement*. At most he does no more than make a witty reference to the political institution, and perhaps catch something of its tone in one of the heated debates of the period.

CHIEF SOURCES

(a) Le Roman de la Rose

Chaucer's lifelong debt to the *Roman de la Rose* is well known. It is probable that the first 1705 lines of the Middle English translation of the *Roman* (referred to here as the *Romaunt*) are by Chaucer himself, and a reading of the first 5810 lines in particular of the *Romaunt* is more illuminating for the tone and quality of Chaucer's earlier verse than any amount of modern discussion. Wherever possible in this edition references to the *Roman* are made in terms of the *Romaunt*, easily available to readers in Robinson's or Skeat's editions.

The *Roman* was written by two authors: by Guillaume de Lorris in the early thirteenth century up to line 4058, and the rest by Jean de Meun some forty years later.[1] The

---

[1] The whole poem was edited by E. Langlois, SATF (Paris, 1914–24, 5 vols.). The best short account of it in English is still that by C. S. Lewis, *op. cit.*, pp. 119ff; cf. also Brewer, *op. cit.*, pp. 27ff, and especially A. M. F. Gunn, *The Mirror of Love* (Texas Tech Press, 1951), who makes a stimulating reinterpretation of the whole poem.

peculiar quality of the poem is largely due to the different natures of the two authors. Guillaume's portion is essentially a courtly love-vision, with the usual conventions (though far better done than in the later love-visions). It is, however, unlike the later love-visions in that it presents two hostile ' confrontations ' of *fine amour*. First, outside the garden of the god of Love is a set of images of Old Age, Crime, Poverty, etc., which represent qualities incompatible with *fine amour*. Secondly, after the lover has received a rebuff, the allegorical figure of Reason points out to the lover the pain and folly of love (*Romaunt*, ll. 3189ff). She condemns love without qualification. Soon after this Guillaume's poem abruptly breaks off.

When Jean de Meun continued, he soon introduced Reason again. This time she speaks differently. She makes a distinction. Good love is allowable. It is engendered of a true heart, is just, and secret (*Romaunt*, l. 5090), and is concerned with begetting offspring. ' The world must be peopled ' (cf. ll.4856ff). What is condemned is love which is concerned merely with fleshly pleasure (l. 5092). The god of love must be banished (l. 5109). It is however cardinal to the argument (and here is the relation of the *Roman* to such scholastics as are represented by Aquinas) that ' good love ' is accompanied by legitimate pleasure (l. 4869–71), and may well be courtly and ' debonaire ' (l. 5081). In fact, Reason re-admits by the back door that *fine amour* which she began by throwing down the front steps. All refinement of love is allowable, provided its chief aim is the continuation of life, of God's plan for the universe, the fulfilment of the ' principle of plenitude '. Thus, in terms of the *Parlement*, the suitors of the formel are well entitled to be courtly, because, as we may see from Nature's approval of them, and from the implication of other remarks, they expect to breed.[1]

Reason's remarks are taken up again and amplified much later in the *Roman*, in the dialogue between Nature and her priest Genius (who signifies fertility).[2] In this dialogue Genius describes at length the ' good park ', which draws

[1] Cf. *Parlement*, 612–15 and Brewer, *EC* 5 (1955), 407ff.
[2] *Roman*, ll. 16272ff.

for its imagery on descriptions of the Earthly Paradise, and which is a figure of heaven. Those who have loved well and have lived a good life will enter this park.[1]

Jean contrasts the goodness of this park with the badness of the earlier garden of Deduiz (Mirth), as described by Guillaume, which symbolises the *fine amour* condemned by Jean.[2] To enter the good park Genius says you must ' think how to honour Nature; serve her by working well '.[3]

There is, of course, a vast amount of other material, satirical, scientific, philosophical, in the *Roman*, but the elements emphasised above may be considered as its core, and they are all reflected in the *Parlement*. Central to each poem is the debate about the nature of love, explicit in the *Roman*, implicit in the *Parlement*. The chief philosophical sources of the *Roman* are Alanus and Boethius. Both these authors are remembered by Chaucer in the *Parlement*, and it was probably his reading of the *Roman* which first introduced him to them, as it must also have introduced him to the name of Macrobius, who is cited at the very beginning of the *Roman* as an authority for dreams. The two confrontations of love in Guillaume's part of the *Roman* are paralleled in the *Parlement* by the summary of the Dream of Scipio. The *Roman* solves the problem of love by the dual concepts (in Jean's section) of Reason and Nature, who speak with much the same voice.[4] So Chaucer resolves the problem of love in the *Parlement* by the concept of Nature. The ' good park '

[1] *Roman*, ll. 19931ff. It does not matter for the purpose in hand that much of what Genius says seems tainted, if Paré (*Les Idées*) is right, by the Averroist heresy which, in the interests of fertile ' plenitude ', advocated sexual promiscuity. Chaucer avoids the heretical passages.

[2] *Roman*, ll. 20279ff.   [3] *Roman*, ll. 20637–8.

[4] The speech of Reason (*Romaunt*, ll. 4615ff) is mainly drawn from Alanus's representation of Nature. The Nature of Alanus, and the Reason of Jean de Meun, do not advocate sexual promiscuity. Since such promiscuity is not advocated till late in the *Roman* it is clearly a development in Jean's thought that occurred during the years he was writing his immense portion of the *Roman*, and which led him away from the orthodoxy of Alanus. The implications of Chaucer's Nature are those of Jean's Reason and of the Nature of Alanus. Chaucer is perfectly orthodox.

of the latter part of the *Roman*, within the description of
which occurs the contrast to the false garden of Deduiz, is
paralleled in the *Parlement* by the good park to which
Africanus leads the poet in dream, which has set within it
the contrasting Temple of Venus. The timeless nature of
the good park in the *Roman* is reflected in the timeless nature
of the park in the *Parlement*, where the leaves last for ever
(173) and night never comes (209–10). The contrast pointed
out in the description of the good park in the *Roman* between
the healing properties of its fountain and the deadly properties
of the ' perilous fountain ' of the garden of Deduiz [1] is
reflected in the two messages on the gate into the park of
the *Parlement* even down to the water-imagery. The
favourable message on this gate talks of the ' well of grace '
(129). The unfavourable message, after the reference to
Disdain and Danger (which recalls such guardians of the
Rose, as Danger, Shame, Jealousy, Wicked-tongue), speaks
of the stream which leads to the sorrowful weir (138–9).

Chaucer knew the *Roman* extremely well, and it is no less
than the *matrix* of the *Parlement*. The remarks of earlier
editors that the influence of the *Roman* is slight are quite
mistaken. It is possible that what prompted the composition
of the *Parlement* itself was Chaucer's discovery of Macrobius'
Commentary incorporating the Dream of Scipio. His mis-
take about ' King Cipioun ' in the *House of Fame* (l. 916),
repeating the very mistake of the *Roman* (cf. *Romaunt*, l. 10),
indicates that he had not yet read the Dream of Scipio when
he composed the *House of Fame*, which was therefore
probably written before the *Parlement*. Chaucer's interest
in the Dream was coloured with concern, since although it
is referred to in the *Roman* it has nothing to do with love.
When he had finished it he was thus ' fulfyld of thou3t
& busy heuynesse ' (89), and carried his meditation about love
further, guided still by the *Roman* in his general thought and
in his search for further authorities, and led by the *Roman*
to Alanus in particular.

Profound as the influence of the *Roman* was, however,

---

[1] *Roman*, ll. 20465ff.

Chaucer still retained his independence of thought and judgment. He did not follow Jean into what has been claimed to be his Averroistic heresy. Here, apart from the Dream of Scipio itself, the *De Planctu* and, finally, Boccaccio were his safeguards—in a word, the orthodoxies of Christian teaching preserved him.

(b) *The Dream of Scipio* and Macrobius' *Commentary* [1]

The Dream of Scipio was written by Cicero and originally formed part of the *De re publica*, Book vi. The larger work was lost for centuries, but the Dream of Scipio was preserved in the Middle Ages in the vastly longer commentary upon it by Macrobius, who lived about A.D. 400. The joint work had immense prestige and influence throughout the Middle Ages.

The Scipio of the title is the younger Scipio Africanus, whom Cicero describes as visiting Massinissa, king of Numidia, in 150 B.C. They talked of the elder Africanus, uncle and grandfather by adoption of the younger, and the younger dreamt of his grandfather that night.

Chaucer summarises the Dream of Scipio to bring out its chief ideas with great skill. The literal translation in Appendix III is offered for the reader's convenience in making his own comparison.

Chaucer omits the personal circumstances of Scipio's life and such matters as, for instance, the speech of Paulus, the gist of which (55–6) is attributed to Africanus. He omits or slightly adapts purely pagan concepts, such as the concern for glory and the need to know oneself a ' god '. The summary gives prominence to the ideas of righteousness, the care for ' common profit ', the need to despise the world, and the punishment for sensuality.

Apart from these points, Cicero's emphasis on law, especially as in councils or assemblies, and the position of Africanus as a guide and mentor may have influenced Chaucer, reinforcing and helping to remodel the conventions of guide and debate in the traditional love-vision.

---

[1] See especially Bennett, *op. cit.*, pp. 30ff.

Chaucer probably read some of Macrobius' *Commentary* as well (cf. *Parlement*, l. 28) and he refers to Macrobius' final remark (l. 111). Macrobius is more concerned with elucidating and elaborating the scientific concepts inherent in the Dream than with the moral or theological essence of the work, and introduces Nature half-personified, especially in Book i, Chap. 2, 17.

Chaucer also shares the more general debt of the Middle Ages to Macrobius' *Commentary* for introducing the concept of the ' scale of Nature ' (cf. above, p. 27).

(c) De Planctu Naturae

Chaucer's actual verbal borrowings from Alanus are very slight. It is clear from what has been said about the love-visions that the council of birds with their debate is a traditional part of this type of poem, and the idea that Chaucer took the suggestion of a ' parliament ' from Alanus must be abandoned. Chaucer may have taken the suggestion for the list of birds, and a few characterisations, from the list in the *De Planctu*.[1] But of course the major and vital debt to Alanus was the allegorical figure of Nature, with all that she implies. This has already been discussed in the section on Nature (above, p. 26). Chaucer was probably also indebted to Alanus for the placing of Venus in relation to Nature (*ibid.*).

The chief usefulness of the *De Planctu* to Chaucer was that, more than any other poem, it presented Nature as an allegorical figure, a personification, which could be used on the same poetic plane as the Venus and Cupid of the earlier love-visions. Alanus made it possible for Chaucer to substitute Nature for the god, or goddess, of love in the earlier poetry, and thereby immeasurably to increase the scope and implications of the *Parlement*.

(d) Teseida

Chaucer makes such detailed use of the *Teseida* that it has reasonably been assumed that he owned a manuscript of it

---

[1] Reprinted by W. W. Skeat, *The Works of Geoffrey Chaucer* (1899), i, 74.

himself.[1] His manuscript was probably one of the largest group now surviving, and so was probably without Boccaccio's own notes, the *Chiose*. It was very corrupt.

In the *Parlement* Chaucer uses a highly ornate passage from the *Teseida* to help him realise in the most decorative way possible a theme already suggested by his reading of Alanus. The *Chiose* make it absolutely clear that Boccaccio has precisely the same attitude to Venus as had Alanus;[2] but of course that attitude is clearly implicit in the passage from the *Teseida* itself, just as, for example, Spenser's attitude is clearly implicit in his description of the Bower of Bliss, though a modern reader is sometimes misled by the richness of the decoration. Both Boccaccio and Chaucer, like Spenser after them, wished to describe what they deplored in rich and luxuriant terms as a set-piece of beautiful description. Temptations are presented as highly tempting. Beautiful evil is still beautiful.

Chaucer translates the passage from the *Teseida* fairly closely, and the reader may compare his version with the literal translation in Appendix IV. The demands of verse make the version freer at the end of a stanza than at the beginning, and Chaucer would also seem to have deliberately modified his source in various ways. The major modification is in the order of appearances. Thus, since for Boccaccio, Cupid signifies the more agreeable and courtly aspects of love—though even these are not without folly and vice—and Venus signifies a darker sensual passion, Venus rightly comes at the climax and end of the passage. Chaucer, however, while not denying these symbolic functions, focuses attention on the human victims of Venus. He transposes the conventional list of lovers from a comparatively incon-

---

[1] R. A. Pratt in *SP* **42** (1945), 745ff, *PMLA* **62** (1947), 598ff, and in *Sources and Analogues of Chaucer's Canterbury Tales*, ed. W. F. Bryan and G. Dempster (Chicago, 1941), pp. 82ff. Bennett's comments, *op. cit.*, pp. 74ff, are as usual valuable, though he is probably wrong in supposing that Chaucer knew the *Chiose*, though Pratt himself occasionally presses too hard the argument that he did not; cf. K. Malone, *MLR* **45** (1950), 63ff.

[2] Part of the *Chiose* is translated in Brewer, *op. cit.*, pp. 82ff.

spicuous place to the end of the passage. In order to give
the list greater weight for its more important position he
extends it, adding a couple of lovers (including Troilus) from
his own memory, but using chiefly Dante's list in the Hell
of the Lustful. The place from which he took most of his
additional lovers is of course significant in reinforcing the
general effect of the whole passage, even though his audience
would not have recognised his source. The list of dead but
famous lovers is as it were introduced by Chaucer's own
addition of the ' two ȝonge folk ' crying to Venus, an
addition which again emphasises the human concern of the
passage. He also reinforces the symbolism of the passage by
adding the hill of sand (243) which emphasises the ill-
founded hopes and the insecurity of Patience in the affairs
of love.

(e) The Divine Comedy [1]

The first link with the *Divine Comedy* is an association, not
a borrowing. It occurs at the end of the summary of
Scipio's dream where it is said that breakers of the law and
lecherous folk, when dead, shall whirl about the earth in
pain (79–80). This not merely resembles the general doc-
trine of purgatory. It specifically calls to mind Dante's
second circle of Hell, where the lustful are whirled about
(*Inferno*, v). The *Inferno* having been called to mind,
Chaucer borrowed a line or two from the beginning of the
second canto to help him make his transition (85–6).[2]

But Chaucer's debt is not only casual. Although it is a
convention of the Old French love-visions to provide the
poet with a guide, and Chaucer probably drew his general
concept from the French tradition, he models the un-French,
masculine firmness of his guide, and the guide's relation to
the poet, on Virgil's relation to Dante in the *Divine Comedy*.
Thus, as Dante had studied Virgil so carefully, so had
Chaucer earnestly read the Dream and its *Commentary*, for

---

[1] Cf. Bennett, *op. cit.*, pp. 56ff (where, however, the influence of
Dante is occasionally overestimated).

[2] Chaucer had borrowed from the same canto, 7ff, for a similar
purpose at the beginning of Book ii of *HF*.

which Scipio praises him (109–10). Scipio's comment to the
poet (155–6) echoes those of Virgil to Dante. As Virgil
guides Dante to the gate of Hell with its intimidating
inscription, and pushes him through, and takes his hand, so
does Scipio to Chaucer. But this episode in itself provides
a very clear example of what use Chaucer is making of Dante.
There is no attempt to mimic Dante's great aim and power.
Chaucer's touch is above all lighter, as his aim is different.
The first motto on the gate of Chaucer's park is clearly a
reference to Dante, the very rhythm of whose words has been
caught.[1] But Chaucer's echo is a kind of parody, though
without mockery. The threatening message of Dante's Hell
is echoed in the cheerful promise of the golden letters, before
being echoed by the black; and it is a double motto that
Chaucer uses, not the single one of Dante.[2]

Chaucer also uses Dante to supplement the *Teseida*. In
the description of the beautiful park Chaucer draws a touch
from Dante's description of the Earthly Paradise (201–3).
In particular, as already mentioned, Chaucer drew on
Dante's list of the lustful (*Inferno*, v, 58–69) to supplement
Boccaccio's list. Lists of lovers are extremely common in
medieval poetry, and Chaucer could have easily borrowed
such a list as that of Froissart's in the *Paradys d'Amour* (from
which he had borrowed the opening of the *Book of the
Duchess*). It is significant that he should have chosen Dante's
list, which for all its compassion is a list of those who are
guilty, condemned, and suffering.

[1] D. Everett, *Essays on Middle English Literature* (1955), p. 143;
W. Clemen, *Der Junge Chaucer* (Bochum Langendreer, 1938), p. 175.
[2] The *double* gates were perhaps suggested by the two famous gates
at the exit of Virgil's Hades (*Aeneid* vi, 893), which are, very appro-
priately for the *Parlement*, the gates of sleep, and of which one gave out
true dreams and the other false. The *content* of the mottoes on Chaucer's
gates derives, as has already been suggested, from the *Roman*.

(a) General

Chaucer learnt his art partly from treatises on rhetoric, and partly from other poems; and he brought to his learning a genius which surpassed his lessons and masters. One treatise he certainly knew was the *De Poetria Nova* of Geoffrey of Vinsauf.[1] There were probably others.

(b) The form of the Parlement

In modern terms, the poem is made up of a *Prologue* (1–14), *thesis* (15–112), *prelude to anti-thesis* (113–19), *anti-thesis* (120–692), *epilogue* (693–9). The *anti-thesis* may itself be resolved into smaller sections consisting of an *introduction* (120–68), *subsidiary thesis* (169–294), *anti-thesis* (295–692). The form is composed of a series of contrasts, with transitional passages, the general *thesis* against the *anti-thesis*, and within the general *anti-thesis* the contrast of Venus with Nature; and within Nature's parliament the contrasting attitudes of the various speakers. Contrast was recognised in medieval rhetoric as a figure of speech and a figure of thought, known in each case as *contentio*.

The form is precise and careful, but it develops by means of association and contrast of ideas, often presented in pictorial terms, rather than by logical argumentative process. There is no special emphasis on essentials, while the ' surface ' is decorative and elaborate. It is Chaucer's greatness, however, that what would be in other poems merely traditional decorative ' surface ' passages—such as the lists and other commonplaces—are all related to each other, to the story, and to the basic mood. In linking the commonplaces together the device of the wondering narrator is of the highest

---

[1] Edited by E. Faral, *Les Arts poétiques du XIIe et du XIIIe siècle* (Paris, 1924)—the fundamental work on the subject. J. W. H. Atkins, *English Literary Criticism: The Medieval Phase* (1943) is sometimes useful, but not sympathetic nor always accurate. D. Everett, *op. cit.*, has an invaluable chapter (pp. 149ff) and excellent remarks elsewhere, as have H. S. Bennett, *Chaucer and the Fifteenth Century* (1947), J. A. W. Bennett, *op. cit.*, Clemen, *op. cit.*, Curtius, *op. cit.* Chaucer's knowledge of Geoffrey is clear from *Troilus* i, 1065–9, and *CT* vii, 3347.

importance. It is his presence, and his underlying pre-
occupation, barely more than hinted at, with the nature of
love, that link together the various passages and give them
depth and meaning.

(c) Commonplaces

The poem is a web of commonplaces.[1] The poet's bewilder-
ment at the beginning is Chaucer's characteristic twist of the
device called by Curtius ' affected modesty ' which goes back
to pre-Christian antiquity. The passage on dreams (99–105)
is actually based on Claudian, but many poets wrote similar
passages. The dual nature of love, bitter-sweet, good-and-
bad, is re-iterated from Ovid onwards throughout the Middle
Ages; the grove, the *locus amoenus* (garden, park, or pleasance),
goes back to Greek poetry, as does the device of the list or
catalogue. Lists of birds and trees are common in medieval
French poetry, as are lists of lovers—though Chaucer in
each case makes his list serve some particular and rather
unusual purpose. Descriptions of Venus, Cupid, and Nature
are common in medieval Latin, and are found several times
in medieval French, though Chaucer was the first to describe
them in English. All such descriptions are part of the
general rhetorical tradition.

(d) The nature of the rhetoric

The first stanza of the *Parlement* is a treasure-trove of
rhetorical devices, which need be only briefly noted here.[2]
It begins with a *sententia* or striking apophthegm, which is

---

[1] It is not to be supposed that a commonplace necessarily makes
bad poetry: if it did, much of Shakespeare's poetry would stand
condemned. The importance of the commonplace in medieval poetry
is emphasised by Curtius, *op. cit.*, passim, but especially pp. 79ff; for
the *locus amoenus* see his pp. 183ff. Some of the critical problems raised
are discussed by Cleanth Brooks, *The Well Wrought Urn* (New York,
1947), especially the chapter on Gray; observations on the importance
of stock responses are made by C. S. Lewis, *A Preface to Paradise Lost*
(1942), pp. 53ff.

[2] There are full analyses in H. S. Bennett, *op. cit.*, pp. 89ff and
Everett, *op. cit.*, pp. 103ff.

one of the recognised methods of beginning a poem. The
sententia is in the somewhat unusual form of a *contentio* or
contrast, and is moreover a *circumlocutio*, or roundabout way
of expression. The second line contains a metaphor, which
is also an example of *circumlocutio*. The first three lines are
also an example of *interpretatio*, or different ways of saying
the same thing.

This may sound highly artificial and pedantic. But of
course it is not to be supposed that Chaucer first thought of
several abstract figures of speech before he started to com-
pose. Some figures of rhetoric are inherent in the nature of
human thought and language (e.g. metaphor), and therefore
rhetoric is unavoidable in human speech. Chaucer lived in
an age of especially conscious elaboration of figures of speech.
This rhetorical tradition implies a highly sophisticated,
subtle, and technical attitude to the art of poetry on the part
of Chaucer and his audience. Such an attitude, even more
widespread in Elizabethan times, was only finally lost in the
Romantic revival; to recognise it is vital for criticism.

The devices enumerated in the first stanza of the *Parlement*
are well suited to the needs of an audience which primarily
hears (though it may read as well), and some of Chaucer's
technical brilliance is no doubt to be attributed to his
expectation of a highly critical and well-educated audience
who would have had some technical understanding of such
figures of speech, and who appreciated their use in poetry.[1]
Thus in the first stanza the mind is ' naturally ' led forward
by a combination of information and mild mystification,
which arouses both expectation itself and pleasure in its
ingenuity.

The method employed is fundamentally repetition with
variety, and this method of variation is well suited to the
beginning of a poem which is heard. Variation or some
similar method of ensuring that the listener will understand

[1] It would seem that at least a part of his audience was expected to
have read the *De Planctu* of Alanus (cf. *Parlement*, 316–17) which is in
by no means simple Latin, and to recognise from their schooldays the
quotation from Claudian (ll. 99–105). Rhetorical analysis was part of
their education.

the poet's main point is a necessity in oral poetry—as we may understand from Shakespeare himself.[1] The needs of the listener, whom too concentrated a meaning will fatigue and eventually defeat, explain the fondness for lists, explanations like ' al this mene I be . . .' (4), and the firm and obvious transitions, ' But now to purpos as of this matere ' (26), ' This forseyde Affrycan ', etc.[2] A poet who writes for listeners will also be glad to use the rhetorical device of *repetitio*, repetition of important words, phrases, or syntactical forms, so as to guide his listeners in the development of the story and to establish links that remain either consciously or half-consciously in the mind; thus the repetitions ' Fyrst tellith hit ' (36), ' Thanne tellith hit ' (43), ' Thanne axede he ' (50), etc.; and for a more subtle purpose, the repetition of ' blysful place ' (48, 72, 76–7, 127), and of ' acord ' (371, 381, 668). The use of *sententia*, often proverbs or in proverbial form, is another characteristic of medieval poetry. They are used partly because oral poetry needs familiar phrases, and partly because poetic theory, and the audience too, valued the gnomic, ' clinching ' effect of such phrases, which were felt to be at once decorative, learned, and familiar.[3] The favourite device of amplification, under which many figures of rhetoric fall (and which was the curse of much medieval poetry), is also to be attributed in part to a listener's need for not too concentrated a form. The light touches of dramatic realism in the speeches of the birds are also provided for in rhetorical theory—the fitting of the style

[1] Cf. C. S. Lewis, ' Variation in Shakespeare ', *Rehabilitations* (1939).

[2] E.g. 295–6, 372, 533.

[3] Cf. Curtius, *op. cit.*, pp. 57ff. Poetry that is meant for reading often attempts, quite reasonably, to avoid all these effects. When Boswell pointed out the repetition of the same word within a few lines in Johnson's *Vanity of Human Wishes*, Johnson immediately altered it (*Life*, 19 May, 1778). The use of proverbs or ' sentences ' did not in the Middle Ages mean that a speaker was uneducated—rather,' the reverse (the example of Sancho Panza in *Don Quixote* is misleading here). When in the *Parlement* the turtle dove (518) or the duck (595) use proverbial expressions, the use is not a dramatic expression of a low-class origin. The courtly Pandarus used them; Chaucer stuffed his own *Tale of Melibeus* full of them.

to the speaker (*Poetria Nova*, ll. 1842ff). Again, when Chaucer remarks on the goose's ' facounde gent ' (558) he practises a precept found in the *Poetria Nova* (ll. 431–4)—if you wish to condemn the ridiculous, ' praise, but ridiculously . . . let your speech have teeth '.[1]

METRE

(a) General

Chaucer's earlier long poems are written in the short so-called ' octosyllabic ' verse, but he presumably felt some dissatisfaction with the narrow limits imposed by this metre. As early as *An ABC* (a poem almost certainly written before the *Parlement*, and perhaps even before *The Book of the Duchess*) he used a line of ten syllables, which has been attributed to the influence of Machaut, one of Chaucer's earliest French masters. But the greatest practitioners of a longer line known to Chaucer were Dante and Boccaccio, who use an eleven-syllable line with much elision and (in Dante at least) some variety in the placing of the caesural pause. It is no coincidence that the *Parlement*, which reveals so much Italian influence, is also the first of the regular succession of Chaucer's poems in the longer line.

A modern authoritative treatment of Chaucer's prosody is sorely needed, and the following remarks are tentative. What seems to have happened is that Chaucer imitated the longer line and the syllabic regularity of French and Italian verse. This syllabic regularity did not absolutely insist on the same number of syllables a line. The sort of licence that was freely permitted was the intrusion of an extra syllable before the caesural pause, or an extra syllable at the end of the line.

But in imitating French and Italian syllabic regularity Chaucer inevitably retained something of the rhythmic

[1] Geoffrey's advice comes in a comment on apostrophes, which Chaucer amusingly enough turns against Geoffrey himself in *The Nun's Priest's Tale* (*CT* VII, 3338ff). Even Chaucer's mockery of the famous rhetorician follows that same rhetorician's own rules. This is the extent of Chaucer's ' emancipation ' from rhetoric that was once so talked of.

quality of the older English verse, because English in its very
nature is a heavily stressed language. Probably Chaucer's
greatest innovation was the *regular* use of five stresses in a
line of about ten syllables. This usage developed the
tendency to have five stresses, which was already noticeable
in the traditional alliterative verse. It seems likely, however,
that quite often in Chaucer's verse one of the five heavy
stresses was lighter than the other four. This tendency in
regular English ' decasyllabic ' verse may be frequently
observed. Sometimes, indeed, the fifth stress was missing
altogether, and Chaucer reverted to something very close to
the original native pattern of English verse, of which every
century has its examples. It also seems likely, in the light
of verse written before and after Chaucer, that the caesural
pause in the line was a good deal stronger than anything we
are accustomed to nowadays.[1] The result is that although
Chaucer's verse-line is often closely similar to the regular
English pentameter especially familiar in eighteenth- and
nineteenth-century English literature, it allows of wider
variants. Chaucer established a delicate balance of forces
between syllabic and stress verse, and it is not surprising that
with the additional complication of the disappearing final -*e*
(representing an older, fuller inflection), his fifteenth-century
followers found it almost impossible to imitate him. The
English ' heroic ' line had to be discovered anew in the
sixteenth century.

(*b*) *Details of metrical usage—the line*

The underlying measure in Chaucer's verse may be seen at
its simplest in the following lines:

Be thow myn helpe in this, ‖ for thow mayst best   (116)

The skornynge iay, ‖ the elis fo, heroun   (346)

---

[1] Cf. Skeat, *The Works of Geoffrey Chaucer* (1899), .vi, lxxxiiff, and
C. S. Lewis, ' The Fifteenth-Century Heroic Line ', *Essays and Studies
of the English Association* 24 (1938), 28ff.

But natheles, ‖ in this condicioun (407)

And for these watyrfoulis ‖ tho began (561)

There are many variants on this. The most notable and frequent is the addition of an unstressed final -*e* at the end of the line, which makes the line (apart from its rhythmic quality) extremely close to the Italian endecasyllable; as in the first line of the *Parlement*:

The lyf so short, ‖ the craft so longe to lerne

(The final -*e* of *longe* is merely scribal and is not pronounced. The final -*e* of *lerne* represents the OE full verbal inflexion -*an*, and is pronounced.) In many other lines, normal English speech-feeling tells us that one of the five full stresses has less weight than the others, as in the line

The day gan faylyn ‖ & the derke ny3t (85)

(where ' 3 ' (yogh) corresponds to the modern English digraph ' gh ').

In this line *&* should at most receive a medium stress, and could indeed receive no stress at all, leaving the line with only four stresses, and with a pattern that could be described perfectly adequately in terms of OE prosody; even alliteration is present.

A number of lines are ' headless ', i.e. lacking the first light syllable, e.g.:

Quod the sperhauk, ‖ neuere mot she the! (569)

Compare also 426, 510, 632. Such lines usually occur in connexion with dialogue.

A few lines have an extra final syllable which is not final -*e* (e.g. 44/6, 57/9, 401/3).

A few lines, again usually when it is a question of dramatic emphasis in dialogue, have extra weight on the first syllable, e.g.:

'Lo! ‖ here a perfit resoun of a goos!'   (568)

In this line what would, in the basic measure, be a full stress on *of* is much lightened, and *of* should perhaps be taken as having no particular stress at all.

Some lines have an extra-metrical syllable placed just before the pause, as in French. The pause, according to Skeat, prevented the syllable (which is always unstressed final -*ė*) from being elided with the following word, even when that word began with a vowel. Examples are to be found in 95, 202. However, it may be doubted, in the light of Chaucer's occasional practice of suppression of a final -*ė* (for which see below), whether the extra-metrical final -*ė* in the middle of a line was actually sounded. An example where the final -*ė* before the pause cannot be elided (since it is followed by a consonant) may be found in 391:

May I nat lete ‖ for all this world to wynne!

If the extra-metrical final -*e* is not indeed to be suppressed, it may be easily enough accommodated if the pause is sufficiently long. English easily permits such a variation. In 621 the word *hire* is extra-metrical, and the movement of the line thus varies a little more widely than usual from the basic pattern.

The chief source of the great variety of Chaucer's line is his variation of the place of the pause. This variation is one of the marks of his genius. The most usual place for the pause is, as in the first line of the *Parlement*, after the fourth syllable, that is, after the second heavy stress. But it may be placed almost anywhere else in the line to achieve dramatic effect or logical emphasis. In this, as in practically all matters of English prosody, the meaning and a practised ear will guide us. Examples of its use are: after the first syllable (568, 570), after the second (18, 29), after the third (37, 389), after the fifth (41, 521), after the sixth (10, 14), after the seventh (22, 451), after the eighth (17, 509).

Occasionally the pause is very weak and the line runs on with hardly any perceptible break (e.g. 97, 526); and on a few occasions there may be two pauses (e.g. 15, 522), though this is a more difficult matter to decide.

If the reader remembers the possibilities of variety in the basic measure he will find Chaucer's verse in the present text easy to scan even if he is quite ignorant of Middle English, provided he follows the natural speech rhythm and observes a few conventions. Most of these conventions are familiar enough to any reader of English poetry, except for the use of final -*e*. Etymological final -*e* is usually the last trace of the Old English inflexion of parts of some nouns, adjectives, and verbs, but it may also represent a Latin or French inflexion (e.g. *Naturė* ⟨ Latin *Natura*; *prouė* ⟨ OFr *prouer*). In Chaucer's time it was fast disappearing from the spoken language. In consequence, as it came to be written where it was no longer pronounced, scribes often wrote it in where there could never have been an inflexion, and often left it out where it had, even in Chaucer's day, been pronounced. A final -*e* which does not represent a former full inflexion is termed scribal. The scribe of the manuscript here used as a basic text complicates matters further by inserting an extra -*e*- in odd places in various words. These must be ignored. For the convenience of readers unaccustomed to Middle English I have marked final -*ė* where it was probably pronounced, thus: *erthė*. Its sound is an unstressed obscure vowel [ə]. I have not marked etymological final -*e* where it should be elided or suppressed (see below), nor where it occurs as an extra-metrical syllable at the pause, nor where it occurs at the end of a line, in which last case it should always be pronounced. It must be emphasised that such markings are *tentative suggestions only*. The principles underlying Chaucer's use of final -*ė* are difficult to establish and the reader is free to disagree.

It should also be noted that the genitive and plural inflexions of nouns, -*is*, -*ys*, are usually pronounced as a separate syllable. Some words are to be pronounced with more syllables than their present derivatives, such as *cre-a-ture*; and words ending in -*i-oun*, which is two full syllables.

Some words have a variable accent, e.g. góddésse or goddésse, and in others (chiefly of French origin) the accent falls later than in present-day English, e.g. myráklis, matére, Natúre.

The following notes give examples of the chief conventions to be observed in a metrical reading of the lines.

Elision. A final *-e* may be elided with a following vowel or word beginning with *h-* as in *Th'assay*, 2, *wolde*, 544, *hadde*, 556. Final *-o* of *to* is elided, 648.

Suppression. Etymological final *-e*, though usually sounded, may occasionally be so slurred over as to be disregarded, as in *shulde*, 590, *hadde*, 455 (cf. 90–1 where the final *-ė* must be sounded), *knowe*, 386 (contrast 393, and Gg's addition). Etymological final *-e* is particularly liable to suppression in words of frequent occurrence such as possessive adjectives and auxiliary verbs, especially when it is preceded by *-r-*. It also disappears *within* the set phrase *fro ʒer to ʒeere*, 23.

The vowel in medial or final *-ed*, *-id*, *-yd* in the past tense of weak verbs is sometimes suppressed, as in *shewed*, 572, *louid*, 454.

The vowel of medial *-en-* is often unetymological and may be suppressed, as in *euene*, 149, *owene*, 320.

The vowel of medial *-er-* is sometimes unetymological and may be suppressed, as in *brekeris*, 78; *lykerous*, 79; *euery*, 68, and often elsewhere, as *souereyne*, 416 (contrast 422).

The vowel of final *-er* (*e*) is often suppressed, as in *euer*, 585, 640; *laughtere*, 575; *longere*, 453 (contrast *lengere*, 657); *neuere*, 436 (contrast 439).

The vowel of the plural inflexion of the noun is sometimes suppressed, as in *erys*, 500, *seris*, 541, *instreumentis*, 197.

The vowel of final *-yr* is sometimes suppressed, as in *modyr*, 292; *ouyr*, 123 (contrast 300).

Contraction. Certain forms are often contracted, especially the verbal inflexion *-yth*, as in *comyth*, 25, 61, etc.; *lyuyth*, 328; and auxiliary verbs preceded by *ne*, as in *ne haddė*, 91, which should be pronounced *naddė*. Sometimes the scribe writes the contracted form, as *nystė* (*ne+wystė*), 152.

The form *nouper*, 602, is contracted in pronunciation to

nor. The scribe of the manuscript used as basis for this text did not realise this, and substituted *nat.*

This is is often shortened to *this* as in 411, 620.

Whethir, a dissyllable in 152, is sometimes one syllable, and indeed is written *wher*, 7.

(c) *The stanza*

The stanza form is the rhyme royal, a French verse form, which as far as is known Chaucer was the first to use in English. It was a great favourite with him in his middle years, being used in the *Troilus* and a number of other poems.

(d) *The roundel*

The roundel is another French verse form found in Machaut, Deschamps, and others. Chaucer elsewhere used it only in the poem *Merciles Beaute*, and as far as is known is the first poet to use the form in English. Essentially it consists of eight unlike lines, in three sections of three, two, and three lines respectively, of which the second and third sections are followed by refrains made up of repetition of the first line, or the first and second lines, or the first, second, and third lines. Skeat's reconstruction, which is followed in the present text, adopts the thirteen-line arrangement which came to be considered normal, but the reader may vary the length of the refrains if he wishes. ' There *must* be a full-stop at the end of the third and fifth lines; but the skilful poet takes care that complete sense can be made by the first line taken alone, and also by the first *two* lines taken alone. Chaucer has done this.' [1]

THE TEXT

1   *The manuscripts*

The authorities for the text of the *Parlement* are fourteen MSS and Caxton's edition of 1477–8. They were classified in two groups by Miss Hammond [2] as in the following list (the lettering differs from hers):

[1] Skeat, *The Works of Geoffrey Chaucer*, i, 525.

[2] ' On the Text of the *Parlement* ', *University of Chicago Centennial Publications*, First Series, 7 (1902), 3–25.

Group A	Group B
Gg Cambridge University Library Gg.IV.27	**F** Fairfax 16, Bodleian Library
Ff Cambridge University Library Ff.I.6	**B** Bodley 638, Bodleian Library [1]
H Harley 7333, British Museum	**D** Digby 181, Bodleian Library
R Trinity College, Cambridge R.III.19	**Lt** Longleat 258 (in the possession of the Marquis of Bath)
Hh Cambridge University Library Hh.IV.12 [1]	**T** Tanner 346, Bodleian Library
C Caxton's edition	
P Pepys 2006, Magdalene College, Cambridge [1]	
S Arch Selden B.24, Bodleian Library [1]	
L Laud 416, Bodleian Library [1]	
J St John's College, Oxford, LVII	

This classification agrees with that of J. Koch.[2] Near the beginning of her article (p. 9) Miss Hammond states that Group A is nearer to Chaucer's original, but at the end (p. 25) she favours Group B. The question is incapable of certain decision, but probably Group A, as Miss Hammond's evidence shows, is slightly better. Within Group A, Gg and Ff constitute an important subgroup, with a number of notably superior readings, of which the most striking is l. 363 (see below). All MSS have many errors and omissions, but Gg has fewest; Ff is in general very careless. Gg has therefore been taken as the basis of the present edition.

2 *Characteristics of Gg*

(a) *General.* Gg.IV.27 is a large handsome MS written on vellum about 1420–40.[3] Besides the *Parlement* it contains *The Canterbury Tales* and several other poems by Chaucer, and also Lydgate's *Temple of Glas.* It has the unique version

---

[1] Incomplete. In addition all MSS except Gg, J, D, omit the roundel (680ff).

[2] *Geoffrey Chaucers Kleinere Dichtungen* (Heidelberg, 1928).

[3] *The Text of the Canterbury Tales*, ed. J. M. Manly and E. Rickert (Chicago, 1940), i, 170ff.

of the *Prologue to the Legend of Good Women* (labelled A by Skeat, G by Robinson). One scribe, writing in a formal book hand, wrote the Chaucerian pieces. His version of *The Canterbury Tales* was made under supervision, he made innumerable corrections, and he probably corrected each page as written. Everything goes to show his unusual care, although he occasionally made extraordinary blunders.

He had access to unusual and good texts. In *The Canterbury Tales* about half his text is independent of the other major MSS. Even when he derives from the same ancestor he is free from the usual variants, though he has many of his own. More striking still is his unique text of the *G Prologue to the Legend*. Its unusual metrical and grammatical accuracy is characteristic both of the scribe and his exemplar, although he has also some strange readings. The evidence indicates that he drew directly from Chaucer's unpublished MS of the *G Prologue*, whereas the other extant MSS are all derivative. But many of his unique readings are of doubtful authority.[1]

(*b*) *Gg's text of the Parlement.* Within the general group A, Gg's readings are often closely associated with those of Ff. Manuscript Ff is of very different character, a small paper volume badly written late in the fifteenth century by several scribes; the text of the *Parlement* was written by two of them with many errors and omissions. Ff did not use Gg as exemplar, so they had a common exemplar. Since we know from Gg that this exemplar was good, coincidences of reading between Gg and Ff, even when against the reading of all the other MSS, deserve special attention.

That Gg had an excellent exemplar is to be expected from the evidence of his other texts of Chaucer's poems, and is made clear from such lines as 363, 381, 428, 460, 537, etc., which also show the care with which he copied. His care may also be seen in his corrections, of which there are several, e.g. at the end of 561 he first wrote *goos*, but substituted the correct *began*. This does not prevent him in

---

[1] E. F. Amy, *The text of Chaucer's Legend of Good Women* (Princeton, 1918).

the *Parlement*, as in the other texts, from making one or two extraordinary errors, e.g. in 507.   But these are rare.

Unfortunately Gg's care was such that when he found what he considered to be a mistake in a line, he did his best to correct it.   A clear example in 358 is pointed out by Miss Hammond.   The line in Gg reads:

> The wakyr goos the cokkow most onkynde

The *m* of *most* has been altered from *eu*.   All the other MSS read *euer(e)* instead of *most*.   It is clear that Gg did not realise that Chaucer sometimes used the monosyllabic form of *euer* (see above, p. 56), and so, in the interests of a smoother metre, he substituted a monosyllable.   Gg was unusually sensitive to metre, but did not always understand the pronunciation of final -*è*.   He therefore has a number of lines where he alone, against the evidence of all the MSS including Ff, has inserted an extra word in order to ' preserve ' the metre (e.g. 259, 457, etc.).   Such a tendency to edit must make us suspicious of all Gg's *unique* readings when the other MSS are *unanimous* against him.

But not all Gg's unusual readings can be explained as scribal editing.   A clear example occurs in 363, when all the MSS except Gg and Ff have *rauyns, crowes*.   It is unlikely that Chaucer would change from singular to plural in this line only of the list of birds: *rauenwys* could easily have been misread *rauenys* by the scribes of the other MSS or of their exemplars.   The wrong plural form *rauenys* could easily have contaminated *crowe* by unconscious example.   The correct reading is almost certainly that of Gg.   Here it is noteworthy that Gg's reading is supported by Ff, though Ff, with his tendency to omit, has dropped the adjective *wys*.   Here is further evidence of the excellence of the Gg, Ff ancestor.   Readings of Gg supported by Ff have a special value, even though they are occasionally found united in solitary error (e.g. 80, 344, 400).   Gg, Ff readings have been occasionally accepted as in 363 just mentioned, and also 22 where a plural *sey* is better than a singular *seith*, and in 313, 317, and 396.

Where Gg is quite unsupported by other MSS there is

less chance of his proving right.   Usually he is certainly
wrong.   In a few cases his isolated testimony has been
accepted, most often for metrical reasons (e.g. 428, 460, 551),
though having regard to the nature of Chaucer's metre I
should not like to be dogmatic about most of these.

The most controversial reading in the present text is in 65.
The Gg text reads:

And was sumdel disseyuable and ful of harde grace

A ' critical ' text would read:

And was sumdel ful of hardé grace

This is quite possible, but it is awkward, and moreover a
little feeble.   The reading

And ful of torment and of hardé grace

found in the MSS of Group A less Gg and Ff is smooth
enough, but is an extravagant sentiment difficult to attribute
to Chaucer.   It looks very like a scribal attempt to get over
a difficult line.   Gg's reading as it stands is of course
impossible.   But if he too noticed a metrically awkward line,
it is inconceivable that he would have altered it in the
direction of what was not merely more awkward, but
impossible.   He could easily have inserted *it*, for instance,
after *And* if he had the reading of the ' critical ' text before
him.   In other words, it is unlikely that he himself invented
disseyuable.   The most likely place he would have found the
word was in the margin of his excellent exemplar.   It is
possible that Chaucer first wrote the line as it appears in the
' critical ' text, but was dissatisfied with it, crossed out the
feeble *was sumdel* and wrote *disseyuable* as a substitute in
the margin.   The crossing out and the marginal substitution
may well have been overlooked by other scribes, but not by
Gg's exemplar.   The evidence that Chaucer also had the
Consolation in mind at this point (see 65n) is an additional,
if not entirely conclusive, argument in favour of Gg's reading.

(c) *Dialect and spelling*.   The spelling of Gg differs in
several respects from that of Chaucer: *sch-* and *ch-* are inter-

changed, as are *s*- and *c*-; *be* is written for *by*; -*d*- is some-
times used for -*th*-; -*e*- is preferred to -*i*- as in *wele* for *wil*,
dede for *did*; an epenthetic -*e*- is found in various positions,
e.g. *hondered*, and a merely scribal final -*e* is often added
(these must be disregarded in pronunciation); the past
participle of weak verbs is often formed with -*id*; genitives
and plurals are usually formed with -*is*, -*ys*; the final -*n* of
possessive adjectives is regularly retained before consonants;
the final -*n* of the infinitive and past participle is often
retained. These spellings are closely similar to the spellings
found from 1447 onwards in the Paston Letters,[1] written in
East Anglia. There can be little doubt that the scribe of Gg
came from East Anglia—a part of England with which
Chaucer had numerous business and family connections.[2]

Those unfamiliar with Middle English scribal usage may
note that initial *i*- has often the sound of modern *j*; initial ȝ-
(yogh) has the sound of modern *y*-; medial -ȝ- has a guttural
sound, and as a spelling represents modern -*gh*-; þ (thorn)
has the sound of modern *th*-; *u* and *v* are interchangeable
and each may have the sound either of modern *u* or of
modern *v*. The scribe also often writes *w* for *v*.

(*d*) *Editorial treatment.* Gg is the basis of the text. Its
chief disadvantage is its un-Chaucerian spelling, but it was
thought better not to attempt the hazards of a wholesale
reconstruction of Chaucer's spelling, though a few final -*e*s
have been restored where they seemed necessary to the
metre. In a few cases proper names have been restored to
more recognisable form. Punctuation and the use of capitals
are editorial. Emended words have been assimilated to Gg's
spelling, and alterations italicised. Words omitted from the
MS are supplied in square brackets.

The aim of the textual notes is to show the manuscript
evidence on which the printed text has been based. In lines

---

[1] N. Davis, 'The Language of the Pastons', *Proceedings of the
British Academy* **40** (1954), 119ff.

[2] R. A. Caldwell, 'The Scribe of Gg.IV.27', *Modern Language
Quarterly* **5** (1944), 33ff, proposes the ingenious but unlikely hypothesis
that the scribe of Gg.IV.27 was a Dutchman who did not properly
understand English.

to which there is no textual note it may be assumed that the printed text is exactly that of Gg and that none of the other MSS (including Caxton's printed text) has any significant variation. This does not mean that other MSS may have no mistakes at all in such lines, for they have; but there has been no attempt to record the obviously erroneous and individual variants of careless scribes. The only exception to this is of course Gg, whose every mistake is noted. It should not therefore be thought that Gg is more faulty than other MSS.

Where Gg has gone wrong and the other MSS have various readings, they have all usually been noted; and where an important group of MSS have a reading that may be bad but seems of interest, that reading has been noted even if not acceptable.

Unless otherwise indicated, wherever there is a note the reading of the printed text is usually that of all MSS except those indicated in the note. Thus the note to line 358

euere] *Gg* most

indicates that all MSS (and Caxton's print) read *euere*, except for Gg, which reads *most*. Very occasionally an obvious isolated scribal error (usually by S) has been disregarded, as have also differences of spelling. Where a reading, even when based on Gg, is that of a minority of MSS, the fact is noted thus, as in the note to line 385:

ʒow] *so Gg, Ff, C, L; others* me

which indicates that the reading ʒow is found in MSS Gg, Ff, C, L, and that all other texts read *me*.

The Chaucer Society reprints and Koch's selection of variants have been used for all MSS except Gg. The Chaucer Society reprint of Gg is accurate save in lines 154 (*Ne* for *Me*) and 624 (*not* for *nat*) and that in line 420 it looks more like *leue* than *leve*.

It would perhaps be hardly appropriate in an edition such as the present, even if space allowed, to argue the merits of more than a very few disputable readings. A selection of the evidence of the MSS has been provided, and anyone interested may indulge in the fascinating perplexities of textual criticism. It is important to realise, what is sometimes overlooked or denied, that the reasons for preferring one reading against another may vary with every individual case. The problems of Chaucer's text are a subject in themselves and cannot be decided by methods evolved for dealing with the very different circumstances of the tradition of classical texts. Much weight must naturally be given to the evidence of the ' best ' MSS, but there can be no mechanical reliance on the well-known processes of arriving at a ' critical ' text, any more than these processes can be entirely neglected.[1] One must also take into account individual scribal practice; likely sources of error; metre; grammar; spelling; parallel passages; the original (where it is a case of translation); and not least, Chaucer's own style and possible intentions. The editor's judgment and preconceptions inevitably enter in, whether he realises it or not; to sum up, the construction of a text is not a mechanical operation. There is no purely objective text that is not a mere reprint of one manuscript— and no manuscript, least of all one written in the fifteenth century when standards of copying were so low, is a purely objective rendering of its exemplar.

The present text, therefore, does not claim to be objective: nevertheless, it is hoped that in all except spelling it is closer to Chaucer's original than the texts of earlier editors, from which it differs in a number of small particulars. The manuscripts of the *Parlement* are full of minor corruptions, but there are enough copies to make the task of correction, if not easy, at least not hopeless. Now and again it is impossible to know Chaucer's exact intention, but there is no reason to suspect major error or corruption in our text.

[1] These are well described by E. P. Hammond in *Chaucer: A bibliographical manual* (1908), pp. 106ff.

SELECT BIBLIOGRAPHY

Books and articles cited in the Introduction or Notes to make a particular point are not listed again here.

Bibliographical works

E. P. HAMMOND *Chaucer: a Bibliographical Manual* (New York, 1908). Fundamental.

D. D. GRIFFITH *Bibliography of Chaucer, 1908–53* (Seattle, 1955).

F. W. BATESON *The Cambridge Bibliography of English Literature* (Cambridge, 1940), i, 208ff; and v, *Supplement* edited by G. Watson (Cambridge, 1957), 130ff. Books and articles published up to 1955.

Life of Chaucer

CHAUCER SOCIETY *The Life-records of Chaucer* (1875–1900). The documentary basis of modern knowledge about the life of Chaucer; documents discovered since 1900 are listed in the bibliographies, and some are printed by E. Rickert (see below).

D. S. BREWER *Chaucer* (2nd ed. 1960).

Editions

The Complete Works of Geoffrey Chaucer, edited by W. W. Skeat (Oxford, 1894, 2nd ed. 1899) in six volumes. Out-of-date, though still containing much of value, especially in the Glossary. The *Parlement* is in vol. i, 335ff.

The Works of Geoffrey Chaucer, 2nd ed., edited by F. N. Robinson (Cambridge, Mass., and London, 1957). The standard modern edition; indispensable. The *Parlement* is on pages 309ff.

Geoffrey Chaucers kleinere Dichtungen, herausgegeben von J. Koch (Heidelberg, 1928). Valuable for its full selection of textual notes. The *Parlement* is on pages 8off.

Social background

G. G. COULTON *Chaucer and his England* (1908).

E. RICKERT *Chaucer's World,* edited by C. C. Olson and M. M. Crow (1948). A valuable collection of extracts illustrating the ordinary life of the times, translated into modern English where necessary.

G. M. TREVELYAN *Illustrated English Social History,* i (1949).

Literary background—texts

CICERO *De re publica,* edited and translated by C. W. Keyes (Loeb Classical Library, 1928).

MACROBIUS *Opera,* edited by F. Eyssenhardt (Teubner, 1868).

Macrobius; Commentary on the Dream of Scipio, translated by W. H. Stahl (New York, 1952).

ALANUS DE INSULIS *Opera* (*Patrologia Latina,* edited by J. P. Migne, vol. 210).

'The Complaint of Nature by Alain de Lille', translated by D. M. Moffat, *Yale Studies,* 36 (1908).

GUILLAUME DE LORRIS AND JEAN DE MEUN *Le Roman de la Rose,* edited by E. Langlois, SATF (Paris, 1914-24), 5 vols.

The Romance of the Rose, translated by F. S. Ellis (Temple Classics, 1900), 3 vols.

CH. OULMONT *Les Débats du Clerc et du Chevalier* (Paris, 1911).

Les Arts poétiques du XIIᵉ et du XIIIᵉ siècle, edited by E. Faral (Paris, 1924).

DANTE ALIGHIERI *La Divina Commedia,* edited by H. Oelsner, variously translated (Temple Classics, 1899-1901).

G. BOCCACCIO *Teseida,* edited by S. Battaglia (Firenze, 1938).

A. PIAGET *Oton de Grandson* (Lausanne, 1941).

A. KLEIN 'Die Altfranzösischen Minnefragen', *Marburger Beiträge zur Romanischen Philologie*, Heft 1 (Marburg, 1911).

Literary background—studies

W. A. NEILSON ' Origins and Sources of *The Court of Love* ', *Harvard Studies* 6 (1899). Summaries of love-visions.

W. O. SYPHERD ' Studies in Chaucer's *Hous of Fame* ', *Chaucer Society* (1907). Summaries of love-visions.

W. P. KER *English Literature: Medieval* (Home University Library, 1912, 1945). Brief but masterly, with a most judicious and penetrating chapter on Chaucer.

J. M. MANLY ' What is The Parlement of Foules? ', *Studien zur englischen Philologie* 50 (1913), 279–90. A valuable list of ' questions of love ', and a section on the date of the *Parlement*.

C. S. LEWIS *The Allegory of Love* (1936). Brilliant and stimulating.

A. M. F. GUNN *The Mirror of Love* (Texas Tech Press, 1951). An important study of *Le Roman de la Rose* which frequently challenges the interpretations of C. S. Lewis and earlier scholars.

E. R. CURTIUS *Europäische Literatur und lateinisches Mittelalter* (Bern, 1948); English translation, *European Literature and the Latin Middle Ages* (1953). Essential to an understanding of the learned tradition and nature of much medieval literature.

The Age of Chaucer (vol. i of *The Pelican Guide to English Literature*, edited by B. Ford, 1954). Eccentric but stimulating.

Studies of Chaucer and the Parlement

J. L. LOWES *Geoffrey Chaucer* (1934).

W. CLEMEN *Der junge Chaucer* (Köln, 1938). Has a valuable chapter of detailed commentary on the *Parlement*.

P. VAN D. SHELLY *The Living Chaucer* (Philadelphia, 1940).

H. S. BENNETT *Chaucer and the Fifteenth Century* (1947).   A volume in the Oxford History of English Literature.

N. COGHILL *The Poet Chaucer* (1949).

D. EVERETT *Essays on Middle English Literature*, edited by P. Kean (1955).   Four valuable essays on Chaucer, including one on the interpretation of the *Parlement*.

J. A. W. BENNETT *The Parlement of Foules* (1957).   A valuable extended interpretation of the poem.

(See also works by Ker, Lewis, Brewer above)

Language and metre

B. TEN BRINK *Chaucers Sprache und Verskunst* (Strassburg, 1884); English translation, *The Language and Versification of Chaucer* (1901); third German edition, revised by E. Eckhardt (Tauchnitz, 1920).   Rather old-fashioned, but still very valuable.

H. KÖKERITZ *A Guide to Chaucer's Pronunciation* (Stockholm and Connecticut, 1954).   Intended for the non-philological student and issued in conjunction with recordings.

(See also the editions by Skeat and Robinson, and works by Hammond, H. S. Bennett, and Everett above)

Select Supplementary Bibliographical Note (books only)

Bibliographical:

A. C. BAUGH *Chaucer* (New York, 1968).

W. R. CRAWFORD *Bibliography of Chaucer 1954-63* (Seattle and London, 1967).

Editions:

Chaucer's Major Poetry, ed. A. C. Baugh (New York and London, 1963).

Chaucer's Poetry, ed. E. T. Donaldson, New York, 1958.

Studies:

Chaucer and Chaucerians, ed. D. S. Brewer (London, 1966).

Sphere History of Literature in the English Language, Vol. I, ed. W. F. Bolton (London, 1970).

Chaucer's Mind and Art, ed. A. C. Cawley (London and Edinburgh, 1969).

W. CLEMEN *Chaucer's Early Poetry* (London, 1963).

E. T. DONALDSON *Speaking of Chaucer* (London, 1970).

S. S. HUSSEY *Chaucer, An Introduction* (London, 1971).

C. MUSCATINE *Chaucer and the French Tradition* (Berkeley, 1957).

D. W. ROBERTSON, *A Preface to Chaucer* (Princeton and London, 1963).

D. W. ROBERTSON and B. F. HUPPÉ *Fruyt and Chaf* (Princeton, 1963).

Companion to Chaucer Studies, ed. B. Rowland (London, Toronto and New York, 1968).

Chaucer Criticism II: Troilus and Criseyde and the Minor Poems, ed. R. J. Schoeck and J. Taylor (Notre Dame, 1961).

The Parlement of Foulys

Here begynyth the Parlement of Foulys

THE lyf so short, the craft so longe to lerne,
Th'assay so sharp, so hard the conquerynge,
The dredful ioye, alwey that slit so ȝerne,
Al this mene I be Loue, that myn felynge
Astonyith with his wondyrful werkynge   5
So sore iwis, that whan I on hym thynke,
Nat wot I wel wher that I flete or synke

For al be that I knowe nat Loue in dede,
Ne wot how that he quitith folk here hyre,
Ȝit happith me ful ofte in bokis reede   10
Of hise myraklis & his crewel yre.
Ther rede I wel he wele be lord & syre;
I dar nat seyn, ' his strokis been so sore ',
But, ' God save swich a lord '—I sey na moore.

Of vsage, what for lusté, what for lore,   15
On bokis rede I ofte, as I ȝow tolde.
But wherfore that I speke al this?   Nat ȝoore
Agon, it happede me for to beholde
Vpon a bok, was wrete with letteris olde,
And thervpon, a certeyn thing to lerne,   20
The longé day ful faste I redde & ȝerne.

For out of oldé feldys, as men sey,
Comyth al this newé corn from ȝer to ȝere,
And out of oldé bokis, in good fey,
Comyth al this newé science that men lere.   25
But now to purpos as of this matere;
To redé forth so gan me to delite,
That al that day me thouȝté but a lyte.

71

This bok of which I makė mencioun
Entytlyt was al thus as I schal telle: 30
' Tullyus of the drem of *Scip*ion '.
Chapiteris seuene it hadde, of heuene & helle,
And erthe, and soulis that therynnė dwelle;
Of whiche, as shortly as I can it trete,
Of his centence I wele ʒow seyn the greete.   35

f 481v Fyrst tellith it, whan Scipion was come
In Affrik, how he metyth Massynisse,
That hym for ioie in armys hath inome;
Thanne tellyth he here speche & of the blysse
That was betwix hem thil that day gan mysse,   40
And how his auncestre, Affrycan so deere,
Gan in his slep that nyʒt to hym apere.

Thanne tellith it, that from a sterry place,
How Affrycan hath hym Cartagė schewid,
And warnede hym beforn of al his grace,   45
And seydė what man, lernyd oþer lewid,
That louede comoun profyt, wel ithewid,
He shulde in to a blysful placė wende,
There as ioye is þat last withoutyn ende.

Thanne axede he if folk that *here* been dede   50
Han lyf & dwellynge in anothir place.
And Affrican seyde, ' ʒa, withoutyn drede ',
And that oure present worldis lyuys space
Menyth but a maner deth, what weye we trace,
And rightful folk schul gon aftyr they dye   55
To heuene; and schewede hym the Galaxye.

Thanne schewede he hym the [litil] erthe that
    here is,
At regard of the heuenys quantite,
And after schewede he hym the nynė speris,
And aftyr that the melodye herde he   60
That comyth of thilkė speris thryės thre,
That welle is of musik & melodye
In this world here, & cause of armonye.

Than bad he hym, syn erthė was so lyte,
And disseyuable, & ful of hardė grace, 65
That he ne schulde hym in the world delyte.
Thanne tolde he hym, in certeyn ȝeris space
Ther euery sterre shulde come in to his place
Ther it was ferst, & al schulde out of mynde
That in this world is don of al mankynde. 70

f482r Thanne preyede hym Cypyon to telle hym al
The weye to come in to that heuenė blisse
And he seyde, ' Know thynself ferst inmortal,
And loke ay besyly thow werche & wysse
To comoun profit, & thow shalt not mysse 75
To comyn swiftly to that placė deere,
That ful of blysse is & [of] soulys cleere.

But brekeris of the lawė, soth to seyne,
And lykerous folk, aftyr that they ben dede,
Schul whirle aboutė þ'erthe alwey in peyne, 80
Tyl manye a world be passid, out of drede,
And than forȝeuyn al hire weked dede:
Than shal þey come in to this blysful place,
To whiche to comyn, God [the] synde his grace.

The day gan faylyn, & the derkė nyȝt, 85
That revith bestis from here besynesse,
Beraftė me myn bok for lak of lyght,
And to myn bed I gan me for to dresse,
Fulfyld of thouȝt & busy heuyhesse;
For bothe I haddė thyng [which] that I nolde, 90
And ek I ne haddė [that] thyng that I wolde.

But fynally myn spirit at the laste,
Forwery of myn labour al the day,
Tok reste, that madė me to slepė faste,
And in myn slep I mette, as þat I lay, 95
How Affrican ryȝt in the same aray
That Cipion hym say byfore that tyde,
Was come, & stod riȝt at myn bedis syde.

(2,236) 6

The wery huntere, slepynge in his bed,
To wode aȝen his myndė gȯth anon;   100
The iugė dremyth how hise pleis been sped;
The cartere dremyth how his carte is gon;
The riche of gold; the knyght fyȝt with his fon:
The sykė met he drynkyth of the tunne,
The louere met he hath his lady wonne.   105

f482v Can I nat sėyn if that the causė were
For I hadde red of Affrican byforn,
That madė me to mete that he stod theere,
But thus seyde he, ' Thow hast the so wel born
In lokynge of myn oldė bok *to-t*orn,   110
Of whiche Macrobye roughtė nat a lyte,
That sumdel of thyn labour wolde I quyte.'

Cytherėa thow blysful lady swete,
That with thyn ferbrond dauntist whom th*e* lest
And madist me this sweuene for to mete,   115
Be thow myn helpe in this, for thow mayst best.
As wisely as I seye the north-nor-west,
Whan I began myn sweuene for to write,
So ȝif me myght to ryme & ek t'endyte.

This forseyde Affrican me hente anon,   120
And forth with hym vnto a gatė brouȝte,
Ryȝt of a park, wallid *with* grenė ston,
And ouyr the gat*e* with letteris large iwrowht*e*,
There werė vers iwrete*n*, as me thouȝte,
On eythir *halfe*, of ful gret difference,   125
Of which I schal now seyn the pleyn sentence.

' Thorw me men gon in to that blysful place
Of hertis hele & dedly woundis cure;
Thorw me men gon onto the welle of grace,
Theere grene & lusty May shal euere endure;   130
This is the weye to al good auenture;
Be glad, thow redere, & thyn sorwe ofcaste
Al opyn am I; passe in & sped the faste.'

' Thorw me men gon,' than spak that othir side,
' Onto the mortal strokis of the spere 135
Of whiche Disdayn & Daunger is the gyde,
Ther neuere tre shal freut ne leuys bere;
This strem ʒow ledith to [the] sorweful were
There as the fisch in prysoun is al drye;
Th'eschewing is only the remedye.' 140

f483r These wers of gold & blak iwretyn were,
Of whiche I gan astonyd to beholde;
For with that on encresede ay myn fere,
And with that othir gan myn hertė bolde;
That on me hette; that othir dede me colde: 145
No wit hadde I, for errour, for to chese,
To entre or flen, or me to saue or lese.

Right as betwixsyn adamauntis two
Of euenė myʒt a pece of yryn set
Ne hath no myʒt to meuė too ne fro— 150
For what that on may hale, that othir let—
Ferde I, that nystė whethir me was bet
To entre or leue, til Affrycan, myn gide,
Me hente, & shof in at the gatis wide,

And seyde, ' It stant iwrityn in thyn face 155
Thyn errour, though thow telle it not to me;
But dred the not to come in to this place,
For this writyng is nothing ment bi the,
Ne by non but he Louys serwaunt be:
For thow of loue hast lost thyn tast, I gesse, 160
As sek man hath of swet & byttyrnesse.

But nathėles, althow that thow be dulle,
ʒit that thow canst not do, ʒit mayst thow se.
For manye a man that may nat stonde a pulle,
ʒit likyth hym at wrastelyng for to be, 165
And demyn ʒit wher he do bet or he.
And if thow haddist cunnyng for t'endite,
I shal the shewė mater of to wryte.'

With that myn hand he tok in his anon,
Of whiche I confort kaughte, & *wente in* faste.   170
But Lord, so I was glad & wel begoon!
For oueral where that I mynne eyen caste
Were treis clad with leuys that ay shal laste,
Eche in his kynde, of colour frosch & greene
As emeroude, that *ioyė* was to seene.   175

f483v   The byldere ok & ek the hardy assh,
The pilere elm, the cofere vnto carayne;
The boxtre pipere, holm to whippis lasch;
The saylynge fyr, the cipresse deth to pleyne;
The shetere ew, the asp for shaftys pleyne;   180
The olyue of pes, & ek the dronkė vyne;
The victor palm, the laurer to deuyne.

A gardyn saw I, ful of blosmy bowys,
Vpon a reuer, in a grenė mede,
There as swetnesse eueremore inow is,   185
With flouris whitė, blewė, ʒelwe & rede,
And coldė wellė-stremys, nothyng dede,
That swemyn ful of smalė fischis liʒte,
With fynnys rede & skalis syluyr-bryʒte.

On euery bow the bryddis herde I synge   190
With voys of aungel in here armonye;
So besyede hem here bryddis forth to brynge.
The litele conyes to here pley gunne hye;
And ferthere al aboute I gan aspye
The dredful ro, the buk, *the* hert & hynde,   195
Squyrelis, & bestis smale of gentil kynde.

Of instreumentis of strengis in acord
Herde I so pleye, & rauyshyng swetnesse,
That God, that makere is of all & lord,
Ne herdė neuere betyr, as I gesse.   200
Therwith a wynd—onethe it myght be lesse—
Made in the leuys grene a noysė softe
Acordaunt to the *foul*is song alofte.

The eyr of that place so attemprė was
That neuere was greuaunce of hot ne cold;   205
There wex ek euery holsum spice & gras;
No man may waxė therė sek ne old,
Ʒit was there ioyė more a thousentfold
Than man can telle, ne neuere wolde it nyghte,
But ay cler day to ony manys syghte.   210

f484r   Vndyr a tre, besyde a welle, I say
Cupide, oure lord, hise arwis forge & file,
And at his fet his bowe al redy lay,
And Wil, his doughtyr, temperede al this whyle
The heuedis in the welle, & with hire wile   215
She touchede hem, aftyr they shuldė serve
Some for to sle, & some to wounde & kerve.

Tho was I war of Plesaunce anonryght,
And of Aray, and Lust, & Curteysie,
And of the Craft that can & hath the myght   220
To don be force a wight to don folye
(Disfigurat was she, I nyl nat lye);
And by hemself, vndyr an ok, I gesse,
Saw I Delyt, that stod with Gentilesse.

I saw Beutė withoutyn ony atyr,   225
And Ʒouthė ful of game & iolyte;
Foolhardynesse, Flaterye & Desyr,
Messagerye & Meede & oþer thre—
Here namys shul not here be told for me—
And vpon pileris greete of iasper longe   230
I saw a temple of bras ifounded stronge.

Aboute the temple daunsedyn alwey
Wemen inowe, of whichė some ther weere
Fayre of hemself, & some of hem were gay;
In kertelis, al discheuele wente they there;   235
That was here offys alwey, Ʒer be Ʒeere.
And on the temple of dowis white & fayre
Saw I sittynge manye an hunderede peyre.

Byfore the temple dore ful sobyrly
Dame Pes sat with a curtyn in hire hond,   240
And by hire sydė, wondyr discretly,
Dame Paciencė syttynge there I fond,
With facė pale, vpon an hil of sond;
And aldirnex, withinne & ek withoute,
Byheste & Art, & of here folk a route.   245

f484v   Withinne the temple, of sykys hoote as fuyr,
I herde a swow that gan aboutė renne,
Whiche sikis were engenderede with desyr,
That madyn euery auter for to brenne
Of newė flaume, & wel espyed I thenne,   250
That al the cause of sorwe that they drye
Cam of the bittere goddesse Ielosye.

The god Priapus saw I, as I wente,
Withinne the temple in souereyn placė stonde,
In swich aray as wan the asse hym shente   255
With cri be nyghte & with [his] septure in honde.
Ful besily men gunne asaye and fonde
Vpon his hed to sette, of sundery hewe,
Garlondis ful of froschė flourrys newe.

And in a priuė corner in desport   260
Fond I *Ven*us & hire porter Richesse,
That was ful noble & hautayn of hyre port.
Derk was that place, but aftyrward lightnesse
I saw a lyte—vnnethe it myȝte be lesse—
And on a bed of gold sche lay to reste,   265
Tyl that the hotė sunnė gan to weste.

Hyre giltė heris with a goldene thred*e*
Ibounden were, vntr*e*ssede as sche lay,
And nakyd from the brest vp to the hed*e*
Men myȝthe hyre sen, & sothly for to say,   270
The remenaunt was wel keuerede to myn pay
Ryght with a subtyl couercheif of valence;
Ther *w*as no thikkere cloth of no defense.

The placė ʒaf a thousent sauouris sote,
And Bacus, god of wyn, sat hire besyde,   275
And Ceres next, that doth of hungir boote,
And as I seyide, amyddis lay Cypride,
To wham on kneis two ʒongė folk there cryede
To ben here helpe; but thus I let hyre lye,
And ferthere in the temple I gan espie,   280

f485r That in dispit of Dyanė the chaste,
Ful manye a bowe ibroke hyng on the wal
Of maydenys swiche as gunne here tymys waste
In hyre seruyse; *and* peyntede oueral,
Ful manye a story, of whiche I touchė shal   285
A fewe, as of Calyxte & Athalante,
And manye a mayde of whiche the name I wante.

Semyramus, Candace, & Hercules,
Biblis, Dido, Thisbė & Piramus,
Tristram, Isaude, Paris, & Achilles,   290
Eleynė, Cliopatre, & Troylus,
Silla, & ek the modyr of Romulus:
Alle these were peyntid on that othir syde,
And al here loue, & in what plyte they dyde.

Whan I was come aʒen into the place   295
That I of spak, that was so sote & grene,
Forth welk I tho, mynseluyn to solace.
Tho was I war wher that ther sat a queene,
That as of lyght the somer sunnė shene
Passith the sterre, right so ouer mesure   300
She favrere was than ony creature.

And in a launde, vpon an hil of flouris,
Was set this noble goddesse [of] Nature;
Of braunchis were here hallis & here bouris
Iwrought after here cast & here mesure,   305
Ne there was foul that comyth of engendrure,
That they ne werė prest in here presence,
To take hire dom, & ʒeue hire audyence.

For this was on seynt Valentynys day,
Whan euery bryd comyth there to chese his make 310
Of euery kyndė that men thynkė may,
And that so heuge a noysė gan they make,
That erthe & eyr & tre & euery lake
So ful was, that onethė was there space
For me to stonde, so ful was al the place.   315

f485v   And right as Aleyn in the *Pleynt of Kynde*
Deuyseth Nature *of* aray & face,
In swich aray men myghte hire therė fynde.
This nobil empéressė, ful of grace,
Bad euery foul to take his owenė place,   320
As they were wonyd alwey from ȝer to ȝeere,
Seynt Valentynys day, to stondyn theere.

That is to seyn, the foulis of rauyne
Were heyest set, & thanne [the] foulis smale
That etyn as hem Nature wolde enclyne,   325
As werm or thyng [of whiche] I telle *no* tale;
And watyrfoul sat loueste in the dale;
But foul that lyuyth be sed sat on the grene,
And that so fele that wondyr was to sene.

There myghtė men the ryal egle fynde,   330
That with his sharpė lok persith the sunne,
And othere eglis of a lowere kynde,
Of whiche that clerkis wel deuysė cunne;
Ther was the tiraunt with his federys dunne
And grey, I mene the goshauk, that doth pyne   335
To bryddis for his outrageous rauyne;

The gentyl facoun, that with his feet distraynyth
The kyngis hand; the hardy sperhauk eke,
The quaylis foo; the merlioun that paynyth
Hymself ful ofte the larkė for to seke;   340
There was the douuė with hire eyen meke;
The ielous swan, aȝens his deth that syngith;
The oule ek, that of deth the bodė bryngyth;

The crane [the] geaunt, with his trompis soun;
The thef the *choughe*, & ek the iangelynge pye;   345
The skornynge iay, the elis fo, heroun;
The falsé lapwynge, ful of trecherye;
The staré, that the conseyl can bewrye;
The tamé rodok, & the coward kyte;
The kok, that orloge is of thorpis lyte;   350

f486r The sparwé, Venus sone; the nyhtyngale,
That clepith forth the grené leuys newe;
The swalwé, mortherere of the foulis smale
That makyn hony of flouris frosche *of h*ewe;
The wedded turtil, with hire herté trewe;   355
The pokok with his aungelis *federys* bryghte;
The fesaunt, skornere of the cok be nyghte;

The wakyr goos; the cokkow *euere* onkynde;
The popiniay, ful of delicasye;
The draké, stroyere of his owené kynde;   360
The stork, the wrekere of avouterye;
The hoté cormeraunt, of glotenye;
The rauen wys; the crowe wit vois of care;
The thurstil old; the frosty feldéfare.

What shulde I seyn?   Of foulys euery kynde   365
That in this world hath federis & stature
Men myghtyn in that place assemblede fynde
Byfore the noble goddesse [of] Nature;
And eueriche of hem dede his besy cure
Benygnely to chese, or for to take   370
By hire acord, his formel or his make.

But to the poynt; Nature held on hire hond*e*
A formele egle, of shap the gentilleste
That euere she among hire werkis fond*e*,
The most benygné, & the goodlieste.   375
In hire was eueri vertu at his reste
So ferforth, that Nature hireself hadde blysse
To loke on hire, & ofte hire bek to kysse.

Nature, [the] vicayre o the almyghty lord,
That hot, cold, heuy, lyght, moyst & dreye   380
Hath knyt with euené noumberis of acord,
In esy voys began to speke & seye,
' Foulis, tak hed of myn centence, I preye,
And for ʒore ese, in fortheryng of ʒoure nede,
As faste as I may speke, I wele ʒow speede.   385

f486v   ʒe knowe wel how, seynt Valentynys day,
By myn statute, & thorw myn gouernaunce,
ʒe comé for to cheese—& fle ʒoure wey—
ʒoure makis, as I prike ʒow with plesaunce;
But natheles, myn ryghtful ordenaunce   390
May I nat *lete* for al this world to wynne,
That he that most is worthi shal begynne.

The ters*el* egle, as that ʒe knowé wel
The foul ryal, aboue ʒow in degre,
The wyse & worthi, secré, trewe as stel,   395
Whiche I haue formyd, as ʒe may wel se,
In euery part, as it best likyth me—
It nedith not his shap ʒow to deuyse—
He shal ferst schese, & spekyn in his gyse.

And aftyr hym by ordere shul ʒe chese,   400
Aftyr ʒoure kyndé, eueriche as ʒow lykyth,
And, as ʒoure hap is, shul ʒe wynne or lese.
But which of ʒow that loué most entrikyth,
God synde hym hire that sorest for hym sykyth.'
And therwithal the tersel gan she calle,   405
And seyde, ' Myn sone, the choys is to ʒow falle.

But nathéles, in this condicïoun
Mot be the choys of euerich that is heere,
That she agre to his eleccïoun,
Who so he be that shuldé be hire feere: 410
This is oure vsage alwey from ʒer to ʒeere,
And ho so may at this tyme haue his grace,
In blisful tyme he cam into this place.'

With hed enclyned, & with humble cheere,
This ryal tersel spak, & tariede noht: 415
'Vnto myn souereyn lady & not myn fere
I chese, & shes with wil & herte & thought,
The formel on ȝoure hond, so wel iwrouȝt,
Whos I am al, & euere wele hire serve,
Do what hire lest, to do me leue or sterve;   420

f 487r   Besekynge hire of merci & of grace,
As she that is myn lady souereyne;
Or let me deyė present in this place.
For certis, longe I may nat lyue in payne,
For in myn herte is korvyn euery veyne.   425
Hauynge reward only to myn trouthe,
Myn deerė herte, haue on myn wo sum routhe.

And if that I to hyre be founde vntrewe,
Dishobeysaunt, or wilful necligent,
Auauntour, or in proces loue a newe,   430
I preye to ȝow, this be myn iugėment,
That with these foulis I be al torent
That ilkė day that euere she me fynde
To hire vntrewe, or in myn gilt vnkynde.

And syn that non louyth hire so wel as I,   435
Al be she neuere of louė me behette,
Thanne ouhtė she be myn thour hire mercy,
For othir bond can I non on hire knette.
Ne neuere for no wo ne shal I lette
To seruyn hire, how fer so that she wende.   440
Say what ȝow leste; myn tale is at an ende.'

Ryght as the froschė redė rosė newe
Aȝen the somyr sunnė coloured is,
Ryght so for shame al wexen gan the hewe
Of this formel, whan she herde al this.   445
She neythir answerde wel, ne seyde amys,
So sore abasht was she, tyl that Nature
Seyde, 'Dooughter, drede the nought, I ȝow
          assure.'

Anothir tersel egle spak anon,
Of lower kynde, [&] seyde, ' That shal nat be!   450
I loue hire bet than ȝe don, be seynt Ion,
Or at the leste, I loue as wel as ȝe,
And longere haue seruyd hire, in myn degre;
And if she shulde a louid for long louynge,
To me *allone* hadde be the gerdonynge.   455

f487v I dar ek seyn, if she me fyndė fals,
Vnkynde, iangelere, or rebel onywise,
Or gelous, do me hangyn by the hals!
And but I berė me, in hire seruyse,
As wel as that myn wit can me suffyse   460
From poynt in poynt, hyre honour for to saue,
Tak the myn lif & al the good I haue! '

The threddė tercel egle answerde tho,
' Now, serys, ȝe seen the lytil leyser heere;
For euery foul cryeth out to ben ago   465
Forth with his mak, or with his lady deere,
And ek Nature hireself ne wele not heere,
For taryinge here, not half that I wolde seye;
And but I speke, I mot for sorwe deye.

Of long seruyse auante I me nothing;   470
But as possible is me to deye today
For wo, as he that hath ben languyssynge
This twenty *wynter*; & as wel happyn may,
A man may seruyn bet, & more to pay,
In half a ȝer, althav it were no moore,   475
Than sum man doth that hath seruyd ful ȝoore.

I sey not this by me, for I ne can
Don non seruyse that may myn lady plese,
But I dar seyn, I am hire treweste man,
As to myn dom, and fayneste wolde hire ese;   480
At shortė wordis, til that deth me sese,
I wele ben heris, *whethir* I wake or wynke,
And trewe in al that hertė may bethynke.'

Of al myn lyf, syn that day I was born,
So gentil ple, in loue or othir thyng,   485
Ne herdė neuere no man me beforn,
Ho that haddė leyser & cunnyng
For to reherse hyre cher & hire spekyng;
And from the morwė gan this spechė laste,
Tyl dounward *went* the sunnė, wondir faste.   490

f488r   The noyse of foulis for to ben delyuered
So loudė ronge—' Haue don & lat vs wende! '—
That wel wende I the wode hadde al tos*h*yuered.
' Cum of! ' they criede, ' Allas, ʒe wele vs sh*e*nde!
Whan shal ʒure cursede pletynge hau*e* an ende?   495
How shulde a iugė eythir partie leue,
For ʒe or nay, withoutyn *ony* preue? '

The goos, the cokkow, & the doke also
So cryedė ' kek kek ', ' kokkow ', ' quek quek ' hye,
That thourw myne erys the noysė wentė tho.   500
The goos seyde, ' Al this nys not worth a flye!
But I can shappe herof a remedie,
And I wele seye myn verdit fayre & swythe
For watyrfoul, ho so be wroth or blythe.'

' And I for wermfoul,' *seyde* the fol kokkowe,   505
' *For* I wele of myn owene autorite
For comun *spede*, tak on [me] *the* chargé *n*owe;
For to delyuere vs is gret charite.'
' ʒe may onbyde a whilė ʒit, perde! '
Quod the turtil; ' If it be ʒoure wille   510
A w*ih*t may speke, hym were as fayr ben stylle.

I am a sedfoul, on the onworthieste,
That wot I wel, & litil of cunnynge;
But bet is that a wyhtis tungė reste,
Than entirmetyn hym of su*c*he doinge,   515
Of which he neythir redė can ne *s*ynge.
And whoso doth, ful foule hymself acloyith,
For offys *vncommytted* ofte anoyeth.'

Nature, which that alwey hadde an ere
To murmur of the lewedenesse [behynde],   520
With facound voys seyde, ' Hold ȝoure tungis
    there!
And I shal sone, I hope, a conseyl fynde,
Ȝow to delyuere & from this noyse vnbynde:
I iuge, of euery folk men shul on calle,
To seyn the verdit for yow foulys alle.'   525

f488v   Assentid were to this conclusïoun
The briddis alle; & foulis of rauyne
Han chosyn fyrst, by playn eleccïoun,
The terselet of the facoun, to diffyne
Al here centence, [&] as hem leste, termyne;   530
And to Nature hym gunne to presente,
And she acceptyth hym with glad entente.

The terslet seyde [thanne] in this manere:
' Ful hard were it to proue by resoun
Who louyth best this gentil formele heere,   535
For euerych hath swich replicacïoun,
That non by skillis may been brought adoun.
I cannot se that argumentis avayle;
Thanne semyth it, there muste be batayle.'

' Al redy! ' quod thise eglis tersels tho.   540
' Nay, seris,' quod he, ' if that I durste it seye,
Ȝe don me wrong, myn tale is not ido.
For, seris—ne takith not agref, I preye—
It may not gon as ȝe wolde in this weye.
Oure is the voys that han the charge in honde,   545
And to the iugis dom ȝe motyn stonde.

And therfore, pes!   I seye; as to myn wit,
Me wolde thynke how that the worthieste
Of knygthod, & lengest hath vsed it,
Most of estat, of blod the gentilleste,   550
Were sittyngest for hire, if that hire leste;
And of these thre she wot hireself, I trowe,
Whiche that he be, for it is light to knowe.'

The watyrfoulis han here hedis leid
Togedere, & of a short auysẻment,   555
Whan euerryche hadde his largẻ golẻ seyd,
They seydyn sothly, al be on assent,
How that the goos with hire facoundẻ gent,
' That so desyryth to pronounce oure nede
Shal telle oure tale,' & preyedẻ God hire spede.   560

f489r And for these watyrfoulis tho began
The goos to speke, & in hire kakelynge
She seydẻ, ' Pes! now tak kep, euery man,
And herkenyth which a resoun I shal brynge!
Myn wit is sharp, I loue no taryinge;   565
I seye I rede hym, thow he were myn brothir,
But she wele loue hym, let hym *loue* anothir! '

' Lo! here a perfit resoun of a goos! '
Quod the sperhauk, ' neuere mot she the!
Lo! sich it is to haue a tungẻ loos!   570
Now perdẻ! fol, ȝit were it bet for the
Han holde thyn pes, than shewed thyn nysete.
It lyth nat in his *wit*, ne in his wille,
But soth is seyd, " a fol can not ben stille ".'

The laughtere aros of gentil foulis alle,   575
And right anon the sedful chosyn hade
The *turti*l trewe, and gunne hire to hem calle,
And preyeden hire to seyn the sothẻ sadde
Of this matere, & axsede what she radde.
And she answerde, that pleynly hire entente   580
She woldẻ shewe, & sothly what she mente.

' Nay, God forbede a louere shuldẻ chaunge! '
The *turti*l seyde, & wex for shame [al] red.
' Thow that his lady eueremore be straunge,
ȝit lat hym serue hire [euer], til he be ded.   585
Forsothe, I preysẻ nat the gosis red;
For thow sche deyede, I wolde non othir make,
I wele ben hires til that the deth me take.'

'Wel bordit!' quod the dokė, 'By myn hat!
That men shul*de* louyn alwey causėles,   590
Who can a resoun fynde or wit in that?
Daunsith he murye that is myrthėles?
Who shuldė rekke of hym *that* is rechėles?
3e, *qu*ek,' 3it sey*de* the doke ful wel & fayre,
'There been mo sterris, God wot, than a payre!' 595

'Now *fy*, cherl!' quod the gentil tersėlet,
'Out of the donghil cam that word ful ri3t!
Thow canst nat seen wh*ich* thyng is wel beset.
Thow farst by loue as oulys don by lyght:
The day hem blent, *ful* wel they sen be nyght.   600
Thyn kynde is of so low a wrechednese,
That what loue is, thow canst no*uþer* seen ne gese.'

Tho gan the kokkow putte hym forth in pres,
For foul that etith werm, & seydė bly*ue*,
'So I,' quod he, 'may haue myn make in pes,   605
I rechė nat how longė that 3e stryue.
Lat eche of hem ben soleyn al here lyue!
This is myn red, syn they may nat acorde;
This shortė lessoun nedith nat recorde.'

'3e, have the glotoun fild inow his paunche,   610
Thanne are we wel!' seydė th*e* merlioun;
'Thow mortherere of the heysoge on the braunche,
That broughte the forth, thow reufulles*t* glotoun!
Leue thow soleyn, werm*is* corupcioun!
For no fors is of lak of thyn nature—   615
Go, lewed be thow, whil the world may dure!'

'Now, pes!' quod Nature, 'I comaundė here!
For I haue herd al 3oure opynyoun,
And in effect 3it be we n*eue*re the nere.
But fynally, this is myn conclusïoun: 620
That she hireself shal han *hire* eleccïoun
Of whom hire lest, who [so] be wroth *or* blythe;
Hym that she chesith, he shal hire han a*s* swithe.

For syn it may nat here discussid be
Who louyth hire best, as seyde the tersélet,   625
Thanne wele I don hire this fauour, that she
Shal han [right] hym on hom hire herte is set,
And he hire that his herte hath on hire knet.
Thus iuge I, Nature, for I may not lye;
To non estat I haue non othir ye.   630

f49or   But as for conseyl for to chese a make,
If I werè Resoun, thanne wolde I
Conseylè ȝow the ryal tersel take,
As seyde the terselet ful skylfully,
As for the gentilleste & most worthi,   635
Which I haue wrought so wel to myn plesaunce,
That to ȝow oughte to been a suffisaunce.'

With dredful vois the formel *hire* answerde,
' Myn rightful lady, goddesse of Nature,
Soth is that I am euere vndyr ȝoure ȝerde,   640
As is *euerych othir* creäture,
And m*u*ste ben ȝoures whil myn lyf may dure;
And therfore graunt*e* me myn ferstè bone,
And myn entent ȝow wele I seyn riȝt sone.'

' I graunte it ȝow,' quod she; & riȝt anon   645
This formel egle spak in this degre:
' Almyghty queen, vnto this ȝer be *d*on,
I axè respit for to avisè me,
And aftyr that to haue myn choys al fre.
This al & sum that I wele speke & seye: 650
Ȝe gete no more, althow ȝe do me deye.

I wele nat seruè Venus ne Cupide
Forsothe as ȝit, be no manerè weye.'
' Now syn it may non othirwise betyde,'
Quod tho Nature, ' heere is no more to seye.   655
Thanne wolde I that these foulis were aweye,
Eche with his make, for taryinge lengere heere! '
And seyde h*e*m thus, as ȝe shul aftyr here:
(2,236)   7

' To ȝow speke I, ȝe tersletis,' quod Nature,
' Beth of good herte, & seruyth allė thre.   660
A ȝer is nat so longė to endure,
And eche of ȝow pey*ne hym* in his degre
For to do wel; for God wot, *quyte* is she
Fro ȝow this ȝer, what aftyr so befalle.
This entyrmes is dressid for ȝow alle.'   665

f 490v And whan this werk al brought was to an ende,
To euery foul Naturė ȝaf his make
By euene acord, & on here weye they wende.
But Lord! the blisse & ioyė that they make!
For ech [of hem] gan othir in wyngis take,   670
And with here nekkis eche gan othyr wynde,
Thankynge alwey the noble *goddesse* of Kynde.

But fyrst were chosyn foulis for to synge,
As ȝer be ȝer was alwey *hyre* vsance,
To synge a roundele at here departynge,   675
To don Naturė honour & plesaunce.
The note, I trowė, makid w*as* in Fraunce;
The wordis werė sweche as ȝe may fynde
The nextė vers, as I now haue in mynde.

' Nowe welcome somor with [thy] sonnė softe, 680
That hast thes wintres wedres ovireshake,
And dreuyne away the longė nyghtes blake!

Saynt Valentyne, that ert ful hye olofte,
Thus syngen smale foules for thy sake,
Nowe welcome somor with thy sonnė softe   685
That hast thes wintres wedres ovireshake.

Wele han they causė for to gladen ofte,
Sethe ech of hem recouerede hathe hys make,
Ful blisseful mowe they *syngė* when they wake,
Nowe welcome somor with thy sonnė softe   690
That hast thes wintres wedres ovireshake
And dreuyne away the longė nyghtes blake! '

And with the shoutyng, whan the song was do,
That foulys madyn at here flyght awey,
I wok, & othere bokys tok me to 695
To reede vpon, & ʒit I rede alwey;
I hope, iwis, to redé so sum day
That I shal meté sum thyng for to fare
The bet, & thus to rede I nele nat spare. 699

Explicit Parliamentum Auium in die sancti

Valentini, tentum secundum

Galfridum Chaucer.

Deo gracias.

TEXTUAL NOTES

2 sharp . . . hard] *so Gg, Ff, J, L; others* hard . . . sharp
5 Astonyith] *Gg, J, L* astonyd
7 flete] *Gg* slete; *F, T, Lt* wakc. —synke] *F, T, Lt* wynke; *H* swynk
9 that] *so Gg, R, Hh, L, H; others omit*
12 Ther] *Gg* that
15 luste] *Gg, L, C* lust &; *S* loue
22 out] *Gg* ofte; *Ff, J, L* omit. —sey] *so Gg, Ff; others* seith
24 fey] *so Gg, Ff; others* feith
26 as] *so Gg, J, Hh, L; others omit*
27 so] *so Gg;* I *J, S, Hh, C; others* hit. —to] *(second) so Gg, D, L;*
    P omits; others so
29 make] *Gg, H, J, Hh, L, R, C* make of
30 Entytlyt] *Gg* Entytlt. —thus] *so Gg, S, C; L* here; *others* there
31 Scipion] *Gg* sothion; *others* Cipion, Scipion
33 therynne] *Gg* thereon (o *changed from* y)
34 it] *so Gg, S, L, Hh; J* of; *others omit*
37 metyth] *Gg* metyh
39 speche] *Gg* spche. —of] *so Gg, Ff, J, L; R omits; others* al
40 betwix] *Gg* betwixsyn; *others have dissyllable.* —that] *so Gg, Ff,*
    H, L; others the
46 seyde] *so Gg, Ff, S; others* seyde hym. —oþer] *so Gg; others* or
47 louede] *so Gg, Ff; others* loueth
50 here] *Gg* now
53 that] *so Gg, Ff; R, H, Hh, L, P, D, C* how; *S* how þat here; *others*
    omit. —worldis] *Gg* wordis
54 Menyth] *Gg, C* Nys; *S* Was; *Hh, L, B* Ment; *J* In
55 dye] *Gg* deye
56 Galaxye] *Gg* galylye; *others* galazie, galoxie, *etc., variously*
57 litel] *Gg omits*
65 And disseyuable, & ful] *Gg* And was sumdel disseyuable & ful;
    Group B and Ff omit disseyuable &; *others* And ful of torment ànd
72 blisse] *Gg* blis
75 shalt] *Gg* shat
76 that] *Gg* this. —to] *so Gg, J; others* into (vnto)
77 of *(second)*] *Gg, J, H, and Group B omit*
78 brekeris] *Gg* brekeis. —seyne] *Gg* seyn
80 þ'erthe] *so Group B; Gg, F* þere; *others* the world
82 than] *Gg* that. —al hire] *Gg* is his
83 come] *Gg* comyn
84 the synde his] *so H, L, C; Gg, Ff* synde vs; *J* sende the his; *P* sende

the; *R* vs sende hys; *S* sende vs all; *Hh* ʒe graunt his; *Group B* sende ech lover

85 faylyn] *Gg* folwyn

88 bed] *Gg, Ff* self

90 which] *Gg, Ff, S, P omit*

91 that (*first*)] *R, C* the; *Gg, Ff, S, and Group B omit*

102 carte is] *so Gg, Ff, J, P; others* cartes

107 byforn] *Gg* byforen

110 to-torn] *Gg* byforn

113 Cytherea] *so F, B, D, S, Hh, C; others* Cythera

114 the] *so F, B, T, S, C; others* thow

119 & ek] *so Gg, Hh; Ff* eke &; *R, H, J, C, L, D, S* hyt and; *P, F, B, T* and. —t'endyte] *so Gg; F, B, P, T* to endyte; *S* to wryte; *others* endyte

122 with] *Gg* of

123 gate] *Gg* gatis. —iwrowhte] *so J; others* iwrowht

124 iwreten] *Gg* iwrete; *others* (i)writen. —thouʒte] *so J; others* thouʒt

125 halfe] *Gg, P* side

132 ofcaste] *Gg* ouercaste; *S* outcaste

133 sped] *Ff, Group B* hye

134 spak] *Gg* spat

137 Ther] *Lt* the; *Gg* that. —tre] *Gg* ʒit

138 the] *Ff* that; *Gg omits*

140 Th'eschewing] *Gg* Ther shewing; *R* In eschuyng

141 iwretyn] *Gg* iwetyn

143 with] *Gg* whi

152 bet] *Gg* best

154 Me] *Chaucer Soc. print of Gg* (*erroneously*) Ne

155 stant] *so Gg, R, H, Hh, P; others* stondeth. —iwrityn] *All MSS have* writyn (writen); *cf.* 1.141

158 is] *Gg* nys

160 tast] *Gg* stat

161 hath] *Gg* hat

162/4 dulle/pulle] *Gg* dul/pul

163 ʒit (*first*)] *so Gg, H, J, Hh; R* Though; *P* It; *C* Yf; *S* And; *others omit*

165 ʒit] *Gg, T, D, Lt* It

166 demyn] *so Gg, S; J* to deme; *others* demyth

167 And] *Gg* And there

168 of to] *Gg, R* for to; *Ff* to; *H* of for to; *S* quhar of

170 wente in] *Gg* that as

175 ioye] *Gg* sothe

183 blosmy] *so H, J, P; Gg* blospemy; *Hh* blossummy; *R, C* blossom(e); *others* blossomed

185 as] *Gg* as ther; *J, Hh, P* as that

186 blewe] *Gg* blewe &

188 li3te] *Gg, J, P* lite

192 So] *so Gg, Ff; Group B* That; *P omits; others* Some

195 the (*third*)] *Gg* &; *F omits*

197 Of (*first*)] *Group B, C* On

203 foulis] *Gg, P* bryddis; *H* soules

204 eyr] *Gg* erthe

205 was greuaunce] *so Gg, Ff, C; Group B* was greuaunce ther; *P* was the greuaunce; *others* was there greuaunce

206 gras] *Gg* gres

214 Wil] *Gg* wel; *S* wele; *H* whill; *T, D, Lt* while; *Ff* whiele; *Hh* omits; *others* wyll(e)

216 touchede] *so C, R, B; S* ordanyt; *others* couchede

221 don] *Group B* goo. —be force] *Gg, Ff, Group B* before

223 hemself] *so Gg; Ff* themself; *others* hymself

227 Foolhardynesse] *Gg, Hh* Foolhardynesse &

232 that . . . daunsedyn] *others* the . . . daunsed

251 al] *Gg, H, D, S* alle. —sorwe] *so Gg, J, P, S; others* sorwes

252 Cam] *so Gg; R, H, Ff* Cometh; *C* Comen; *others* Com(e)

256 his] *Ff* a; *Gg, S* omit. —in] *Gg, Ff, P* in his

259 frosche flourrys newe] *Gg* flourrys frosche & newe

261 Venus] *Gg* febus

262 hautayn] *Gg* hauntayn

267 goldene] *so Gg, Ff; P* golden; *S* silkyn; *others* gold(e). —threde] *Gg, B* thred

268 vntressede] *Gg* vntrussede; *Hh* vntrossed

269 vp to] *so Gg, Ff; J, Hh, D* to; *others* vnto. —hede] *Gg, B* hed

273 was] *Gg* nas

276 Ceres] *Gg* sereis

278 two] *S, F, B* the; *R, H omit; Ff* to. —folk] *R, P, S, F, B, T* folkes. —there] *R, H, S, C, P, Group B omit*

279 hyre] *Gg* hem; *S* thame

284 And peyntede] *Gg* ipeynted were; *Ff* and peynted was

285 Ful] *so Gg, Ff, C; others* Of

286 Calyxte] *Gg* Calyote; *C* Caliste

291 Eleyne] *Gg* Elyne. —Troylus] *Gg* Troylis

294 plyte] *Gg* plyt. —dyde] *Gg* deyde

295 into] *Gg, H, Hh* vnto; *S* to

298 that] *so Gg, Hh; S* as; *others omit*

299 lyght] *Gg* lygh. —somer] *Gg, Ff* someris. —sunne] *Gg* sunnys

303 of] *so J, S, F, B, T; others omit*. (*Cf.* 368, 639, 672)

305 iwrought] *Gg* iwrough. —cast] *so Gg, Ff; C* tast; *others* craft. —mesure] *Gg* mesuris

307 they] *so Gg, Ff, C, R, S; others* there. —were] *Gg* were al

309 Valentynys] *Gg* Volantynys (*also* 322, 386)

313 eyr] *so Gg, Ff; others* see

316 right] *Gg* righ
317 Nature] *Gg* Natur. —of] *Gg, S* in. —array] *so Gg, Ff; others* suche array
320 his] *so Gg, Ff; S, Lt* thair(e); *others* her
324 the] *Gg, S* omit
325 hem] *so Gg; Ff* them; *S* thaire; *J omits; others* that
326 of whiche] *Ff* of such; *Gg omits.* —no] *Gg* myn
327 And] *so Gg, Ff, C; others* But
328 But] *R, H, Hh, Group B* And
335 And] *Gg* A
339 merlioun] *Gg* merilioun. (*Cf.* 611)
342 his] *Gg, Ff, S* hire
344 the (*second*)] *Gg, Ff omit*
345 choughe] *Gg, Ff, J* crowe. (*Cf.* 363)
348 stare] *Gg, S* starlyng. —bewrye] *Gg* bewreye
352 grene] *so Gg, Ff, C; others* fresshe
354 of hewe] *Gg, Ff, D* & newe
356 federys] *Gg* clothis
358 euere] *Gg* most
361 the (*second*)] *so Gg, R, H, J, P; others omit*
363 rauen wys] *so Gg; Ff* ravon; *others* rauyns. —the crowe] *so Gg, Ff; others* (the) crowes. —vois] *so Gg, Ff; others* hyr vois
368 of] *Gg, Ff omit.* (*Cf.* 303, 639, 672)
369 eueriche] *so Gg; Ff, J* euery; *S* sche; *others* eche
372/4 honde/fonde] *Gg, R* hond/fond
379 the] *Gg omits.* —vicayre] *Gg* vicarye
381 with] *so Gg, Ff; others* by. —noumberis] *so Gg; Ff* membris; *S* mesure; *others* nombre
382 began] *Gg* gan for; *Ff* thus bygan; *J* he gan
385 ʒow] *so Gg, Ff, C, Lt; others* me
389 ʒoure] *so Gg, Ff; others* With ʒoure
391 lete] *Gg* breke, *Ff* suffre
393 tersel] *Gg* terslet. —knowe] *Gg* knowe ful
394 above ʒow in] *Gg* abouyn euery
396 Whiche] *so Gg, Ff; H* The; *others* The whiche. —wel] *so Gg, Ff; others omit*
400 ʒe] *Gg, Ff* they
401 ʒow] *Gg* ʒe; *S* him
404 sorest] *Gg* soryest
406 ʒow] *so Gg, J, P, S; others* the
410 Who] *Gg, S* What
414 humble] *R, H, C, S, F, B, D, T* full humble
424 I may] *so Gg, J, S, C; others* may I
426 Hauynge] *Gg, C* And hauynge. —reward only] *Gg, D* only reward
427 on] *Gg, S, C* of
428 that] *so Gg; others omit*

432 I be] *Gg* be I
434 vntrewe] *Gg* vntrere
435 non louyth hire] *Gg* hire louyth non
436 Al be] *Group B* Although. —she] *Gg* it that he; *S* it she; *P, C*
that she. —neuere of loue me] *Gg* me neuere of loue; *Lt* of loue
she me neuere. —behette] *Gg* beheette
438 knette] *Gg* arette
439 Ne (*first*)] *so Gg, J, C*; *S* ʒit; *Ff* And; *others* For
444 the] *Gg, P* hire
447 abasht] *Gg* abashat
448 the] *so Gg, J*; *T* not; *others* ʒow
450 &] *Gg omits.* —shal] *so Gg, Ff, J*; *others* shulde
452 loue] *so Gg, S, C*; *others* loue her
455 allone] *Gg* fullonge; *S* al hole
457 Vnkynde] *Gg* Vnkynde or
460 that] *so Gg*; *others omit*
461 in] *so Gg, Ff, H, T*; *others* to
462 the] *so Gg*; *R, H* ye; *D* els; *others* she
465 ago] *Gg has* agon *with* n *expuncted*
471 But as] *S* For als; *Gg* That. —is] *Gg, J, S* is to
473 wynter] *Gg, C* ʒeer. —as] *so Gg, Ff, J, P*; *others omit*
480 ese] *so Gg, Ff, S*; *others* plese
482 whethir] *Gg* were
490 went] *Gg* drow
493 toshyuered] *Gg* toslyuered
494 criede] *Gg* criedyn. —shende] *Gg* shynde
495 haue] *Gg* hauyn
497 ony] *Gg, S* othir
498 the cokkow & the doke] *so Gg*; *others* the doke and the cukkowe
503 I] *so Gg, C, S*; *others omit*
505 seyde] *Gg* quod
506 For] *Gg* And
507 spede] *Gg, J* profit. —me the charge now] *Gg* no charg howe; *R*
the charge now; *J* on me this *etc.*
511 wiht] *Gg* whit. —fayr] *P, Group B* (*less T*) god; *C* better
514 bet] *so Gg*; *others* better
515 suche] *Gg* suhe
516 synge] *Gg* fynde
518 vncommytted] *Gg* onquit; *Ff* vncommaundet; *J* vnconveyid; *Gg*
at first omitted this line and then added it at the foot of the page
520 behynde] *R, H* blynde; *C* by kynde; *Gg omits*
524 of] *Gg* on
526 were] *so Ff, J, C, Group B*; *others* was
527 foulis] *so Gg, Lt*; *others* the foulis. —rauyne] *Gg* lauyne
530 &] *Gg, R, D omit.* —termyne] *so Ff, C, S*; *others* to termyne
532 acceptyth] *Gg* acceptyh

533 thanne] *Ff, J, P* that; *Gg, S omit*
537 non by skillis may] *so Gg*; Lt skillis noon; *others* by skillis may noon
540 thise eglis tersels] *Gg* this Eglis terslet; *R* this Eglis tarsell; *C* these terselis egles; *S* the tercell egle; *J* thes eglis tarcelettis
543 ne] *so Gg*; *others omit*
545 Oure] *so Gg, C; S* Ȝouris; *others* Our(e)s. —charge] *Gg* charg. —in] *Gg, C, D* on
548 worthieste] *Gg* worthiest
551 sittyngest] *so Gg; S* best sittyng; *others* sittyng. —hire] *Gg* he
553 it] *Gg* here; *D* that
558 gent] *Gg* so gent
560 God] *so Gg, R, J, H; others* to god. —hire] *Gg* hym
561 And] *Gg* As
562 hire] *Gg* his
563 She] *Gg* He
564 brynge] *so Gg; others* forth brynge
567 loue (*second*)] *Gg* take
569 she] *Gg* he
571 ȝit] *Gg* now; *J, S* it
572 shewed] *Gg* shewe; *S* told
573 wit] *Gg* mygh
576 right] *Gg* righ
577 turtil] *Gg* tersel
578 preyeden] *so F, B, D, T; Gg* preyede; *R, Ff, Lt* prayed; *S* preying; *others* preyd(e). —to] *Gg* for to
579 radde] *Gg* rardde
581 shewe] *Gg* it shewe; *C* declare
583 turtil] *Gg* tersel. —al] *Gg omits*
585 euer til] *so Ff, F, R, H, S, C, T; J, B, D, Lt* euir-more tile; *P* til; *Gg* til that
588 hires] *Gg* hire
590 shulde] *Gg* shul
593 Who shulde rekke of hym that] *Ff, H, R, Hh, C, L, J* (shall), *Group B* Who shulde recche of that; *P, S* Who shulde recche of hym that; *Gg* What shulde I rekke of hym that
594 Ȝe quek] *Ff, H, Hh, C, L, J, F, B, Lt, T* Ȝe queke; *Gg* kek kek; *R* Ee kekyll; *S, D* Ȝa (Ye) queke queke; *P* Yet quek. —ȝit] *so Gg, Ff, H, S; others omit.* —seyde] *Gg* scith; *P, F, B* quoth (quod); *T omits*
596 fy] *Gg* sey; *R* sygh. —terselet] *Gg* terslet
598 which] *Gg, S* what
600 ful] *Gg* but; *C omits.* —nyght] *Gg* nygh
602 nouþer] *Gg, C* nat
604 blyue] *Gg* blythe
611 the] *Gg* thanne a

613 reufullest] *Gg* reufulles; *P* rowthfull; *others* rewfull
614 wermis] *Gg* werm
616 whil the] *Gg* whil that the
619 neuere] *Gg* not
621 hire] *Gg, C* the
622 who so] *Gg* & who. —or] *Gg* &
623 as] *Gg* a
624 syn] *so Gg; J* sithens; *others* sith
625 seyde] *Gg* seyth. —terselet] *Gg* terslet
627 right] *Gg omits*
628 knet] *Gg* knyt
629 Thus] *so Gg, J; others* this
630 ye] *Gg* eye
632 I] *so Gg, P, Group B; others* hit. —thanne] *Gg* certis thanne
637 to ʒow] *so Gg, C; R, H* hit to ʒow; *B* it (ought to be) to ʒow; *others* to you it
638 hire] *Gg* tho; *P* omits
640 is] *Gg* ist
641 euerych othir] *Gg* anothir lyuis; *J* eny othir; *C* euerych ylk
642 muste] *Gg* mot. —ʒoures] *Gg* ʒoure. —myn] *Gg, Ff* that myn
643 graunte] *Gg* grauntyth; *R, H, Ff, T, D* graunt
644 ʒow wele I] *so Ff, P, F, T; Gg* that wele I; *B* I shal yow; *others* I wyll yow. —riʒt] *Gg* wol; *R omits*
645 riʒt] *Gg* that
647 don] *Gg* gon
650 This] *so Gg, Ff, F, B; others* This is
655 tho] *so Gg, H; others omit*
658 hem] *Gg* hym; *Ff* omits
661 is] *Gg* ne is
662 peyne hym] *Gg* peignynge
663 quyte] *Gg* what
664 Fro] *Gg, P, T, D* For
665 for] *so Gg, J, C; others* fro(m)
669 But] *so Group A, F, B; others* And
670 of hem] *Gg omits.* —wyngis] *Gg, Ff, H, Lt* his wyngis
672 goddesse] *Gg* queen
674 hyre] *Gg* the
676 Nature] *Gg* to Nature
677 trowe] *Gg, Ff, R, H, B* trow. —makid] *Gg* imakid; *R, J, Lt, Ff, C, D* made. —was] *Gg* were
678 fynde] *so Gg; others* here fynde
680–92 *Only complete in Gg, though in different later fifteenth-century hand. Some lines in J, D; others omit. Lines in italics represent reconstructed form, following Skeat*
680 thy] *so D; Gg, J omit*
682 longe] *so J, D; Gg* large

684 smale] *Gg* smal
689 synge] *so J, D*; *Gg* ben
694 That foulys] *R, Lt*, The foulys; *Gg* That the foulys
697 I] *Gg* In
699 nele] *so Gg, Ff, T*; *others* wyl

NOTES

1. This well-known proverb goes back ultimately to Hippocrates. Cf. Skeat, *E.E.Prov.*, p. 57, no. 135. See also Introduction, p. 48, for comments on the rhetorical opening.

2–3. Cf.:

> The peyne is hard, out of mesure,
> The joye may eke no while endure.
>
> *(Romaunt, 3279–80)*

The bitter-sweet quality of love is a very frequent commonplace from Ovid onwards. Of several instances known to Chaucer, *De Planctu*, col. 455, and *Romaunt*, 2295ff, are good examples.

7. **flete or synke.** A rhyming tag, found also in *CT*, I, 2397; *Pity*, 110; *Anelida*, 182.

8. After the *BD* Chaucer usually represents himself as an outsider in the affairs of love; cf. *HF*, 628; *Troilus*, i, 16; *ProLGW*, F 490.

10–13. The impossibility of resisting love, its pain, the lordliness and cruelty of the God of Love, and mention of his arrows are all commonplaces of literature about love from Ovid onwards. Cf. *Ars Amatoria*, i, 9; *Metamorphoses*, i, 453; *Remedia Amoris*, 28, etc.; frequent references in religious writers are noted by Rousselot, p. 65ff. For a description of the God of Love, cf. *Romaunt*, 877ff and *ProLGW*, F 226ff, G 158ff.

15ff. The poet's love of books is also mentioned *HF*, 657 and *ProLGW*, 29–39.

22. **As men sey.** See variant readings; *men* could here be a singular, the weakened form of the indefinite pronoun *man=one*, found elsewhere in Chaucer, and so taken here by editors. But in l. 25 *men* must be a plural, as the form of the verb *lere* shows; the parallel between ll. 22 and 25 make a plural form more likely in l. 22. The singular form *seyth* is thus wrong. The readings *men sey*, and *fey* (l. 24), are thus probably instances of the superiority of Gg and Ff in combination against the other MSS. *As men sey* seems to indicate a proverb; no such proverb is recorded, but a ' proverbial flavour ' was an adornment. See Introduction, p. 50. For the image used, apparently found only in Chaucer, cf. *ProLGW*, F 1–36, 73–6.

26. **matere.** The normal word for subject-matter, as opposed to the method of handling it; cf. l. 168.

31. Tullyus, i.e. M. Tullius Cicero, who wrote the ' Somnium Scipionis ', part of the longer *De re publica*. The *De re publica* (partly recovered in 1820) was unknown in the Middle Ages, but the ' Somnium Scipionis ' was preserved in a long commentary upon it by Macrobius. It was particularly valued as an authority on dreams, and was the literary progenitor of a long line of accounts of dreams and visits to the sky. It is referred to in the *Roman de la Rose* (cf. *Romaunt*, 6–10), *BD*, 286,

HF, 916 (each case having 'king Scipion'). It is also referred to in the *Nun's Priest's Tale* (*CT*, VII), 3123-4, by Chanticleer, who attributes the dream of the 'worthy Cipioun' to Macrobius. See Introduction, p. 42, and Appendix III. Gg's form *sothion* was probably due to the scribe reading *ci* of *scipion* as *o*, and the *p* as *þ*, which he then wrote as *th*.

32. The division into chapters varies in different MSS and editions.

47. **comoun profyt,** 'the general good'. *Comune profit* was a phrase often used in the proceedings of contemporary English parliaments. Here, as in the parliamentary sense, it signifies, in Cicero's words, 'saving, helping, enlarging the country'. Cf. *Rot. Parl.*, p. 29, etc.

56. **Galaxye,** the Milky Way, as Chaucer himself explains *HF*, 936-7, thought of here as the path to heaven (cf. Appendix III). See textual variants; the unfamiliar technical name puzzled the scribes. Chaucer's use in *HF* is the earliest instance recorded in *OED*.

57-8. Cf. *Boece* II, pr. 7, 'al the envyrounynge of the erthe aboute ne halt but the resoun of a prykke at regard of the gretnesse of hevene'; and, 'the whiche litel regioun of this world' (*ibid.*). This whole *prosa* of the *Consolation* is based on the Dream of Scipio (which is referred to later) and was probably in Chaucer's thought while summarising the Dream. Cf. l. 65n.

59-63. Cf. Appendix III, where Cicero makes eight moving spheres produce seven notes. The notion of the music of the spheres is common in literature up to Milton's time. It is referred to by Alanus, *De Planctu*, col. 434-5, and by Jean de Meun, *Roman*, ll. 16948ff.

65. **disseyuable.** See textual variants, and Introduction, p. 61. Cicero has no equivalent for l. 65. A further justification for the reading *disseyuable*, referring to the world, may be found in *Boece*, where Fortune is *disceyuable*, and Fortune and 'the world' may easily appear to be the same thing. Thus: *desceyuable hard* Fortune (ii, m.); Fortune's *grace* (e.g. ii, pr. 2). Fortune has a 'proper stablenesse in the chaungynge of hirself' (ii, pr. 1), and the world also 'with stable feyth varieth accordable chaungynges' (ii, m. 8). Finally, to clinch the *disseyuable* nature of this earth, Philosophy sings, 'Cometh alle to gidre now, ye that ben ykaught and ybounde with wikkide cheynes by the *desceyuable delyt* of *erthly* thynges' (iii, m. 10).

67-8. This refers to the Great or Mundane Year, which is the period in which all the heavenly bodies depart from and return to a given position. According to Macrobius, *Commentarium*, ii, 11, 1l, it was 15,000 ordinary years; the *Roman* (l. 16816) makes it 36,000 years.

73-7. Cf. Appendix III. Cicero is here 'christianised'.

78-84. This passage in some ways resembles the doctrine of Purgatory. Macrobius (*Commentarium*, ii, 17, 13-14), like Cicero, considers that the whirling souls eventually reach Paradise (cf. Bennett, *op. cit.*, p. 43).

85-6. Imitated from *Inferno*, ii, 1-3, 'The day was departing, and the dark air released from their toils the souls that are on earth.' Cf. Introduction, p. 45.

90-1. See textual variants. Gg makes the lines octosyllabic. The meaning is no doubt deliberately enigmatic, and is variously interpreted.

Perhaps, ' I had an answer (i.e. the injunction to despise the world) to my wondering about love, which I did not want, and I still had my bewilderment about love.' Cf. Introduction, p. 19. The couplet may, however, be no more than a familiar expression of discontent. It derives from Boethius (*Boece*, iii, pr. 3). Chaucer uses it several times, always in love-poetry. It occurs in expanded form in *Pity*, 99–104 (' I have not what I desire (i.e. the pity of my lady), and I have everything that may make me miserable '), and in the *Complaint to his Lady*, 43–5. Cf. *Anelida*, 203, and *Troilus*, iii, 445.

91. Scan *n'haddè*.

99–105. The theme of this stanza is a commonplace. The same idea occurs near the end of the Dream of Scipio itself, and Skeat and Robinson note many parallels. The stanza itself, however, is translated from Claudian's poem, *De VI Consulatu Honorii Augusti*, ll. 1–10. R. A. Pratt has shown (*Speculum* 22 (1947), 419ff) that part of this poem, including these lines, was used in the *Liber Catonianus* (a well-known medieval school-book) as the preface to Book iii of Claudian's *De Raptu Proserpinae*. The passage would therefore be familiar to those in Chaucer's audience who had had any schooling. The modern text does not differ in any essentials from the medieval text, which is here literally translated :

All desired things which are pondered over with the waking sense, kindly repose brings back to the sleeping mind. The hunter lays his tired limbs upon the bed, yet his mind returns to the wood and to his quarry. Sleep (brings back) lawsuits to judges, and the chariot (*currus*) to the charioteer, and the shadowy turning-point is avoided by the horses of the night : the lover rejoices in what he has stolen, the shipman makes exchange of goods, the miser watchfully grasps at elusive riches, and to sick and thirsty men all-pervading sleep offers in vain sweet draughts from a cool spring.

Chaucer has substituted a knight for the uncourtly shipman or merchant, has shortened some parts, has made the lover's achievement less morally equivocal, and has placed the lover at the climax of the stanza. The whole stanza is artfully placed to justify and emphasise Scipio's dramatic appearance in l. 98, and to heighten the sense of expectation.

102. See textual variants. The version of Gg and Ff and two others has been preferred as closer to the sense of the source. But it is not clear if Chaucer understood the reference to chariot-racing, and *currus* could grammatically be plural.

111. Macrobius concludes his commentary by saying of the Dream, ' Truly it ought therefore to be said that there is nothing more perfect than this work, in which the whole of universal knowledge (*philosophiae*) is contained.'

113. **Cytherea,** a frequent name for Venus. In the *Teseida*, indeed, Boccaccio seems to use it more frequently than the name Venus itself. Chaucer refers here to the planet, under the form of a personification, as l. 117 makes clear, even though in the next line he refers to the ' firebrand ', attributed to mythological Venus in the *Roman* (*Romaunt*, 3705ff). Cf. Introduction, pp. 30. Dante refers to the planet as Citerea (*Purgatorio*, xxvii, 95), seeming ' always burning with the fire of love ' (*ibid.*, 96) and appears to attribute to ' her ' influence a dream. Chaucer

invokes Venus as Cipris, *HF*, 518, and (following Boccaccio) as Venus, *Troilus*, iii, 1ff; cf. especially iii, 41, and iii, 1255ff.

swete. See l. 274n.

With this line the verse takes on a more vigorous note.

114. Cf. *Merchant's Tale*, *CT*, IV, 1777, referring to Venus's firebrand.

117–18. **north-nor-west.** This is the earliest recorded use of the phrase, which is probably to be taken literally and not (as in *Hamlet*, ii, 2, 396) metaphorically. According to Manly in *Studien zur Englische Philologie* 50 (1913), 279–90, Venus is never strictly north-north-west, but may easily be thought to be so when it reaches its extreme northern point. Venus was visible at this point in May in 1374, 1382, 1390. The first date is too early (as pointed out, Introduction, p. 3) for it to be a reasonable date for the composition of the poem. The third date is too late, since the *Parlement* is mentioned as already composed in the first *Prologue to the Legend of Good Women*; and in any case such a date is on stylistic grounds in the highest degree unlikely. We are left with 1382, which fits in well with all that is known of Chaucer's development. Thus it would seem that Chaucer began to write his poem in May 1382, presumably for presentation on St Valentine's Day 1383. It is interesting to note that the fifth Parliament of the reign of Richard II was also in session at Westminster in May 1382, and in great haste to finish.

120. Affrican performs the function of the guide in the love-visions; cf. Appendix I.

122. **grene stone** is usually taken to mean ' mossy stone ', which may be right. But in the *Fablel* (see Appendix I) the enclosing wall is of porphyry and ivory (st. 13) and possibly Chaucer may here have some semi-precious stone in mind. The colour green might also possibly suggest fertility and everlastingness; cf. l. 130, ll. 173–5.

127. **Thorw me men gon** translates Dante's famous and thrice-repeated ' Per me si va . . .' (*Inferno*, iii, 1–3). The sense of the Dante passage is however far different from Chaucer's. ' Through me one goes into the sorrowing city; through me one goes into eternal grief; through me one goes among those who are lost. Justice moved my high Maker. Divine Power, highest Wisdom, primal Love made me. Before me nothing was created that was not eternal, and I endure for ever. Abandon every hope, you who enter.' Dante, moreover, does not describe a double gate. Two gates, through which issued true and false dreams, were described at the exit of Virgil's Hades (*Aeneid*, vi, 893ff). The bitter-sweet, or antithetical, nature of love (cf. above, 2–3n) suggests the contrary nature of the two messages. The earlier part of the *Roman* also has the *pros* and *cons* of love (*Romaunt*, 2289ff, 3295–8).

133. **opyn.** Pronounced as a monosyllable. Chaucer perhaps wrote *ope*.

136. **Disdayn and Daunger** recall the personifications of the *Roman*, where *Daunger* appears, though not *Disdayn*. In the *Roman*, *Daunger* is a ' churl ', who rushes out and rebuffs the lover (cf. *Romaunt*, 3015ff).

138–9. The plight of a lover is compared to a fish in a weir in *Troilus*, iii, 35, and to a fish without water in *Troilus*, iv, 765; in one of the Harley Lyrics the state of mind of an unhappy lover is compared to water in a weir (Sisam, *Fourteenth Century Prose and Verse*, p. 166).

140. A proverbial statement. Cf. *Owl and Nightingale*, l. 176; Skeat, *E. E. Prov.*, p. 57, no. 136.

141. The message of hope was written in gold, that of despair in black. The inscription in Dante was written in a dark colour (*Inferno*, iii, 10).

142. Dante also represents himself as unable to understand (*Inferno*, iii, 12), though Chaucer has a characteristically heightened statement.

154. Affrican treats his charge with less dignity than any other guide treats a poet, except the eagle in *The House of Fame*. However, *shof* had not its modern associations.

155–6. A somewhat similar situation often occurs in the *Divine Comedy*, e.g. *Paradiso*, iv, 10–12 (which is not however verbally close).

159. serwaunt (*w* written for *v*) is as it were the technical name for a man in love, found in Shakespeare and later; cf. *Knight's Tale* (*CT*, I), 1814. Cf. 419n.

161. swet. Cf. 274n.

165. wrastelyng. Although Sir Thopas seems to be mocked for his ability in wrestling (*CT*, VIII, 740) and it is the accomplishment of the Miller (*CT*, I, 548) it may also have been a courtly pastime. Capgrave describes courtiers wrestling and putting the stone (*Life of St Katharine*, EETS 100, 1893, I, l. 763). Compare the court wrestling-match in *As You Like It* (i, ii), where the chief fighter is a lower-class professional, but where courtiers watch the sport, and the nobly-born Orlando actually takes part.

169. Virgil also comforts Dante by taking his hand (*Inferno*, iii, 19). This is the last reference to the guide who, dreamlike, disappears without further mention. But it may be noted that Virgil also leaves Dante after bringing him to the edge of the Earthly Paradise (*Purgatorio*, xxvii, 131), though there it is explained why.

173. The everlasting leaves of the trees have a reminiscence of the paradisal park in the *Roman*, 19949ff, and of the Earthly Paradise of Dante where ' spring is everlasting ' (*Purgatorio*, xxviii, 143).

174. Eche in his kynde. The phrase ' after his own kind ' occurs nine times in Genesis i, in the description of the creation of what became later known as the Earthly Paradise.
    frosch. This peculiar spelling is regular in Gg though not recorded elsewhere. According to *MED*, Chaucer appears to be the first to apply *fresh* to leaves, flowers, etc., and this is the earliest instance, not quoted in *MED*. The usage, however, is not uncommon in the late fourteenth century.

176. Lists of trees are a well-known convention. Skeat and Robinson quote many examples. Lists of names give natural pleasure in poetry, as Homer, Marlowe, Spenser, Milton, and the makers of nursery rhymes all knew. W. H. Auden would make appreciation of lists a test of a true love of poetry (*Making and Judging*, 1956). Chaucer's list here exemplifies the richness of the park, and enables him to make his transition to the garden set within it. The trees are described in terms of usefulness to men; the epithets give energy to the description.

There is a list of trees in the *Roman* (*Romaunt*, 1349ff) which prefaces the description of a garden, in which is the God of Love, with his arrows (*Romaunt*, 1327ff). Boccaccio's garden (cf. 183n) is based on this garden in the *Romaunt*, although Boccaccio does not describe the trees. Chaucer, when he followed Boccaccio, had also the *Roman* (or the Middle English *Romaunt*) in mind (cf. 186n).

176. byldere ok. Original. **hardy assh,** '*fraxinus audax*' in Joseph of Exeter's *Iliad* (a book also drawn on in the *Troilus*), i, 509. One epithet is literary; the other derives from everyday knowledge and use.

177. pilere elm. The epithet is original, but there are many references in Latin literature to the elm supporting the vine.
cofere vnto carayne, original; coffins were usually made of elm.

178. boxtre pipere, *cantatrix buxus.* See Joseph, *ibid.* But box was still used for pipes or horns in Chaucer's day; cf. *Nun's Priest's Tale* (*CT*, VII), 3398.
holm to whippis lasch. Original.

179. saylynge fyr. Cf. *apta fretis abies,* 'fir suitable for the sea' (for masts), of Claudian, *De Raptu Proserpinae,* ii, 107.
cipresse deth to pleyne, *cupressus flebilis,* in Joseph, *ibid.,* 505. But the association of the cypress with death is familiar in literature.

180. shetere ew. Original. The yew is also Chaucer's own addition in the *Romaunt* (1385).
asp for shaftys pleyne. Original.

181. olyue of pes, *oliua conciliars,* Joseph, *op. cit.,* 506.
dronke vyne, *ebria vitis,* Joseph, *ibid.,* 510.

182. victor palm. An obvious commonplace, but cf. Ovid, *uictoris praemia palmae* (*Met.* x, 102), copied by Boccaccio, *Teseida,* xi, 24.
laurer to deuyne, *interpres laurus,* Joseph, *op. cit.,* 505, and *venturi praescia laurus, De Raptu Proserpinae,* ii, 109. For the details of this tree list see R. K. Root, *MP* **15** (1917–18), 1ff, and R. A. Pratt, *PMLA* **62** (1947), 598ff. See also Curtius, *European Literature and the Latin Middle Ages,* p. 195.

183–294. Partly translation, partly adaptation, from *Teseida,* vii, 51–66; see Appendix V and Introduction, pp. 43.

183. blosmy. See textual variants. Chaucer uses **blosmy** elsewhere only in *Troilus,* ii, 821, and *Merchant's Tale* (*CT*, IV), 1463, which are the only instances recorded in *OED* before Coleridge. The word gave the scribes some trouble, because they did not recognise it. Gg's rendering has a characteristic and inexplicable oddity.

186. ʒelwe is applied to flowers in the *Romaunt,* 1433 (in which the garden noted above, l. 176n, is being described), and which was consciously or unconsciously in Chaucer's mind as he translated and adapted Boccaccio. Yellow flowers are however also mentioned in *CT*, I, 1929, signifying jealousy, and by Dante in his description of the Earthly Paradise (*Purgatorio,* xxviii, 55); **blewe** may be a reminiscence of the violet and periwinkle mentioned in the *Romaunt,* 1431–2.

191. The comparison of birdsong with the song of angels is probably a commonplace (cf. *Romaunt,* ll. 671–2, and *Owl and Nightingale,* l. 916).

196. gentil. See Glossary and Appendix IV. Chaucer's text of the *Teseida* may have corruptly read *carissimi*.

201–3. The wind and the song of birds may be another reminiscence of Dante: ' A light air, unchanging in itself, struck me on the forehead with no stronger blow than a soft wind, at which the branches, readily trembling, all bent towards that part where the holy mountain casts its first shadow; they did not however part so far from their natural straightness that the little birds ceased to practise all their arts; but singing with full delight in the early hours,' etc. (*Purgatorio*, xxviii, 7–17). This is, however, part of the stock description of the *locus amoenus*; cf. Curtius, *op. cit.*, p. 195.

204–10. This stanza has no counterpart in the *Teseida*, but is made up of reminiscences of the *Roman* and *BD*.

204–5. Chaucer had already written in the *Book of the Duchess*:

> Blew, bryght, clere was the ayr,
> And ful atempre for sothe hyt was,
> For nother to cold nor hoot yt nas.
>
> (340–2)

206. Cf. in the garden of the *Romaunt*, ' Ther was eke wexyng many a spice ' (1367), and a list of medicinable spices follows. Medieval gardens and flowers were valued for their medicinal and culinary uses as well as their beauty; spices were the most precious plants, and were thought to have the richest scents. Cf. *Pearl*, ed. E. V. Gordon (1953), ll. 43–4, and note thereto, which has many references.

207. After drinking from the well of the paradisal park of the *Roman* it is said that ' they will live just as they wish, without being ill or dead ' (ll. 20396–7).

208. The same sentiment as quoted in 207n occurs a little later in the *Roman*, and the further comment is added, ' thus they go in joy ' (l. 20655).

209–10. In the paradisal park of the *Roman*, ' Night is never born there, so that there is only one day alone; but there is no evening, nor can morning begin.' The passage goes on at some length, and refers to the ' eternal springtime ' of the park (ll. 20001–36).

209. nyghte. This meaning of the verb is first recorded by *OED* in *Troilus*, v, 515.

211. In the *Teseida* there is no tree, but in the *Roman* (l. 1434) the well is under a pine-tree (cf. *Romaunt*, l. 1456), and again, in the paradisal park (l. 20345).

212. Cupide, oure lord. This is the lordly God of Love of the *Roman*, and not the boy of classical or Renaissance mythology. Cf. Introduction, p. 32, and also Cupid's remark in the *Romaunt*, ' Pore men han maad her lord of me ' (5993), though there is no suggestion here that Chaucer is thinking of himself as poor. Cf. also ll. 10–13n above.

214–28. In the corresponding passage in the *Teseida* Boccaccio mentions sixteen personifications (counting *Arts* in st. 55 as one); Chaucer has eighteen, if we count the ' other three ' (228). Chaucer also makes other alterations, as a comparison immediately shows. There is no exact correspondence; Chaucer was not attempting a literal translation. In both texts there is an implication of disapproval.

214. **Wil.** See textual variants, and cf. *Teseida*, vii, 54. Some MSS of the *Teseida* instead of *Voluttà* (Sensual Desire) read *Voluptade* (same meaning) or *Voluntade* (Will). Whichever word was in Chaucer's MS it is clear that a proper noun is wanted to translate it, and that the adverb *wel* (read by Skeat) will not do. If Chaucer wrote *Wil*, Gg's form *Wel* could easily be accounted for by his dialectal preference for *-e-* rather than *-i-*; cf. Glossary s.v. *wele* (will), etc. Chaucer would have recognised the form *Wel*, though it is not usual with him, for he uses it himself, in the prepositional case *welle*, when he needs a rhyme for *telle* (*CT*, I, 3037). However, in the present text the form *Wil* is preferred for clarity and convenience, and because all other occurrences of the word in the poem have *-i-*. The meaning ' carnal desire ' for *wil* in Middle English is well attested and suits Boccaccio's meaning. Cf. R. A. Pratt, *SP* 42 (1945), 745ff; K. Malone, *MLR* 45 (1950), 63; and E. P. Hammond, *MLN* 31 (1916), 121. Cf. also below, l. 573n.

215. **heuedis** is a dissyllable.
wile, ' file '. In Gg's dialect *f-* apparently became voiced to *v-*, and Gg here as elsewhere wrote *w* for *v*.

216. **touchede.** See textual variants; *c* and *t* are easily confused in the script of this period. It is curious, however, that only three MSS, of which none is remarkably good, have preserved what seems to be the correct reading; I can find no meaning for *couchede* (the reading of most MSS including Ff and Gg) when used with ' file '.

217. The two types of arrows of the God of Love as described by Ovid (*Met*. i, 468–71), and many others, are gold (causing love), and lead (causing hatred). These appear in the *Roman* (*Romaunt*, 937ff). But the distinction Chaucer has in mind derives from the non-Ovidian remarks, in the same passage of the *Roman*, to the effect that the arrows of gold, e.g. that called Faire-Semblaunt, inflict less grievous wounds than others. For the effect of these see *Romaunt*, 1715ff.

220. **Craft.** Boccaccio has a plural, *Arts*, by which, as he explains in the *Chiose*, he means magical arts. But Chaucer perhaps means no more here than ' skill ' in the bad sense of ' cunning ', employment of wiles to gain love. ' Craft ' was sometimes used in contrast to ' nature ', for example in Trevisa's translation (*c*.1400) of the *De Proprietatibus Rerum* of Bartholomaeus Anglicus, published 1535 and 1582, Book IV, Chapter vii.

221. **To don be force.** See textual variants. That the reading of all MSS of the A group except Gg and Ff is correct is proved by reference to the *Teseida* (see Appendix IV). The full reading of the B group of MSS is *to go before*, where some common ancestor having misread *be force* as *before* has altered the previous word *don* to *gon* in order to make what seemed better sense. The ancestor of Gg and Ff similarly mistook *be force* for *before*, but Gg has preserved the correct *don* and shown his general adherence to the A group and the superior reading.

222. **Disfigurat** corresponds to Boccaccio's *sfigurate*, and, according to *OED*, is a nonce-word.

225. Not quite as Boccaccio describes her. Cf. my ' Ideal of Feminine Beauty ', *MLR* **50** (1955), 259.

I saw Beute withoutyn ony atyr. Boccaccio merely says she was without any adornment (*Teseida*, vii, 56, p. 138 below). Chaucer is probably thinking here unconsciously of the personification of Beauty in the *Roman* (ed. Langlois, ll. 989ff, corresponding to what is probably Chaucer's own translation, *Romaunt*, ll. 1006ff). In the *Roman* Beauty is described as being bright as moonlight, her flesh tender, her face the colour of lily and rose; she is slim, and her yellow hair reaches to her heels. Medieval sculpture sometimes (e.g. at Moissac) shows Eve naked but covered entirely with her own hair, and probably Beauty is so thought of in the *Roman* and in the *Parlement*. In the *Roman* it is also said that she uses no make-up, and in the *Romaunt* it is further added that she does not pluck her eyebrows.

228. A good example of Messagerye and Meede (which are not mentioned by Boccaccio) is to be found in Absolon's wooing of Alison in the *Miller's Tale* (*CT*, I, 3375). Note particularly the contemptuous implication in such a line as, ' And, for she was of toune, he profred meede ' (*CT*, I, 3380). Bennett (*op. cit.*, p. 89) suggests that the *other thre* may refer to the three Graces, associated with Venus.

230–1. **pileris . . . of iaSper . . . temple of bras.** Chaucer has substituted jasper for Boccaccio's copper columns, and has made the *whole* temple of brass. In so doing he has increased the richness of the picture. Elaborate descriptions of temples and palaces are found in the French love-visions and in earlier Latin poetry; for example, Claudian in the *Epithalamium de Nuptiis Honorii Augusti* describes in detail the palace of Love, which is built of precious stones and gold, and whose thresholds are of jasper. Another elaborate description which may have been unconsciously in Chaucer's mind is the description of the New Jerusalem (Rev. xxi), where the ' building of the wall ' and the ' first foundation ' are of jasper.

In the Middle Ages all precious stones were thought to have special powers, and of jasper among other qualities it is recorded in the London Lapidary that whoever looks at it before daylight shall describe dreams (*English Lapidaries*, EETS 190, p. 23).

Brass was thought of as being much the same as copper (for what the Middle Ages called brass was the alloy of copper and tin which we now call bronze). R. A. Pratt shows (*SP* **42** (1945), 745ff) that there was some confusion between brass and copper. So although copper is usually the metal of Venus, as in the *Teseida*, and in *HF*, 1486–7 and *CT*, VIII, 829, *bras* may equally be regarded as the metal of Venus. There is precedent for a goddess's temple made of brass in *Aeneid*, i, where Juno's temple is made of *aes* (modern copper or bronze). Chaucer's *bras* would have been a perfectly good translation for *aes*. Notice that the *bras* is not a substitute for Boccaccio's copper columns (for which Chaucer has columns of jasper) but an additional detail.

232. See textual variants. This is a fascinating example of how Gg can be unique and right. All normal textual theory would encourage the reading of all the other MSS, which was in fact adopted in the first edition of this book. *Daunsedyn* is an almost unique form. But Gg's reading is made likely by the fact that *daunseden* actually occurs in *The Cuckoo and the Nightingale* (ed. Skeat, *Supplement to the Works of Geoffrey Chaucer*, 1897), l. 77.

Its occurrence in this poem which is much influenced by the *Parlement* and was probably written by an associate of Chaucer's, Sir John Clanvowe, who died in 1391 (see Kittredge, *MP* **1** (1903)), authenticates Gg's form and suggests that the line may well be better read

Aboute the temple daunsedyn alwey.

Gg's line is also more pleasingly metrical and helps to confirm the belief that Chaucer wrote metrical, not stumbling, verse.

233. Wemen inowe. The *Teseida* has youths as well.

234. gay probably refers to their clothing (cf. *Teseida*, st. 57, and the reference to the Knight, *CT*, I, 74), but it could be taken in its usual sense.

235. discheule. This is the earliest recorded instance of the word. In the *Romaunt*, 776–9, when two damsels ' full of semelyhede ' are dancing, they go ' faire tressed every tresse '. In the *Parlement* the dancers are not so seemly.

237. dowis has *w* for *v*. Doves were traditionally associated with Venus, being considered lecherous. This dove is the *culver*, not the same as the turtle dove; cf. l. 341n.

243. hil of sond. Chaucer's addition. It perhaps symbolises an insecure foundation (cf. Matt. vii:26) and barrenness, the implication being that the patience of a lover who is a follower of Venus will not necessarily lead to success, or if it does, success is barren.

246–52. Cf. *Knight's Tale* (*CT*, I, 1918ff), which is a more summary treatment of the temple of Venus, giving it a different signification.

253–9. Chaucer has expanded the reference to Priapus in the light of the passage in Ovid (*Fasti*, i, 415ff). ' But crimson Priapus, glory and guard of gardens, lost his heart to Lotis. . . . [*He crept up to her when all were asleep*]. . . . He joyed, and drawing from off her feet the quilt, he set him, happy lover! to snatch the wished-for hour. But lo, Silenus' saddle-ass, with raucous weasand braying, gave out an ill-timed roar! The nymph in terror started up, pushed off Priapus, and flying gave the alarm to the whole grove; but ready to enter the lists of love the god in the moonlight was laughed at by all (*at deus obscena nimium quoque parte paratus/omnibus ad lunae lumina risus erat*).' Translated by J. G. Frazer, *Fasti* (1929), i, 29.

259. The garlands are Chaucer's own addition. ' Chaplets of flowers are much more frequently mentioned than chaplets of leaves, and were associated regularly with festivals of light love. Venus and Cupid are generally represented as crowned with roses ' (G. L. Marsh, *MP* **4** (1906–7), 155, where many references are given).

261. The usual porter (following the *Roman*) is Idleness. Cf. *Romaunt*, l. 593. The next three stanzas are transposed from their place in the *Teseida*. See Introduction, p. 44.

266. The ' timeless ' nature of park and garden is forgotten here as in l. 490. Such minor inconsistencies are not noticed in poetry that is primarily meant to be heard.

272. subtyl. This seems to be the earliest recorded instance in this sense, but Wyclif is also quoted with the same usage in 1382.

valence. This, and a quotation from Lydgate (c. 1430), are the only two instances quoted in *OED*, which shows no connection with modern English *valance*.

couerchief. A dissyllable.

274. sote. In the fourteenth century *sote* (*var*. s(w)o(o)te) is normally used to describe smells and ' nature ' (i.e. showers, grass, leaves, air, etc.) and is occasionally used in the sense of ' gentle ', ' agreeable '; its general sense is therefore ' fragrant and agreeable ' *Swete* is not used in such çases. *Sote* is very rarely used of taste or noise, and never of the gracious or beloved qualities of persons, for which *swete* is used. (Cf. J. H. Fisher, *JEGP* **50** (1951), 326ff). Of Chaucer's 170 uses of the word *swete*, 97 refer to persons.

275–6. Terence's proverb ' Without Ceres and Bacchus (Libero) Venus is cold ' (*Eunuchus*, iv, v, 732), was employed by Fulgentius in the sixth century in the description which set the stamp on the ' mythological Venus ' for the rest of the Middle Ages. See Introduction, p. 30.

277. Cypride. Another name for Venus, deriving from her worship in Cyprus. Among others, Alanus uses it in e.g. *De Planctu*, col. 457.

281. Perhaps scans

$$\text{That in dispit} \mid\mid \text{of Dyanè the chaste.}$$

Dyane = Diana.

283–94. The list of lovers whom love brought to grief is a favourite commonplace of medieval writers. Chaucer uses it several times, e.g. *HF*, 388ff. *LGW* is itself an expansion of the *topos*, but cf. also *ProLGW*, F 249ff. Among those which Chaucer certainly knew is a list by Machaut in *Le Dit dou Lyon* (which may be the source of Chaucer's lost work, ' the book of the Leoun ', mentioned in the Retractations to the *Canterbury Tales*), ll. 1315ff); a list by Froissart in the *Paradys d'Amour* (of which Chaucer borrowed the opening lines in the *Book of the Duchess*), ll. 971ff; and the celebrated list by Dante, *Inferno*, v, 58–69. With the list in the *Teseida* Chaucer has combined Dante's list, and other reminiscences of his reading. His list is more miscellaneous and less unified than Boccaccio's, though it still illustrates the disastrous effects of love.

286. Calyxte. According to Ovid (*Fasti*, ii, 156ff and *Met*. ii, 409ff) she was one of Diana's maidens who was raped by Jupiter, bore a son, incurred Diana's rage, was turned into a bear by the equally angry Juno, and was finally stellified by Jupiter. She is the ' woful Calistopee ' of *Knight's Tale* (*CT*, I), 2056ff.

Athalante. She is the Atalanta famous for running. She appears here, however, because she and her husband committed a crime by making love in a sacred place and were turned into lions. Cf. *Met*. x, 560ff.

287. manye a mayde was perhaps suggested by Boccaccio's reference to ' that other haughty one ' whom Boccaccio does not name (she was another Atalanta); Boccaccio's oblique reference defeated Chaucer, who could have found her story in *Metamorphoses*, viii, 318ff.

288. Semyramus. Chaucer probably interpreted Boccaccio's reference in the light of Dante's account, where it is told that she led so vicious a life that she made a law condoning sexual licence, to remove the blame she was incurring. In the *Chiose* Boccaccio tells that she committed incest with her son. I have not been able to see L. Samuel, ' Semiramis in the Middle Ages ', *Medievalia et Humanistica* (Boulder, Colorado) 2 (1944), 32.

Candace. Ovid's Canace, who loved her brother, bore a child to him, and was made to kill herself by her father; cf. *Heroides*, xi. Gower tells the story (*Confessio Amantis*, iii, 143ff). Chaucer mentions the tale with disgust (*CT*, II, 78–9). Canace is not mentioned in any of the possible immediate sources of this passage, and may have occurred to Chaucer in association with the incest of Semiramis or Biblis. Her inclusion is another clear indication of the disastrous nature of love in the temple of Venus.

Hercules. Not in the *Teseida*. He fell in love with Iole. In order to win him back his wife Deianira sent him the shirt of Nessus, believing it to be a love-charm, but it caused him to die in horrible agony. Cf. *Heroides*, ix and *Metamorphoses*, ix, 1ff.

289. Biblis fell in love with her own brother, and when repulsed went mad. Cf. *Metamorphoses*, ix, 453ff.

Dido. Not in the *Teseida*. She loved Aeneas, and when deserted by him killed herself. Cf. *Aeneid*, iv; *Heroides*, vii. Chaucer tells her story in *HF* and *LGW*. She is mentioned not by Boccaccio or the French writers but by Dante, who describes her as ' she who broke faith with the ashes of Sicheus ' (her husband) (*Inferno*, v, 62, developed from *Aeneid*, iv, 552).

Thisbe and Pyramus loved each other, but their parents forbade their marriage. Pyramus, mistakenly thinking Thisbe dead, killed himself: Thisbe, finding his body, also killed herself. Chaucer found the story in Ovid, *Metamorphoses*, iv, 55–166, and tells it in *LGW*.

290. Tristram, Isaude, Paris, & Achilles very often appear in the French poets, and are also mentioned, except for ' Isaude ', by Dante. They are not in the *Teseida*. The tale of Tristram and Isaude (var. Yseult, Isolde) is one of the most famous tragic love-stories of the Middle Ages. A late version of the tale appears in Malory's *Morte Darthur*. Yseult was married to King Mark, Tristram's uncle, but she and Tristram unwittingly drank a love-philtre which made them infatuated. He was eventually killed by Mark.

Paris' seduction of Helen, leading to the siege and destruction of Troy, was a story very well known in the Middle Ages. Chaucer knew the story in Virgil, Ovid, and Benoît de Sainte-Maure's twelfth-century *Roman de Troie*, where Paris's death at Troy is told.

The Middle Ages knew Achilles especially as the lover of Polyxena. Dante says he fought finally with love (*Inferno*, v, 66). Benoît de Sainte-Maure, source of most of the later Middle Ages' knowledge about Troy, relates how bitterly he suffered for love, and how he was treacherously slain by Paris, lured by his love into an ambush (*Roman de Troie*, ed. L. Constans, SATF, 1904–12, 17531ff, especially 21982). Cf. also *Heroides*, iii. Achilles' fate is mentioned by Chaucer (*BD* 1067–71), and by Gower, who has a list of lovers come to a Parliament in the *Confessio Amantis*, viii, 2450ff, where Achilles is described as the' worthy Greek ', ' which for love deide '.

291. Eleyne, Helen. Not in the *Teseida*. She is mentioned by Dante as she ' through whom so many evil years were spent ' (*Inferno*, v. 64–5).

She was known, of course, wherever the story of Troy was known, and medieval writers almost always disapproved of her.

Cliopatre is not in the *Teseida*, and not, as far as I know, mentioned by French poets. Dante calls her the ' lustful Cleopatra '. Her love for Antony led to loss of empire, and to their deaths. Apart from Dante's reference, Chaucer at some time in his life knew her story from Boccaccio's *De Casibus*, or *De Claris Mulieribus*, and he tells it at greater length in *LGW*.

Troylus. Not in the *Teseida* nor in the *Inferno*. He is frequently mentioned by the French poets as a famous lover, whose love brought him to grief. Chaucer tells his story at length in the *Troilus*, based chiefly on Boccaccio's *Il Filostrato*, but using Benoît and other sources.

292. **Silla** (Scylla) appears in no other list of lovers that I know. She betrayed her father and his kingdom for the love of Minos, who repulsed her with horror for her deed. After torments she was changed into a bird; cf. *Metamorphoses*, viii, 6–151. The other, now more famous, Scylla mentioned by Ovid in *Metamorphoses*, xiii–xiv, did not love anyone and is not likely to be referred to here.

the modyr of Romulus, Rhea Silvia, is also unique in a list of this kind, and her presence may suggest that the list was more historical and less ' romantic' to Chaucer than might be imagined. The earliest and fullest note of her story is in Livy (i, 3–4), but Livy was little known in England in the later Middle Ages (cf. F. Wormald and C. E. Wright, *The English Library before 1700* (1958)), and Chaucer shows no other sign of knowing his work. The passing reference to her in *Aeneid*, vii, 660, seems hardly enough to have suggested her presence here. The likeliest source is the third-century *Historiae Philippicae* of Justinus, which was widely read in the Middle Ages, and where Chaucer might also have read of the fates of Semiramis and Dido. Justinus (43, 2, 2) tells how Rhea, being a Vestal virgin, gave birth to the twins Romulus and Remus, of uncertain father. As a punishment she was laden with fetters, which caused her to die. She is thus yet another who suffered disastrously because she broke ' Diana's law ' with unlawful love.

294. Probably suggested by Dante's line referring to those ' whom love parted from our life ' (*Inferno*, v, 69). Their deaths are not mentioned in the *Teseida*. The translation from the *Teseida* finishes here.

295–7. A verbal echo of *Romaunt*, 621–2.

298. It is not true, as shown in the Introduction, that the subsequent part of the *Parlement* is based upon the *De Planctu* of Alanus, though Chaucer owes primarily to Alanus his concept of Nature, and may have taken from Alanus a few hints about the birds (cf. Appendix I). The debate by the birds is based on the French love-visions. Alanus says the birds are depicted upon Nature's garments. For Nature in general, see Introduction, pp. 26ff.

queene. Nature is so called by Alanus, in e.g. *De Planctu*, col. 440, etc.

299–300. This comparison is proverbial. Cf. E. P. Hammond, *English Verse between Chaucer and Surrey*, p. 452. It may, however, be remarked that planets were often, as now, called stars, and that therefore Venus is a star.

302. This is not as Nature is described in the *De Planctu*, though in the *Anticlaudianus* her dwelling-place is upon a mountain.

303. Nature is called a goddess in the *Roman*, l. 16278, etc.

305. **cast.** See textual variants; *cast* seems inherently the better reading, and again shows Gg and Ff in a class apart from other MSS, though C is practically in agreement.

306. **engendrure.** Chaucer excludes, significantly enough, birds which are not normally procreated, as e.g. the phoenix.

309–10. **seynt Valentynys day.** See Introduction, p. 36, and cf. Grandson, *Songe* (Piaget, 139ff and 309ff): ' Such was their custom, every year, at that feast, that each of them, head for head, chose for his mate (*per*) in his own rank, her who best pleased him. And they lived together, equal in heart and love ' (ll. 86–92).

310. Cf. Bartholomew: ' Among all beasts that bee in order of generation, birdes and foules bee most honest of kinde. For by *order of kinde* males seeke females with businesse, and loue them when they be found, and fight and putte them in perill for them, and bee ioyned to them onely as it were by couenant, and wedding loue. . . . And birds and foules gendering keep couenable time: for in springing time, when the generation commeth in, birdes crie and sing, males drawe to companye of females, and desire each other of love ' (f. 175). The famous thirteenth-century encyclopaedia, *De Proprietatibus Rerum*, by Bartholomew the Englishman was translated into English by Trevisa about 1400. Trevisa's version was edited (with some clearly marked additions disregarded here) by Stephen Batman, and printed in 1582, and cited thence here. There is no evidence for or against Chaucer's knowledge of Bartholomew's work, which is cited here and in the following notes as indicative of the possible knowledge of educated men in Chaucer's day. Quotations are all from Bartholomew's Book 12, by folio from the edition cited.

313. **eyr.** See textual variants: *eyr* seems to make better sense. Again, Gg and Ff stand apart from the other MSS and are clearly superior.

316. **Aleyn.** Alanus de Insulis (1128?–1202). He was best known in the later Middle Ages as author of the *Anticlaudianus* and *De Planctu Naturae*, but he was also the author of a number of other, especially theological, works. He was a member of the twelfth-century ' School of Chartres ', notable for its classical learning, its Neoplatonism, and its recognition of the beauty and goodness of creation. Cf. C. H. Haskins, *The Renaissance of the Twelfth Century* (1928), Curtius, *op. cit.*, Lewis, *op. cit.*, and G. Raynaud de Lage, *Alain de Lille* (Montreal and Paris, 1951).

319. **ful of grace**; a phrase from the Salutation of Mary. Cf. Introduction, p. 29. Chaucer also uses it of Pallas, *Anelida and Arcite*, 5.

323–9. This division of birds is probably adopted from Vincent of Beauvais, whose encyclopaedia Chaucer certainly knew at some time in his life (cf. Introduction, p. 32). All quotations from Vincent are by chapter from the *Speculi Maioris*, vol. I, Book 16. ' Some birds (it is said) feed on flesh. Some on seed. Others on various food, haphazardly. . . . But some feed on worms, like the sparrow. . . . Some live on the banks of the waters of lakes or seas, and feed from them ' (Chap. xiv, partly repeated from Chaps. iii and vi). Bartholomew makes the same distinction, rather more explicitly, without that touch of vagueness in Vincent, which is echoed by Chaucer (ll. 325–6). For the degree in which the birds represent social classes, see Introduction, p. 34.

330–64. The list of birds is a typical rhetorical adornment; examples may be found in the *Roman* (*Romaunt*, 661ff) and in Alanus, *De Planctu*, col. 435 (quoted by Skeat, *Works of Chaucer*, i, 74).

330. **ryal.** The eagle is often referred to as the king of birds; e.g. by Vincent, Chap. xxii, Bartholomew, Chap. i, 176*v*.

331. ' For in the Eagle the spirit of sight is most temperate, and most sharpe in act and deede of seeing and beholding the Sunne ' (Bartholomew, Chap. i, 176*v*). The same belief was expressed in the Bestiaries; cf. J. Hall, *Early Middle English Texts* (1920), p. 177. Skeat gives further references.

332. Examples of the lower kinds of eagle are the *goshawk*, *facoun*, *sperhauk*, *merlioun*.

333. **clerkis.** The ' clerk ' Vincent mentions 16 different kinds of hawk, Chap. xx.

334. **tiraunt.** Perhaps suggested by Alanus' comment ' demanded tribute from his subjects with violent tyranny ' (*De Planctu*, col. 435); but see next note.

335–6. Bartholomew quotes the opinion that the goshawk is cruel to its young, taking food from them when they are fledged, and driving them out of the nest (Chap. ii, 178*r*).

337. **gentil facoun.** Almost a technical term. Bartholomew has ' gentle fawlcon ' (Chap. i, 177*v*, 187*v*, etc.). It is ' a royall fowle, and desireth praye, and vseth to sit on his hand that beareth him ' (Chap. xx, 184*v*). The line has twelve syllables, though it is perfectly acceptable. Scan

$$\overset{\times}{\text{The}} \ \overset{/}{\text{gen}} \overset{\times}{\text{tyl}} \ \overset{/}{\text{fa}} \overset{\times}{\text{coun}} \ \| \ \overset{\times}{\text{that}} \ \overset{/}{\text{with}} \ \overset{\times}{\text{his}} \ \overset{/}{\text{feet}} \ \overset{\times}{\text{dis}} \overset{/}{\text{tray}} \overset{(\times)}{\text{nyth}}.$$

339. In Bartholomew, Chap. iii, 178*v*, it is said of the *alietus*, by which is meant chiefly the sparrow-hawk, but also the merlin and hobby, that ' small birds be his meate and his praye '.

341. **douue.** Not the same as the turtle dove. The dove was associated with Venus from classical times. Fulgentius describes Venus accompanied by doves (*columbas*) because they are ' fervent in coition ' (*op. cit.*, p. 40). Alanus speaks of the *columba* ' drunk with the sweet evil ' (*De Planctu*, col. 436). Bartholomew speaks of their lecherousness, and says they are ' milde birds and meeke ' (Chap. vi, 180*r*). In English they are *doves* or *culvers*.

342. That the swan sings at its death is an extremely common notion. Alanus refers to it (*De Planctu*, col. 435), as does Vincent (xlix–l), quoting Pliny, and Bartholomew (Chap. xi, 182*v*). Chaucer refers to the belief, *Anelida*, 346ff, and *LGW*, 1355ff. Vincent says that the swan is ' of choleric complexion, and hence irritable ' (*loc. cit.*). Jealous in this sense of ' angry ', ' irritable ' is evidenced in *OED* 1382–1661.

343. Skeat's references, including that to Alanus, show only the owl as a ' prophet of misery '. Cf. Bartholomew, ' The crieng of the Owle by night, betokeneth death ' (Chap. v, 180r), and *The Owl and the Nightingale, passim.*

344. ' A Crane is called Grus, and hath that name of her own voice, for she cryeth with such a voice, as Isidore saith. And is a bird of greate winges ' (Bartholomew, Chap. xv, 183r). So Vincent, Chap. xci. Alanus refers to the crane's ' gigantic ' size (*De Planctu,* col. 436).

345. **choughe.** See textual variants. Gg and Ff (with J) are clearly in the wrong, which indicates that the common ancestor of Gg and Ff was also wrong. Alanus refers to its thieving, though as ' praiseworthy theft ' (col. 436). Belief in the chough's thievishness was common and traditional; cf. Pliny, *Historia Naturalis*, x, 29.
   iangelynge. A commonplace referred to by both Alanus and Vincent.

346. **skornynge.** The jay is said to mock at owls, but so do other birds; this may rather refer to its raucous voice.
   elis fo. Vincent quotes Isidore, ' Herons, foes of serpents '. Cf. also Alexander Neckam, *De Naturis Rerum*, Book I, Chap. lxiv, ed. T. Wright (Rolls Series, 1863). This late twelfth-century encyclopaedia became widely known, and is a repository of common ideas about the natural world, which were subjected to moralised interpretations. It serves to illustrate common ideas, some of which Chaucer shared, but there is no evidence that he made any actual use of it.

347. The lapwing feigns a broken leg or wing to draw intruders away from its nest. Whether or not for this reason it had a reputation for falseness: Skeats quotes, ' to seem the lapwing and to jest, Tongue far from heart ' (*Measure for Measure*, I, iv, 32–3; cf. also *Much Ado about Nothing*, III, i, 24–5; *Comedy of Errors*, IV, ii, 27).

348. **bewrye** is proved by the rhyme, and usually means ' conceal '. It is a possible form in Chaucer (cf. F. Wild, ' Sprache d. wichtigeren Chaucer-Mss.', *Wiener Beiträge* 44 (Leipzig, 1915), 312). Cf. *dye*, l. 55. As is well known, starlings can be taught to speak (cf. I *Henry IV*, I, iii, 224), but I can find no references to starlings which explain this allusion. But it is possible that Chaucer may have meant *bewrye* (<be-+wrien, <O.E. wriȝian) meaning ' distort ', which is quoted in *OED* as a nonce-word in Gavin Douglas, *Aeneid*, 1513.

349. **tame rodok.** I have found no references to the robin in writings known to Chaucer.
   coward kyte: ' A kite is . . . a coward & fearefull among great birds ' (Bartholomew, Chap. xxvi, 186r). Vincent says three kites will fly from one sparrow-hawk (Chap. cviii).

350. **orloge.** Alanus refers to the cock, ' common astrologer ', with the *horologio* of his voice. Cf. *Troilus*, iii, 1415, and *CT*, VII, 2853–4. The present instance is the earliest record of *orloge* in a figurative sense; and the earliest record in any sense is Wyclif in 1382.

351. **Venus sone.** The sparrow ' is a full hot bird and lecherous ' (Bartholomew, Chap. xxxii, 187v). It is libidinous, says Neckam (*De Naturis Rerum*, Book 1, Chap. lx). Cf. *General Prologue, CT*, 1, 626.

nyhtyngale. Always associated with spring, especially in Old French poetry. Cf. *The Owl and the Nightingale, passim.*

353. Vincent, Chap. xvii, and Neckam, *De Naturis Rerum*, Book 1, Chap. lii, note that swallows eat bees.

    foulis. Bees were classified as birds, as in Bartholomew (Chap. iv, 178*v*). Cf. Cook, *MLN* **21** (1906), 111, and **22** (1907), 146.

355. **wedded turtil.** ' The Turtle . . . followeth chastity, and if he leeseth his make, he seeketh not companye of any other, but goeth alone, and hath minde of the fellowship that is lost . . . she eateth not carrion, but for meate for her birdes, she seeketh out cleane grains, and gathereth them in cleane places ' (Bartholomew, Chap. xxxiv, 188*r*). The turtle dove's love and faithfulness are referred to by Neckam (Chap. lix), by the M.E. Bestiary (*Early Middle English Texts*, ed. J. Hall, 1920, p. 194) and by Alanus (col. 436).

356. M. Griffin, *Studies on Chaucer and his Audience* (Hull, Quebec, 1956), pp. 49ff, gives examples of representations of angels adorned with peacock's feathers. Examples of copes with such portrayals are to be found in the Victoria and Albert Museum. It was an ancient and common artistic motif.

357. Vincent says that the pheasant is *gallus syluaticus* (Chap. lxxii); Alanus refers to the *gallus syluestris* (the wild cock which Chaucer presumably took to be the same bird, though Alanus mentions the pheasant separately) as scorning (*deridens*) the sluggishness (*desidiam*) of the domestic cock. It is also said that the pheasant will breed with the common hen.

358. **wakyr goos.** The watchfulness of the goose was proverbial, and the story of how the wakeful geese saved the Roman Capitol is told from Pliny by Vincent (Chap. xxix) and by Neckam (Book 1, Chap. lxxi).

    euere. See textual variants, and Introduction, p. 60.

    onkynde. Because it does not look after its own young, but lays its egg in the nest of other birds. The newly-hatched cuckoo ejects the foster-parents' young; cf. l. 612. Referred to by Neckam, Book 1, Chap. lxxii. Cf. *King Lear*,

> The hedgesparrow fed the cuckoo so long
> That it had it head bit off by it young
>
>   (I, iv, 238–9)

which appears to be a snatch of an old song.

359. The parrot had a reputation for wantonness, ' in wine especially lascivious ', says Vincent (Chap. xv), and again, ' very lecherous, and drinks wine ' (Chap. cxxxv).

360. Vincent says that drakes sometimes kill the female in the fury of their wantonness (Chap. xxvii).

361. The belief that the stork kills its female if she is found unfaithful was widespread. Thus Vincent, Chap. xlviii, Bartholomew, Chap. viii, 181*v*. Skeat gives many other references.

362. The cormorant is ' a bird of great gluttony . . . and is enimie namely to Eeles ' (Bartholomew, Chap. xxviii, 186*v*).

363. See textual variants, and Introduction, p. 60. The raven is wise because of its predictions: ' the Rauen hath a manner vertue of meaning and betokening of diuination ' (Bartholomew, Chap. x, 182*r*). According to Neckam (Book 1, Chap. lxi) it lives in towers, foretells the weather, shows how the mind should be raised to higher things, and symbolises the clergy.

According to Bartholomew (Chap. ix, 181*v*) crows also ' betoken rayne with greding and crieng *Corax, Corax*, as this verse meaneth. *Nunc plena Cornix pluuiam convocat improba voce* [*Georgics*, i, 388]. That is to understand, Nowe the Crowe calleth rayne with an eleinge [i.e. dreary] voyce, and is a iangling bird & vnmilde, and grieuous to men there they dwell '.

364. **old.** I do not understand the reason for this epithet, unless it be a reference to the somewhat hoary appearance of the missel-thrush.

This line concludes the list of birds, which has a richness of meaning far beyond any comparable list in any other poet.

366. **stature.** The earliest recorded occurrence of this word in this sense in *OED* is *LGW*, 2446.

369–71. Cf. Grandson, *Songe*, ' They made their acceptances, each one there chose as his mate the one who seemed equal to the other ' (44–6). Cf. also ll. 309–10n above.

370. **benygnely:** for the sense ' kindly, graciously ', *OED* quotes Wyclif first, *c.*1380.

370–1. **or . . . or:** probably not so much alternatives of action as alternative expressions, in fact *repetitio*, or *amplificatio*, an expansion. Cf. Introduction, p. 50. There may however be implied a difference between *formel*, female of the eagle, and *make*, the more general term. Cf. l. 466.

374. It was usual to say of a medieval heroine that she was Nature's best work. Bennett compares the description of Virginia, *Physician's Tale*, *CT*, VI, 7ff. Cf. also (what may be an imitation of the present passage) *Complaynt d'Amours*, 51–4.

379. **vicayre,** ' vicar ', i.e. ' deputy '. Chaucer found the term applied to Nature in the *De Planctu* (cols. 453, 476, 479), and in the *Roman* (16782, 19507); he uses it again, in a passage which usefully describes his idea of Nature (*CT*, VI, 19ff). He addresses the Virgin as ' vicaire and maistresse Of al the world ' in *An ABC*, 140–1, where it is not in the French original as printed by Skeat.

380. For the scansion, cf. *Paradise Lost*, ii, 621. Hot, cold, etc. were considered to be the basic elements which make up the physical universe. From Aristotle the idea extends to the late seventeenth century; cf. G. Sarton, *A History of Science* (1952), pp. 247, 339, 371, etc.

380–1. This extremely common idea is expressed in the *Roman* (16957ff), where the *stars* control hot, cold, moist, dry, in accordance with the scientific truth as conceived in the Middle Ages, of which truth the figure of Nature is the allegory. The general meaning is, ' that has bound the elements together by equal numbers which agree together '. Cf. *acorde* and *euene* in Glossary, and Bennett, *op. cit.*, p. 133. Paré (*Le Roman*, pp. 73ff) gives many references, including Macrobius and Boethius (*Boece*, IV, m. 6), where the control is exercised by the love of

God. Chaucer perhaps had in mind *Boece*, III, m. 9, ' Thow byndest the elementis by nombres proporcionables '; the similarity of this phrase to the reading of Gg and Ff once again shows that Gg's text is superior when supported by Ff, even though here Ff has made a small mistake (see textual variants). Important statements of the idea in Chaucer's poetry are to be found in *Troilus*, iii, 1744ff, and *Knight's Tale*, *CT*, I, 2987ff, each based on Boethius. Alanus also of course refers to it, but not in very specific terms (*De Planctu*, col. 443), as the *quatuor elementorum concors discordia*, ' the harmony of discord of the four elements '.

383–404. Nature's speech corresponds to the opening speech of the Chancellor at the beginning of a Parliamentary session. See Introduction, p. 37.

387, 390. **statute, ordenaunce**, are technical words in constitutional law. The fundamental distinction between them is that the statute is primarily a legislative act, the ordinance primarily an executive act. The statute is a law enacted by the king in Parliament, not to be altered, repealed, or suspended, without the authority of Parliament; it claims perpetuity and the sacred character of law. The ordinance is a regulation made by the king (or his council) and liable to be recalled by the same authority. Although in constitutional practice of the fourteenth century statute and ordinance were sometimes difficult to distinguish, nevertheless by the end of the century parliamentary practice seems to have clearly recognised the general and perpetual quality of the statute, in contrast with the more particular and less necessarily perpetual quality of the ordinance. Parliament sometimes considered Richard II's ordinances as contrary to the law, i.e. to the ancient customs and statutes of the land: a petition was presented by the Commons in 1390 requesting that the Chancellor and council should not ordain such; hence, perhaps, Chaucer's phrase *ryghtful ordenaunce*, where the adjective would have been unnecessary as applied to the statute. Chaucer makes a clear distinction. Nature's *statute* has the sacred character of law, and refers to the general mating; her *ordenaunce* is a particular act or decision within the scope of the *statute*, and is a mode of putting it into practice. See W. Stubbs, *The Constitutional History of England* (fourth edition, vol. ii, section xvii (1896), 292), and E. A. Jolliffe, *Constitutional History of England* (1937), p. 378.

389. Cf. Reason's speech, *Romaunt*, 4845ff, where the duty of begetting children is emphasised; note especially:

> Therfore sette Kynde therynne delit
> (4865)
> Thus hath sotilled dame Nature
> (4871)
> For her desir is for delyt
> (4874)

392. Nature approves of the eagles as the most honoured.

395. This series of epithets sums up the traditional qualities of the courtly lover, which are frequently mentioned. They are in themselves self-explanatory, except that *secre* does not mean ' secretive ', ' furtive ', and does not imply that his love is illicit and hence must be kept quiet. It rather implies that the lover does not publicly discuss private and personal matters, i.e. he is discreet. There is obviously no secret made

of love itself in the *Parlement*. Cf. *Romaunt*, in Reason's speech just quoted above:

> Good love shulde engendrid be
> Of trewe herte, just and secre,
> And not of such as sette her thought
> To have her lust and ellis nought.
>
> (5089–92)

Reason is the daughter of God, and speaks with authority. In a *Balade* of instruction to lovers Grandson tells them to be ' secret, cautious in speech, not speaking enviously, fleeing pride, loving courtesy and honour, valuing good men and seeking their company ' (Piaget, p. 305). Again, he speaks of a lovable lady, ' loyally loving, without folly, beautiful, good, gracious, full of all value, sage, courteous, secret, truly loving ', etc., etc. (Piaget, p. 366). A similar list of qualities is given, p. 375. Sometimes, of course, it was necessary to conceal love, no doubt because it was often illicit, in which case, however, the usual word seems to have been *celant*, ' concealing '. Cf. Klein, pp. 43, 46, 59, 62. In *Troilus*, i, 744, Chaucer refers to the necessity of not telling what in love ' oughte ben secree '; the opposite of *secre* is being *avauntour*, or *iangelere*; see *Parlement*, ll. 430, 457. A list of lover's qualities is applied to Chauntecleer in the *Nun's Priest's Tale* (*CT*, VII, 2910ff).

407ff. Cf. Gower's Valentine poem in the *Cinkante Balades*: ' St Valentine, Love, and Nature had all birds in governance; each of the birds chose a companion agreeable to his desire, fitting to his degree, completely with one accord and one assent.' *Works*, ed. G. C. Macaulay (1899), i, 365.

410. **feere.** Chaucer uses *feere* to mean ' wife ' in *Troilus*, iv, 791.

411. **This is.** Read *This*, as often in later ME verse. Cf. ll. 620 and 650, where the verb is actually omitted.

416ff. The first suitor's speech is an admirable statement of *fine amour*. There is a contrast here with Grandson's Valentine poems, for although both the royal tercel and Grandson emphasise the lady's superiority, Grandson does not hope to win her (Piaget, pp. 256 and 309ff, especially ll. 239–42). For the sentiments of the first suitor's speech, cf. Chaucer's shorter poems in general, as well as the specific points quoted below.

419. The essence of *fine amour*, and the reason for the debate later among the lower birds, is the extreme emphasis on absolute loyalty. Thus in the *Romaunt* the God of Love says:

> And for thou trewe to love shalt be,
> I wole, and comaunde thee
> That in oo place thou sette, all hool,
> Thyn herte. . . .
> Therefore in oo place it sette,
> And lat it *nevere* thannys flette.
>
> (2359–72)

Cf. Chaucer's *Womanly Noblesse*, 9, *Complaynt d'Amours*, 90–1. So Grandson; cf. Piaget, who comments on Grandson's insistence on loyalty (p. 141). It is this view (with which Chaucer sympathises in this poem), that once love is given it can never honourably be retracted, which places the eagles in their predicament. No doubt in real life matters were arranged differently. By Shakespeare's time even in literature it was felt that some such arrangement as the coarser lower birds recommend was perfectly reasonable: hence Orsino's change in *Twelfth Night*. Even so, Shakespeare has to manage the matter with tact.

serve was almost the technical word in *fine amour* for ' to love '. It emphasises the lady's ' sovereignty '. Cf. 159n, and Chaucer's *Complaint to his Lady* (61), *Pity* (60), *Mars* (167, 187, etc.), *Complaint of Venus* (20), *Complaynt d'Amours* (75).

420. Cf. *Complaynt d'Amours*, ll. 34–5, 90–1, *Troilus*, iv, 447–8, all rhyming *serve/sterve*.

421, 427. The lover could not arrogate to himself sufficient merit to ask for more than the lady's ' pity ', or ' mercy '. Grandson, for example, asks that *Danger* (i.e. ' Refusal ', ' Fear ', ' Harshness ') in his lady may be turned to *mercy*, and from *mercy* to *grace* and *pity* (Piaget, p. 202). Cf. Chaucer's *Pity*, especially l. 92; *Complaint to his Lady*, especially l. 17; *Womanly Noblesse*, ll. 20, 22 (this last poem is especially near in temper to the royal tercel's speech). Cf. also *Complaynt d'Amours* (a Valentine poem), especially l. 6; and *Troilus*, iii, 1170–6; the Knight's wife in the *Franklin's Tale* marries him for pity (*CT*, V, 740).

426. A ' headless ' line, i.e. one lacking the usual first unaccented syllable. Chaucer seems to comment on his use of this metrical variant in *HF*, iii, 1098.

428. See textual variants. It is quite possible that this too should be a headless line, which Gg has taken upon himself to ' improve '. Cf. l. 460.

437. **Thanne ouhte she be myn.** This sentiment has been taken by some commentators to be uncourtly, rude, or even ridiculous. But a similar sentiment occurs elsewhere in courtly medieval literature. It seems to be especially frequent in thirteenth-century French poems. Thus in the *Roman*, the God of Love says:

> Wommen wel *ought* pite to take
> Of hem that sorwen for her sake.

> (*Romaunt*, ll. 2671–2)

In *De Venus* (see Appendix I), the lover says ' She (his lady) is of very wicked heart if she lets me die ' (153a). Venus says, ' Cursed be the body of God our Lord, if [a lady] does not love her lover, if she is loved *paramours* ' (178 c–d); the lover in the *Fablel* says of his lady, ' As I believe, if she is so hard against me, it is a great crime ' (102c–d); in a debate poem printed by A. Jeanroy (*Les origines de la poésie lyrique* (3rd ed., 1925), pp. 468–70) of two ladies arguing about the respective merits of two lovers, one says that a beautiful lady *ought by right* to love a good knight if he is of fine spirit, and loyal to her. In the fourteenth century, Gower, in a poem on loyalty, says that it is not fair he should give all and receive nothing (*Cinkante Balades*, xvii; cf. *Romaunt*, 2379–80); even Grandson reproaches his lady, ' If I die, will you not have done wrong to allow me to suffer death for serving well? ' See Piaget, p. 458 (*Lay de Plour*, 705–7), and cf. p. 448, ll. 492–5, and ' *ought I not* to be recomforted? ' (p. 480, l. 2371). In Chaucer's own poetry, apart from the present instance, the clearest example is in *Mars*:

> And ye, my ladyes, that ben true and stable,
> Be wey of kynde, ye *oghten* to be able
> To have pite of folk that be in peyne.

(281-3)

The royal tercel's remark is therefore perfectly natural, and usual in a 'courtly lover'.

450ff. The second tercel is less elaborate in speech, and is more down-right, but there is nothing rude or absurd in his speech.

455. **gerdonynge**, i.e. reward of love. Cf. the *Romaunt* :

> But, in love, fre yeven thing
> Requyrith a gret guerdonyng.

(2379-80)

457. *iangelere.* Cf. 395n above.

458. **do me hangyn by the hals.** This seems to have been the usual way of killing unwanted animals. Neckam tells a story of how a king ordered a goshawk to be hanged (Book 1, Chap. xxiv). For human beings hanging was of course a shameful death.

460. Cf. 428.

461. **in.** See textual variants.

479. **man.** See Glossary. Troilus also says he will be Criseyde's 'man, while he may dure' (i, 468); cf. iv, 447, which has the same usage.

485, 495. **gentil ple.** Grandson, in particular, emphasises that a lover, to succeed, must speak well (Piaget, p. 371, ll. 17-19).
    Chaucer praises the speeches of the eagles, without any irony. Their fine speech is a 'cursed pletynge' to the lower birds, however.
    It does not seem likely that *ple, pletynge, verdit,* have a legal flavour. I have not noticed the use of specifically legal terms in any of the love-poetry with which Chaucer was familiar, and the words quoted are found in many medieval debate poems.

487. A 'headless' line.

490. Cf. 266n.

491. **delyuered** may have been a technical parliamentary term; cf. 'They wished to dissolve (*delivrer*) the said parliament as soon as they could' (*Anonimalle Chronicle*, ed. V. H. Galbraith, p. 83; quoted by Bennett, *op. cit.*, p. 166).

498. See textual variants. Gg's word order corresponds to the cries in the next line, and gives smoother metre, but may be suspect for these very reasons.
    goos. Chaucer thought poorly of the goose; cf. *Troilus*, iii, 584, where Criseyde refers contemptuously to *goosish poeples speche*, where the meaning of *goosish* is 'silly'. Later the goose becomes proverbial for silliness, but apart from Chaucer there are no references before the sixteenth century.
    cokkow. Cf. 358n, and the proverb, 'He can synge noon other songe but of hymself', cited from a manuscript by P. Hodgson, *RES* 24 (1948). 8. The cuckoo is selfish and self-willed. Chaucer calls the cuckoo a fool, l. 505.

502. **remedie** is a word used frequently in the parliamentary proceedings, especially in November 1381; cf. *Rot. Parl.*, pp. 101–2.

507. **charge** is also a frequent parliamentary word, e.g. in the November Parliament of 1381 (*Rot. Parl.*, pp. 100, 102, also pp. 5, 73, 89). It means 'matter to be discussed'.

If the present reading of the line is correct it is another example of a twelve-syllable line.

508. **delyuere.** Cf. 491n.

510–11. 'If it be *your* wish for anyone to speak, it would be as good for him to be silent' (Skeat). That is, anything said that you approve of might just as well not be said (because it would be rubbish). The line should probably be read thus :

$$\overset{\diagup \ \ \times \ \diagup \ \times}{\text{Quod the turtil;}} \ \Big\| \ \overset{\diagup \ \times \ \diagup \ \diagdown \ \ \diagup(\times)}{\text{' If it be ȝoure wille}}$$

517. **acloyith.** The earliest recorded instance of this sense of the word.

518. A version of a common proverb; cf. Skeat, *E.E. Prov.*, p. 121, no. 285. In the *Canon's Yeoman's Tale* (*CT*, VIII), 1066–7, it runs, ' profred servyse Stinketh '. Dante refers to ' officio non commesso ' (*Purgatorio*, x, 57), of which the phrase here looks very like a reminiscence. The word ' uncommitted ' is not recorded elsewhere in this Italianate sense, and the first quotation in *OED* in any sense is 1598. The scribe of Gg did not understand it, and made an inept attempt to give the line some meaning.

520. **lewedenesse** shows the poet's attitude to the ill-bred impatience of the lower birds.

526. The dignified style of this passage and the method of election contrast sharply with the way in which the choice of goose and cuckoo is made.

530. **termyne** perhaps has a parliamentary flavour. In 1377 a schedule was presented by the Commons to the Lords asking among other things that petitions ' might be " rehearsed " before Lords and Commons and debated in a friendly way, and that they might be decided (*terminez*) according to good faith and reason. . . . These things having been decided (*termynez*) in just manner ', the money grant was ' in short time assented to, to the honour and pleasure of God, and the advantage (*profit*) of the King and all the people ' (*Rot. Parl.*, pp. 14–15).

531–2. **presente . . . acceptyth.** Perhaps parliamentary language. Cf. Bennett, *op. cit.*, pp. 140, 168.

534. **resoun.** See Glossary. *Ratio* was originally, like *ordo* and *dispositio*, applied to oratory and legal pleading. It is used so here. Cf. l. 632n.

539. The settlement of a legal question by personal combat was still not uncommon. Grandson met his end in such a battle. In the Parliament of November 1381 Richard of Clyvedon offered to prove his rights in a dispute ' by his body, by the law of arms, and other manner as the Court [i.e. Parliament] may command him, or otherwise by verdict (*verdit*) of jurors ' (*Rot. Parl.* pp. 105–6). Cf. *The Knight's Tale* (*CT*, I), 2111ff :

> Ye knowen wel that every lusty knyght
> That loveth paramours and hath his myght,
> Were it in Engelond or elleswhere,
> They wolde, hir thankes, wilnen to be there
> To fighte for a lady, benedicitee.

Cf. C. T. Flower, *Transactions of the Selden Society* 62 (1943), 113–22.

541–3. The speaker is very polite.

543. **seris, ne.** See textual variants. In this poem *seris* seems to be a monosyllable (cf. ll. 464, 541).

545. **voys.** The earliest date in *OED* for the sense ' right to decide ' is 1433.
  charge. See 507n.

547. **Pes.** According to *OED* Chaucer is the first to use this word as a verb, in the *Prologue to the Wife of Bath's Tale*.

551. **sittyngest.** See textual variants. Of the other MSS, S alone has *best sittyng*, the remainder have no superlative, and thus produce a very lame line, even if one metrically just possible. But the preceding superlatives, and the general sense, call clearly for a superlative here. It is not impossible that scribes either omitted the word *best* or *most* (as they often drop words out) or that they left off the ending of a word they had already begun to write. Gg may have noticed the omission in his exemplar and edited the line, producing by his emendation Chaucer's sense, if not his exact wording. Where all is guesswork, it is best to retain the wording of Gg, the best MS, though no other example of this superlative form is recorded. Another instance where Gg alone has preserved a necessary superlative seems to occur in l. 613. Gg's reading of *he* for *hire* merely shows his frequent misunderstanding of the construction of impersonal verbs.
  It is usual for a Chaucerian heroine to give her pity, and hence her love, to the most worthy suitor; cf. *EC* 5 (1955), 407–13, and 421n above.

556. **gole,** a contemptuous word.

558. **facounde gent.** See textual variants. The final *-e* was probably pronounced (Fr. *facounde*, Lat. *facundia*). But Gg's variant would give precisely the jingling, derisive note which is implicit in Chaucer's use of *gent*. The word *gent* is associated with the English tail-rhyme romances and such early lyrics as the Harley lyrics, which Chaucer mocks in the *Miller's Tale*, where he uses *gent* (*CT*, I, 3234) and in *Sir Thopas*, where he uses *gent* (VII, 715). These are the only uses of the word *gent* in Chaucer except for *Romaunt*, l. 1032, which is the only non-derisive use of the word, and even if by Chaucer is probably an early work. For Chaucer's mockery of earlier popular English verse, see E. T. Donaldson, ' Idiom of Popular Poetry in the Miller's Tale ', *English Institute Essays* (1950), ed. A. S. Downes, pp. 116–40, and L. H. Loomis, ' Chaucer and the Auchinleck MS ', *Essays and Studies in Honor of Carleton Brown* (New York, 1940).

568. The goose's desire for a mate is referred to in proverbial terms in the *Wife of Bath's Prologue* (*CT*, III, 269–70).

573. **his wit . . . wylle.** Wit and will signify respectively the rational and irrational parts of a man. The conjunction of the two words in a phrase is found from the early thirteenth century to the seventeenth.

Cf. B. Dickins, ' The Conflict of Wit and Will ', *Leeds Eng. Language Texts and Monographs* 4 (1937), 8ff. Cf. 214n. Perhaps the reference is to the suitors, each of whom cannot help himself loving, but it is more likely that it is to the fool, who has neither intelligence nor desire to keep himself quiet.

574. A common proverb. See Skeat, *E. E. Prov.*, pp. 58f, no. 139. It occurs in the *Roman*, ll. 4733–4 (*Romaunt*, l. 5265).

582–8. The turtle dove symbolised loyalty in love; cf. 355n. But that she is a speaker here seems to show that Chaucer considered that such loyalty was not, or should not be, the characteristic of only the upper classes.

593. See textual variants: *that is* should be scanned *that's* and the whole line scans:

$$\text{W}\overset{\times}{\text{h}}\text{o}\ \overset{/}{\text{shuld}}\overset{\times}{\text{e}}\ \overset{/}{\text{rekke}}\ \|\ \overset{\times}{\text{of}}\ \overset{/}{\text{hym}}\ \overset{\times}{\text{that}}\ \overset{/}{\text{is}}\ \overset{\times}{\text{rech}}\overset{/}{\text{e}}\text{les}\ ?$$

with a very light pause after *rekke*, or none at all. Gg's reading:

What shulde I rekke of hym that is recheles ?

though superficially plausible looks suspicious in the light of other MS readings; nor does it fit the general context, which is concerned with the behaviour of the loyal but unrewarded lover. The scribe of Gg presumably thought Chaucer's metre awkward because he did not recognise that the final -*e* in *shuldē* must be sounded; so he ' improved ' the line by inserting *I*, which necessitated changing *Who* to *What*. But along with the scribes of P and S he rightly preserved *hym* which the other MSS dropped. The other MSS may have dropped *hym* to help the scansion, not realising that *that is* could be scanned as one syllable. If *hym* is omitted no satisfactory sense can be given to *recheles*.

595. Proverbial. Cf. ' There's as good fish in the sea as ever was caught ', and Skeat, *E. E. Prov.*, p. 59, no. 140.

599–600. Whether or not a point of personal observation, this is also a reminiscence from Boethius: ' thei ben lyk to briddes of whiche the nyght lightneth hir lokynge and the day blendith hem ' (*Boece*, IV, pr. 4).

602. **nouþer.** Pronounced *nor*. See Introduction, p. 56.

609. **lessoun . . . recorde.** See Glossary. But the meaning might be ' learn by heart (by way of preparation, as a child learns its lesson) ', as in *Troilus*, iii, 51, *recordyng his lesson*.

612. Cf. 358n.

613. **reufullest.** See textual variants. Editors emend to *rewtheles* ' ruthless ', which except for a suggestion from P has no MS support, and is not satisfactory in meaning. The merlin's contempt has nothing of the hatred which would be implied by ' ruthlessness ' The MSS have again here lost a necessary superlative ending, as they seem to have done in l. 551. Gg has characteristically omitted a final -*t* (cf. *lyght, myght, ryght, wrought*, in Glossary), but the scribe's care for the metre has led him either to preserve or restore what it seems most probable that Chaucer wrote. It should, however, be noted that, as with l. 551, the majority reading of *rewfull* is metrically just possible,

and that with such a reading, and the sounding of the final *-e* of *broughte*, the line would have ten syllables. Cf. also l. 232 and note.

615. Part of the interest in the mating derives from the concern for the duty of procreation. The formel is expected to breed.

619. **in effect.** *MED* quotes Chaucer as earliest among his contemporaries to use this phrase with this meaning, in *CT*, I, 319.

620. **this is.** Read *this*. Cf. 411, 650.

621. This is in fact what the tercel advised in ll. 552–3.

622. **who so be wroth or blythe.** Another rhyming tag; cf. l. 504.

630. The meaning of this line seems to be: ' I have no regard other than what I should have for any worldly position ', i.e. ' I give no special favours '.

632. A headless line, which Gg, followed by modern editors, wrongly emends; cf. 426n above.
  Resoun. This word has many senses in ME, as has the Latin *Ratio* which it translates. ' Reason ' was often personified, as in the *Anti-claudianus* of Alanus, where *Ratio* is the chief counsel of *Natura*; and in the *Roman*, where she was made by God in Paradise (cf. *Romaunt*, ll. 3189ff), she is concerned with the duty of procreation (cf. *Romaunt*, l. 4822), is the daughter of God (*Roman* ll. 5816ff), and comes to man direct from God, being independent of Nature, who cannot give man reason (ll. 19055ff). ' Discussion as to the exact function of Reason in the universe is endless; she is considered, generally speaking, a kind of divine principle governing all things. . . . Reason is also the judging faculty of the soul, as in *Piers Plowman*,

> And whan I deme domes, and do as treuthe techeth,
> Thanne is Racio my riȝt name, Resoun an Englisshe.
>
>   (B XV, 27–8) '

(R. C. Goffin, ' Chaucer and " Reason " ', *MLR* **21** (1926), 13ff). Gower says a reasonable man must love in good fashion according to reason (*Cinkante Balades*, xlix; cf. also, for the association of what is natural with what is reasonable, *ibid.*, l, li).

641. Another ' headless ' line; cf. 426n above.

648–9. The boon asked for is the year's respite. After that she expects to have the free choice already implicit in Nature's promise, ll. 407–10.

650. **This.** Cf. ll. 411n and 620.

652. **Venus . . . Cupide.** ' To serve Venus or Cupid ' is simply an elaborate expression for ' to love '. *Venus* is frequently used in classical and medieval Latin poetry as a mere synonym for *amor*, while *Cupid* is often in medieval literature (as at the beginning of the *Parlement*) a half-realised personification of *love*. The formel is saying in courtly language that she is not yet prepared to have anything to do with love. There is no reference to the precise symbolism of the earlier passage about Venus in the *Parlement*. If Chaucer had intended such a reference he would hardly have made it so casual. It would be an important point, demanding an emphasis (especially in poetry which was meant primarily to be heard) which is not here.

660. Cf. 419n. The kind of ' service ' a lover performed was seen in his behaviour, of which a useful summary is to be found in *Troilus*, i, 1072–85, where Troilus is described as becoming the friendliest, noblest, most generous, most provident and best of knights, leaving aside all mockery, cruelty and aloofness. The Squire in the *General Prologue* had borne himself well, ' In hope to stonden in his lady grace ' (*CT*, I, 88).

668. **euene acord.** See 381n. Chaucer again uses *acord*, ' loving agreement ', in *ProLGW*, F, 159.

672. **goddesse.** See textual variants. An interesting example of Gg's editing in favour of a smoother metre.

675. **roundele.** Cf. Introduction, p. 57.

677. **note.** Some MSS have written above the place of the roundel *Qui bien aime a tard oublie*, which is a medieval French proverb (see Morawski, *Proverbes Français* (Paris, 1925), p. 67, no. 1835). These words can hardly indicate the tune since they form an octosyllabic line. Nor have they any apparent relevance to the text. I do not understand their function.

678. See textual variants. Gg's line seems metrically more desirable, and the *here* of the other MSS is quite unnecessary. If Gg is wrong, either the line has twelve syllables (two each to *wordis*, *were*, *here*) or *wordis* and *were* are to be regarded as monosyllables; either is quite possible.

680ff. See textual variants. Cf. the song of the birds in *ProLGW*, F, 170, *Welcome, somer, oure governour and lord.* Previously in the F prologue, the birds have sung:

> Blessed be Seynt Valentyn
> For on this day I chees you to be myn, etc.
>
> (145–6)

although the *Prologue* is about May. The whole passage in the *Prologue*, F, 139–70 (of which 152–70 were omitted in the revised version G), is interestingly parallel to the *Parlement*, and should be consulted.

688. **recouerede.** *OED* gives this as the sole instance of the meaning ' to get back or find again (one who has been lost or absent) ', which is plainly wrong. The more frequent sense ' to get or obtain ' is more likely the meaning here; it is recorded from 1398 to *c.* 1661. However, the use here may be a legal term, ' to obtain possession of, or a right to, by legal process ', which is evidenced from *c.*1380 onwards.

APPENDIX I

LOVE-VISIONS [1]

(a) *Le Fablel dou Dieu d'Amors, and associated poems*

THE earliest extant ' love-vision ' is *Le Fablel dou Dieu d'Amors*,[2] which however is probably a combination and working over of two earlier poems.

The poet falls asleep and dreams that he awakes in a beautiful meadow on a May morning with the birds singing. He describes a stream of magical power, flowers and trees which no winter has harmed, and an orchard surrounded by a wall of porphyry and ivory, with a moat paved with the same. There is a drawbridge which no *vilains* (i.e. one of low birth) but only a man who is *courtois* can pass. The god of love rules the orchard. The poet enters without opposition and sits down under a fine tree, which has magical curative powers. A nightingale sings of love, then summons all the birds together and complains of the degeneration of love. The hawk is the first to reply: he says the degeneration is due to *vilainne gent* (low-bred people) who have no care for *drois* and *mesure*; only knights and ' clerks ' (i.e. educated men, who would almost all be in some kind of religious orders) should love. The thrush disagrees; the jay says that if a man loves, and is loved in return, he is as brave as a knight and wise as a ' clerk '. The nightingale agrees, and dismisses the birds, who are once referred to as barons (*li baron*, 32*b*); the lover awakes disconsolate. Here probably ended the first of the original poems—an early form of the celebrated debate between *clerc* and *chevalier*, in which the *vilains* was set against both the others (cf. *Romaunt*, l. 4030). Class distinctions in regard to love were early noticed though Chaucer is perhaps the first poet to represent them, as he does in the *Parlement* with any degree of lively realism.

The *Fablel* continues and the poet falls asleep again. He dreams that the lady for whose love he is suffering visits him, says she loves him and takes him to the castle of the god of love, which is described allegorically: the moat is of tears; clothing and building material are of songs, sighs, kisses, etc. This kind of fancifulness never attracted Chaucer, and the story from here onwards is not significant for the *Parlement*.

The *Fablel* was itself worked over to make another poem, *De Venus La Deese d'Amor*.[3] The lover-poet as usual sleeps and dreams of the meadow and the birds. The birds debate as before, the hawk again

---

[1] Mainly reprinted from *MLR* 53 (1958), 321ff. I am indebted to the Editor for permission to use this material.

[2] Written about the middle of the thirteenth century: ed. I. C. Lecompte, *MP* 8 (1910–11), 63ff and Ch. Oulmont in *Les Débats du Clerc et du Chevalier* (Paris, 1911). See also W. A. Neilson, ' Origins and sources of the Court of Love ', *Harvard Studies* 6 (1899) (valuable, but not always quite accurate), and W. O. Sypherd, ' Studies in Chaucer's *Hous of Fame* ', *Chaucer Society* (1907).

[3] Ed. W. Foerster (Bonn, 1880).

taking precedence. After a good deal of protestation and swooning with sorrow by the lover, Venus the goddess of love appears to him (she is shown as a fine lady, quite without mythological attributes; her approach reminds one of that of Alcestis in *The Legend of Good Women*). Venus and the lover have a long conversation, in which the beloved is praised much as Chaucer's formel might be: she is of noble heart and body, humble, courtly, simple, beautiful and of good speech, wise and understanding (155 *a-c*). Venus says that the lover is like a hawk who relentlessly pursues his prey. At last she promises to take the lover to the court of the god of love, which is described much as in *Le Fablel*, though the story itself diverges, and is not relevant here.

De Venus also takes over some ninety lines from *Dou vrai chiment d'amours*,[1] a dull, pious poem which concludes that though God wishes us to love everyone, He not merely allows, but even wishes and permits that one single person may be loved more than a hundred others, if it be without guile or deceit. The poem is interesting as emphasising the Christian orthodoxy which is present in much medieval French love-poetry, and as showing again that *fine amour* may be legitimate as well as adulterous.

Associated with these poems are the famous series of *débats* about the respective merits of *clerc* and *chevalier* as lovers.[2] The first of these seems to have been the Latin *Altercatio Phyllidis et Florae*. Phyllis and Flora, two fine ladies, sit in a May meadow and debate the worth of their lovers, one a knight, one a ' clerk '. They take the quarrel to the court of the god of love, which is much as described in *Le Fablel*. There are a number of French versions of varying degrees of closeness to the *Altercatio*. In *Florence et Blancheflor* the god calls a parliament of his barons, who are birds, and they debate the question. The hawk as usual takes precedence; the other birds vary in different manuscripts of the poem. Finally the question is decided by trial of battle between nightingale and parrot, clad in armour of flowers. Two similar poems in French were written in England. One of these, *Blancheflour et Florence*, was first written in English (presumably about the end of the thirteenth or beginning of the fourteenth century) and then translated. The poet enters a garden full of fresh smells and music. There is a list of instruments, of precious stones, of trees, of birds. There is the usual argument, and the usual debate by birds at the castle of love. The other poem written in England, *Melior et Idoine*, is more original in setting, but centres on the usual problem, which is debated by birds. Although neither of these poems is a dream-poem they show the general tradition well established in England, and they (especially the latter) have a touch of freshness and realism which is perhaps a little due to naïvety, but which also shows the direction in which Chaucer was to move.

In the fourteenth century a number of dream-poems were written. *La Panthere d'Amours*, by Nicole de Margival,[3] begins with a brief reflection on the truth of dreams, followed by an account of how the poet dreamed he was carried away on 14 August to a forest full of beasts. His lady is symbolised by the panther, most beautiful of beasts. The god of Love comes with music to help the lover. In *La Messe des Oisiaus et li Plais des Chanonesses et des Grises Nonains*,[4] the poet,

---

[1] Ed. A. Långfors, *Romania* 45 (1918–19), 205ff.
[2] The chief poems are edited by Oulmont, *op. cit.*
[3] Ed. H. A. Todd, SATF (Paris, 1883).
[4] Ed. A. Scheler, *Dits et Contes* (Brussels, 1866).

Jean de Condé, tells how he dreamt one May that he sat in a beautiful forest, and just before dawn heard the birds singing overhead. A messenger announces the goddess of love, and calls on the birds to prepare a welcome. A gorgeous throne is set up on which Venus takes her seat to dispense justice and receive adoration. Many complaints are brought up for her decision, but she insists that she must dine first. Then the cannonesses lodge a complaint against the grey nuns for stealing their lovers.

Other dream-poems about love certainly known to Chaucer were written by Machaut and Chaucer's contemporaries and acquaintances Froissart and Deschamps. But the poems develop away from the specific form and content of the earlier love-visions.

(b) Oton de Grandson

The one fourteenth-century poem which is in any respect close to the Parlement is Le Songe Saint Valentin, by Oton de Grandson.[1]

It has usually been accepted that this poem by Grandson influenced Chaucer in the Parlement. But there is no firm evidence of such influence. The chronology of Grandson's poetry is very uncertain. He was an exact contemporary of Chaucer, and of a number of specifically Valentine poems the Songe may well be the latest. It is therefore quite possible that Chaucer influenced Grandson, especially since the cult of Saint Valentin is as much English as French, or more so. Grandson was well known in the English court, and three of his poems served as a basis for Chaucer's late poem The Complaint of Venus, where Grandson is referred to as ' flour of hem that make in Fraunce '. The parallel between the Parlement and Le Songe is striking enough to make a comparison necessary.

Le Songe begins with six lines of which the initial letters form an acrostic on ISABEL, the name of the lady, variously identified by modern scholars, to whom Grandson addressed many of his plaints. The poet remarks how pleasant or unpleasant thinking may be, and says that waking thoughts may affect dreams. So it happens with him on the morning of one St Valentine's Day. Various thoughts have kept him awake all night, but at last he falls asleep. He dreams he goes to look in an orchard for two jewelled rings he lost the day before. In the orchard he sees an assembly of birds, each come there to choose a mate (per). Over them presides an eagle, a female, who has her own mate by her. The poet understands the talk of the birds, each of whom chooses as a mate the one he likes best in his own rank, and they then live together, equal in heart and love (Et font ensemble le demour Pareille de cuer et d'amour, ll. 91–2; cf. Parlement, ll. 400–10). One falcon pelerin, however, is solitary. The eagle asks him why he has not kept up the custom and chosen un pareil (123ff). He replies that he has chosen one from whom he will never part, but she is superior to all others in every way, and it would be a great crime, folly and oultrage for him in his rank to ask for her as mate. He reiterates his loyalty to her, however, and discourses on the pain of separation. Then he flies away. The eagle commends his loyalty. The other birds having chosen their mates all fly away. The dreamer awakes and meditates for some 150 lines on the ease with which the birds were able to choose as they

[1] Ed. A. Piaget, Oton de Grandson (Lausanne, 1941). Apart from this the chief study is H. Braddy, Chaucer and the French Poet Graunson (Louisiana, Baton Rouge, 1947).

wished. With men it is often different, though when their love *is* successful its joy is beyond compare. Men should not be blamed for loving; *Amour est chouse naturelle* (340) with them as with birds and beasts, but love among birds and beasts, who have no sense, does not demand so much as it does among men. Birds are not afraid of shame, and cannot tell good from bad. The poet grieves for the grief of lovers, and wishes they may all be successful.

Obviously the poem is curiously similar in some ways to the *Parlement*; yet in spirit and much else it is very different. *Le Songe* is humourless, lacking in variety and descriptive force. There is no debate. The muddled reflections at the end occupy quite a third of the poem and discuss chiefly the contrast between birds and men. Yet the only bird (apart perhaps from the presiding eagle) which is individualised is the falcon, representing the poet himself, who, however, is also present in his own person as spectator and narrator.

Nevertheless, the assembly of birds on St Valentine's Day to choose a mate under a presidency of the female eagle is strikingly close to the central situation of the *Parlement*. Such similarity cannot be equalled even in the other Chaucerian Valentine poems. Even so, the similarity casts remarkably little light on the *Parlement*. Grandson's poem certainly illustrates some of the typical courtly attitudes current at the end of the fourteenth century, and furnishes some further evidence of the Valentine cult, but there the matter may rest. It is possible that the similarity between the central situations of the two poems arises from the attempt of each poet to render in poetry the same courtly custom, and thus it may be that whichever poem was first written it had small influence on the other.

APPENDIX II

An extract translated from the charter of foundation of the Cour Amoureuse,
The original is printed by A. Piaget, Romania **31** *(1902), 602*

Item, because the highness of love is inconceivable, and because all nobles and others who are worthy of being in love should adorn their hearts with virtues and graces, each according to his power, in order to arrive at good fame; and on the other hand, because, as has been said, our court of love and its lordship are principally founded on the two virtues of humility and loyalty, for the honour, praise, and recommendation of all ladies and demoiselles, we [i.e. the Prince of Love] after mature and deep deliberation, have commanded, and by these presents do command, all our amorous subjects, of whatever power, lordship, or estate that they may be, without any exception, that they do not make, nor cause to be made by any other person, ditties, complaints, roundels, virelays, balades, lays, or anything else in the manner and shape of rhetoric, rimed or in prose, to the dishonour, reproach, detriment [*amenrissement*], or blame of any lady or ladies, demoiselle or demoiselles, or altogether of any women, religious or other, dead or alive, for whatever cause, however serious, dolorous, or displeasing it may be . . . (etc.).

APPENDIX III

THE DREAM OF SCIPIO

The Dream has been translated into English by C. W. Keyes, *Cicero; De re publica* (Loeb Classical Library, 1928), and by W. H. Stahl, *Macrobius; Commentary on the Dream of Scipio* (Records of Civilisation, Sources and Studies, New York, 1952). In making the following literal translation I have used them constantly as guides and have gladly used the phrasing of one or other of them whenever I could; I am much indebted to them.

1. When I arrived in Africa under the consul Manius Manilius, as military tribune in the fourth legion (as you know), my greatest wish was to meet Massinissa, a king for excellent reasons most friendly to my family. When I came to him the old man embraced me and wept greatly, and after a little while looked up to heaven and said, ' I thank thee, O highest Sun, and you other celestial beings, that before I depart from this life, I see in my kingdom and under this roof, Publius Cornelius Scipio, at whose very name I am refreshed; for the memory of that excellent and invincible man never leaves my mind.'

Then I asked him about his kingdom, and he asked me about our commonwealth, and with much to say on each side we spent that day. Moreover, after having been entertained with regal splendour, we prolonged our conversation far into the night. The old man would speak of nothing but of Africanus, and remembered not only all his deeds, but also his words. After we parted to go to bed, sleep seized me more strongly than usual, both because of the journey and because I had stayed up so late. Then (I believe for this reason, that we had talked [about him]—it often happens that our thoughts and conversations produce something in sleep such as Ennius writes of in connection with Homer, whom he very often used to think and talk about when he was awake) Africanus appeared to me in that form better known to me from his portrait [*imagine*; see Stahl, *op. cit.*, p. 70, note 6] than from himself. When I recognised him, truly, I shuddered; but he said to me, ' Be of good courage, Scipio, and lay aside fear, and hold in your memory what I shall say.

2. Do you see that city, which, compelled by me to submit to the Roman people, is renewing former hostility, and cannot remain at peace? ' and from a certain place high up, glorious and bright, set thick with stars, he pointed out Carthage. ' You have now come, little higher in rank than a private soldier, to fight against it. In two years' time, as consul, you will destroy it, and will earn that surname for yourself which up to now you have had as an inheritance from me. When you have destroyed Carthage and celebrated your triumph, you will be censor, and will go as legate to Egypt, Syria, Asia, and Greece; you will be chosen consul again in your absence, and will bring to an end a great war, and destroy Numantia. But when you arrive at the Capitol in your chariot you will find the commonwealth disturbed because of the policies of my grandson. Then, Africanus, it will be necessary for you to show to your country the brilliance of your mind, talents, and judgment. But at that time I see your way wavering between two destinies, as it were. When your age has completed seven times eight

recurring circuits of the sun, and these two numbers have made up your destined sum in natural circuit, the whole state will turn itself to you alone and to your name; to you the senate, all good men, the allies, the Latins, will look; it will be you alone on whom the safety of the state will depend, and, in short, as dictator it will be necessary for you to set the commonwealth in order, if you escape the wicked hands of kinsmen.'

At this Laelius cried out, and the others groaned deeply, but Scipio smiling gently said, ' I beg you not to wake me from sleep, and to be silent; hear the rest.'

3. ' But that you may be the more zealous, Africanus, in safeguarding the commonwealth, believe this; for all who have saved, helped, or enlarged their country (*patriam*) there is a particular place marked off in heaven, where the blessed enjoy themselves eternally.   Nothing that happens on earth is more acceptable to that supreme God who rules all this universe (*mundum*) than assemblies (*concilia*) and associations of men, bound by the rule of law, which are called commonwealths; the governors and preservers of these proceed from here and return here.'

At this point, although I was terrified, not so much by the fear of death as by the fear of the treachery of my kinsmen, I nevertheless asked whether he and my father Paulus and others whom we think of as dead, were living.   ' Most certainly yes,' he said; ' those are alive who have sprung forth from the fetters of their bodies as from a prison; indeed, what is called your life, is death.   Why, look up, and see your father Paulus coming to you.'

When I saw him I poured out a flood of tears.   He, however, embraced me and kissed me, and forbade me to weep.   As soon as I could stop weeping and begin to speak I said, ' I beg you, best and most revered father, since this is life, as I hear Africanus say, why do I linger on earth, why do I not hurry to you here? '

' Not so,' he said.   ' Until that God, whose temple is all this that you see, has freed you from the fetters of the body, the approach here cannot lie open to you.   For men are created under this law, that they should look after that globe which you see in the middle of this temple, and which is called earth; the soul (? *animus*) has been given to them from those eternal fires which you call stars and planets; which globes and spheres, alive with divine minds, complete their circuits and orbits with marvellous speed.   Wherefore, Publius, you and all dutiful men must keep your souls in the custody of your body; nor must you leave the life of men except at the command of him by whom it was given to you, lest you should seem to have deserted the duty assigned to men by God.   But, Scipio, cherish (*cole*) justice and duty (*pietatem*) as your grandfather and I who begot you did; to do this, is of great importance where parents and kinsmen are concerned, but greatest in matters concerning your country.   Such a life is the way to heaven and to the company of those who have already lived, and freed from the body inhabit that place which you see (it was a circle of brilliant splendour shining out amidst the blazing stars) which you, as you have learnt from the Greeks, call The Milky Way.'

As I looked out from this place, everything appeared to me surpassingly brilliant and wonderful.   There were also stars which we never see from this spot [i.e. from the earth], and the magnitude of them all was such as we have never imagined.   Of these the smallest was farthest from heaven and nearest the earth, and shone with a borrowed light.   Indeed, the globes of the stars easily surpassed the size of the earth. Then the earth appeared to me so small that I was ashamed of our empire, which is, so to speak, but a point on its surface.

4. As I looked more carefully Africanus said to me, 'How long, pray, will your mind be fixed on the ground? Surely you perceive into what regions (*templa*) you have come? All things are connected in nine circles, or rather spheres, of which the outermost which contains all the rest is the celestial, and is itself the supreme God, enclosing and holding together the others. In that are fixed, and revolve, the eternal courses of the stars; beneath it are the seven other spheres, which revolve in a contrary direction to that of the celestial sphere. That planet which on earth they call Saturn possesses one of these spheres; then comes that shining light, favourable and beneficial to the race of men, which is called Jupiter; then the ruddy one, terrible to the earth, which you call Mars; next beneath the Sun holds almost the middle region, lord and king (*princeps*) and regulator of the other lights, the mind and guiding principle of the universe, of such magnitude that he reveals and fills all things with his light. The Sun's companions, so to speak, follow him—the spheres of Venus and of Mercury; and in the lowest sphere the Moon revolves, kindled by the rays of the Sun. But below there is nothing but what is mortal and subject to decay, except for the souls given to the human race by the bounty of the gods. Above the moon all things are eternal. The central and ninth sphere, however, is the Earth, which does not move and is lowest of all, and towards which all bodies (*pondera*) are drawn by their own inclination.'

5. I gazed in astonishment, and when I came to myself I said, 'What is this, this great sound which so fills my ears and is so sweet?'

'That,' he said, 'is produced by the onward rush and motion of the spheres themselves; their separation into unequal but carefully proportioned intervals, blending high notes with low, produces various harmonies; for such mighty motions cannot be so swiftly carried on in silence; and Nature brings it about that the spheres at one extreme sound with a low note, and at the other with a high. Therefore, that highest sphere of heaven, the star-bearer, whose turning is faster, is moved with a high, loud note, while the lowest, lunar, sphere has the deepest note; for the ninth sphere, the Earth, remaining motionless, fixed in one position, always clings to the middle place of the universe. But the other eight spheres, two of which [Mercury and Venus] move at the same speed, produce seven distinct notes—a number which is the key to almost everything. Learned men, by imitating these harmonies on stringed instruments and in songs, have opened a way back to this place for themselves, as have others who have pursued divine studies with outstanding ability during earthly life. The ears of men, quite filled with this sound, have become deaf to it (for there is no duller sense [than hearing] in you) just as at that place called Catadupa, where the Nile hurls itself down from highest mountains, the people who live near by have lost their sense of hearing because of the greatness of the sound. But indeed, so great is the sound of the whole universe, turning at the highest speed, that the ears of men cannot catch it, just as you cannot look straight at the sun, and as your sense of sight is overpowered by his beams.'

I was amazed at these wonders (*hæc admirans*) but nevertheless kept turning my eyes back to the earth.

6. Then Africanus continued: 'I see that you are still looking at the region and home of men; if it seems (as it is) small to you, fix your

gaze always on these heavenly things, and despise those that are human. For what fame can you get from the speech of men, or what glory that is worth the seeking? You see that the earth is inhabited in only a few places, and those very small, while vast deserts lie between those inhabited 'spots' as we may call them; and those who inhabit the earth are not only so separated that nothing can pass amongst them from one to another, but some of them live in parts that are oblique, transverse, or even directly opposite to you; certainly, from such you can expect no glory. You will also notice that the earth is girdled and surrounded with certain belts, of which you see that the two which are farthest apart and lie under the opposite poles of heaven are stiff with cold, while the belt in the middle, which is the greatest, is scorched by the heat of the sun. Two are inhabitable; one of them, the southern, the men of which set their feet against yours, is nothing to your people. But of this northern zone, which you inhabit, see how small a part belongs to you Romans. For the whole land which is inhabited by you, narrower at the ends, broader at the sides, is only a small island, surrounded by that sea which is called on earth the Atlantic, or the Great Sea, or the Ocean. Now you see how small it is, for all its big name. Has your name, or the name of any of us, been able to pass from these known and settled lands across the Caucasus, which you see there, or swim across the Ganges? Who shall hear your name in those other lands of the rising or setting sun, or in the farthest parts of north or south? With all these left out, surely you see into what narrow confines your glory is eager to spread? And how long will even those who speak of you now, continue to do so?

7. But even if the children of future men should wish to hand down in succession to their posterity the praises of each one of us which they have received from their fathers, nevertheless because of the floods and fires which necessarily happen at particular times on earth, we cannot achieve even long-lasting glory, let alone eternal. But what difference does it make that those born after you should speak of you, when there was no mention made of you by those who lived before, who were no less numerous, and were certainly better men? Especially as no one of them who may hear our names can retain any memory for a single year. For men commonly measure a year solely by the return of the sun, that is, of a single star; but when all the stars return to the same place from which they all at first set out and have restored the same configurations over the great distances of the whole heaven, then truly can the returning cycle be called a year; how many generations of men may be contained in that year I hardly dare say. For as once the sun seemed to men to fail and be extinguished when the soul of Romulus entered these very regions (*templa*), so when the sun shall again be eclipsed in the same quarter and at the same season, and all the constellations and stars returned to their first positions, then you may consider the year complete. You must understand, indeed, that not a twentieth part of such a year has yet passed.

Wherefore, if you despair of returning to this place, in which all things are given to great and eminent men, of how little value is that glory among men which can hardly last for a tiny part of a year? Therefore, if you will look on high, and contemplate this resting place and eternal home, and neither concern yourself with the talk of the common herd, nor place your hope in human rewards for your exploits, Virtue herself must draw you with her charms to the true glory. What others say about you is their own concern; they will say it in any case.

But all their talk is limited to those narrow regions which you see; it is buried in the death of men and extinguished in the oblivion of posterity.'

8. When he had said these words I replied, ' If, indeed, Africanus, a path as it were to heaven is laid open by serving one's country well, I will strive much more zealously with such a great reward held out before me, though even from boyhood I have walked in your steps and in those of my father, and have not failed to emulate your glory.'

He answered, ' You must strive indeed; and believe this, that you are not mortal, but only this body. For what the outward form reveals is not you, nor is the figure which can be pointed to with a finger, but it is the mind of a man which is he himself. Know, therefore, that you are a god, if indeed that is a god which quickens, feels, remembers, foresees, and which governs, restrains and moves the body over which it is set, just as the supreme God does this universe (*mundum*). And as the eternal God moves the universe which is mortal in part, so an immortal soul (*animus*) moves your frail body.

For what always moves is eternal, but that which communicates motion to something else, but is itself moved by another force, necessarily ceases to live when this motion finishes. That alone, therefore, which moves itself, never ceases to be moved, because it is never deserted by itself: indeed it is the source and beginning (*principium*) of motion of all other things which are moved. The beginning itself has no origin; for all things arise from a beginning, but that beginning itself cannot be born from something else, for that would not be a beginning which originated from something else. And since it never had a beginning, then indeed it will never have an ending; for if a beginning were destroyed it could neither be reborn from anything else, nor could it create anything else from itself, if, indeed, everything has to arise from a beginning. Thus it happens that the beginning of movement derives from that which is self-moved and that can neither be born nor die, otherwise the whole heaven must fall and all nature come to a standstill, finding no force to stir them to motion again.

9. ' Since, therefore, it is clear, that what is self-moved is eternal, who is there who will deny this to be the nature of souls? For everything which is moved by an outside force is inanimate, but that which has soul is moved by its own inner force, for this is the particular nature and property of souls. If the soul is unique in that it moves itself, it has certainly not been born, and is eternal.

Use it, therefore, for the best things. The noblest tasks concern the wellbeing of your country; a soul busy and occupied in such matters will speed the more swiftly to this resting place, its home; and this flight will be still more swift if the soul, while still shut up in the body, will rise above it, and in contemplation of what is beyond, detach itself as much as possible from the body. For the souls of those who have given themselves up to the pleasures of the body, and have become as it were the slaves of the body, and who at the instigation of desires subservient to pleasure have broken the laws of gods and men, when they have left their bodies fly around the earth itself, and do not return to this place except after many ages of torment.'

He departed, and I awoke from sleep.

APPENDIX IV

TESEIDA

Book vii, stanzas 50-66

The text which is translated here is that of S. Battaglia (Firenze, 1938), pp. 197–210. It does not differ significantly in this section from that printed by A. Roncaglia (Bari, 1941). The text reprinted with a line-by-line translation by Skeat (*Works*, i, 68–73) is corrupt, but occasionally gives readings which seem nearer to those which must have been in Chaucer's own text, which was also very corrupt; such readings are noted here as variants and are placed in brackets. References at the ends of stanzas are to the relevant lines of the *Parlement*.

50. As the prayer of Arcita sought out Mars, so that of Palemone went to merciful Venus on Mount Cithaeron, where, somewhat in the shade, among very tall pines, the temple and mansion of Citherea [i.e. Venus] was placed; when she [i.e. the prayer personified] drew near there, Loveliness (*Vaghezza*) was the first she saw in that high place.

51. Going forward with her, she saw that place to be agreeable and delightful to every view, in form of a leafy and beautiful garden, and full of greenest plants, fresh grass, and every newly-blossomed (*novello*) flower; and she saw clear springs (*var.* clear and living springs) arise there, and amongst the other plants, it seemed to her that myrtle was more abundant than any other there. (183–9)

52. Here she heard almost every kind of bird singing sweetly among the boughs, upon which also, likewise, she saw them with delight making their nests; next, among the fresh grasses, she saw rabbits going quickly here and there, and timid deer and fawns and many other kinds of little creatures (*varii bestiuoli: var. carissimi bestiuoli*, dearest little creatures). (190–6)

53. Likewise, she seemed to hear every instrument and delightful song; wherefore, passing with pace not slow, looking about intently, somewhat undecided in herself, at the high place and the beautiful adornment, she saw it in almost every corner full of spirits, which, flying here and there, went to their appointed places. While she was looking at these, (197–8)

54. among the bushes, beside a spring, she saw Cupid making arrows, having placed the bow at his feet; when the arrows were selected his daughter Sensual Desire (*Volutta, var. Voluptade, Voluntade*) tempered them in the water; and placed by them was Ease (*Ozio*) whom, together with Memory (*Memoria*), she then saw tip the arrows with the metal heads (*ferri*) which she [i.e. *Volutta*] first tempered. (211–16)

55. Then, as she passed, she saw Gracefulness (*Leggiadria*) with Adorning (*Addornezza*) and Friendliness (*Affabilitate*) and Courtesy (*Cortesia*) who was quite lost; and she saw the Arts which have power to force others to commit folly (*di fare altrui a forza far follia*), in their appearance much disfigured from the likeness of us; and Vain Delight (*Van Diletto*) she saw stand alone with Nobility (*Gentilezza*). (218–24)

56. Then near her she saw Beauty (*Bellezza*) pass, without any adornment, looking at herself; and with her she saw Attractiveness (*Piacevolezza*), each one commending herself to the other; then she saw Youth (*Giovanezza*) standing by them, lively and adorned, making

holiday (*molto festeggiando*); and on the other side she saw mad Foolhardiness (*Ardire*), with Flattery (*Lusinghe*) and Pimpery (*Ruffiania*) walking together. (225–9)

57. And in the middle of the place she saw a temple on high columns of copper (*rame*), and saw youths and ladies dancing about it, this one beautiful in herself, and that one (masculine) dressed in fine clothes, ungirt in hair and gowns, barefoot, and spending the day in that alone; then above the temple she saw flying many swallows and murmuring doves (*passere molte e colombi ruccare; var. E posarsi colombe e mormorare*, and doves sit and coo). (230–8)

58. And near the entrance of the temple she saw my lady Peace (*Pace*) sitting quietly, holding lightly in her hand a curtain over the door; near her, wretched to see, Patience (*Pazienza*) discreetly sat, pallid in look; and on all sides she saw about her Promises and Artfulnesses (*Promesse e Arte*). (239–45)

59. Then when she had entered the temple she heard a tumult of sighs there, which whirled about all fiery with hot desires; this lit up all the altars with new flames born of torments, of which each one dripped with tears caused by a cruel and wicked woman, called Jealousy (*Gelosia*) whom she saw there. (246–52)

60. And she saw Priapus hold the highest place in that temple, in such habit as whoever might wish to see him could do so on that night when by braying the dullest animal woke Vesta, to care for whom he was not a little inclined, and towards whom, in that fashion, he was going; and likewise she saw throughout the temple many garlands of diverse flowers. (253–9)

61. Here she saw many bows of the company of Diana hung up and broken, among which was that of Callisto, who became the Arctic Bear, and the apples of proud Atalanta were there, who was sovereign in racing, and also the arms of that other haughty one, who gave birth to the beautiful Parthenopaeus, grandson to the Calidonian King Oenus. (281–7)

62. She saw stories painted there all about, among which, of finer work, she saw all the acts made clear of the wife of Ninus [i.e. *Semiramis*]; and she saw at the foot of the mulberry-tree Pyramus and Thisbe, and the mulberries already stained; and great Hercules she saw among these in the lap of Iole, and Biblis, sad and piteous, beseeching Caunus. (288–9)

63. But as she did not see Venus, it was told her (nor did she know by whom), ' She stays in delight in a more secret part of the temple; if you want her, enter quietly through that door.' Wherefore, without other hesitation, meek in manner as she was, she approached it to enter in to her, to perform the mission entrusted to her. (260–1)

64. But first as she came there she found the door guarded by Riches (*Richezza*) who seemed to her much to be reverenced; and when she was allowed by her to enter in, the place was dark to her at the first steps, but after, as she remained, a little light appeared to her, and she saw her [i.e. Venus] lying naked on a great bed which was very beautiful to see (*bello; var. bella, referring to Venus*). (261–6)

65. She had golden hair, fastened around the head without any tress (*rilegati intorno al capo sanza treccia alcuna*); her face was such that in comparison those who are most praised have no beauty at all; the arms and breast and raised apples were all seen, and the other part was covered with a garment (*veste*) so thin (*sottil*) that almost nothing, hardly, was hidden [*Skeat's text varies widely here*]. (267–73)

66. The place was fragrant with full a thousand odours; on one side

of her Bacchus was seated, on the other, Ceres, with her savoury foods (*savori*); and she [i.e. Venus] held Lasciviousness (*Lascivia*) by the hand, and held also the apple which she, preferred above her sisters, won in the Idean valley. And having seen all this, she [i.e. the prayer] made her request, which was granted without denial.   (274–6)

APPENDIX V

ALANUS' DESCRIPTION OF NATURE

(*De Planctu Naturæ*, ed. Wright, pp. 445ff, Migne, *PL* 210, cols. 439–40. Translated by C. S. Lewis, *Allegory of Love* (1936), pp. 106ff)

The virgin, as I have before signified, at her first coming forth out of the coasts of the heavenly region into the hovel of the world passible, was borne in a glassy coach, and was drawn of Juno's own birds, not managed with any yoke, but joined thereto of their proper will and election.   A certain man also that with his height overtopped both the virgin and her coach, whose countenaunce smacked not of vile earthliness but rather of the Godhead's privity, as though he should succour the insufficiency of her sex feminine, did guide its course with measurable regiment.   To the beholding of whose beauty when I had (as it were) drawn together the soldiers of mine eyes, that is, the rays visual; the same, not daring to issue out in the face of so great a majesty, and being blunted with the strokes of his splendour, betook themselves for fear into the tents of mine eyelids.   At the coming of the said virgin you would a thought that all the elements, as though they then renewed their kinds, did make festival.   The heaven, to lighten (as it were) the maid's journey with his candles, gave order to his stars that they should shine beyond their wont; wherefore methought the daylight marvelled at their hardihood who durst so insolently be seen in his presence. Phoebus also, putting on a jollier countenance than he was used, poured forth all the riches of his light and made a show of it to meet her; and to his sister (from whom he had taken away the garniture of his beaming), giving her back again the garment of jocundity, he bade that she should run to meet such a queen as was now come among them.   The air, putting off his weeping clouds, with serene and friendly cheer smiled upon her where she came, and whereas he was before grieved with the raging of Aquilo, now popularly took his ease in the bosom of Favonius.   The birds, moved by a certain kindly inspiration, rejoicing with the plausive playing of their pinions, showed unto the virgin a worshipping countenance.   Juno forsooth that before had scorned the kissings of Jupiter, was now with so great joy made drunken, that by a darting prologue of her glances she set her husband on fire for pleasing passages of love.   The sea also that before was enraged with stormy waves, at the maid's coming made an holiday of peace and swore an everlasting calm; for Aeolus, lest they should move their wars (more than civil) in the virgin's presence, bound in their prisons the tempestuous winds.   The fishes, even, swimming up to the eyebrows of the waves, so far forth as the lumpish kind of their sensuality suffered them, foretold by their glad cheer the coming of their lady; and Thetis, being at play with Nereus, bethought her that time to conceive another Achilles.   Moreover certain maidens, the greatness of whose beauty was able not only to steal away the reason from a man but to make those in heaven also to forget their deity, coming forth out of places where streams sprang, brought unto her gifts of pigmentary's nectar, making as they should offer tithes to their newcome queen. And truly, the earth, that before lay stripped by winter's robbery, of her garnishments, made shift to borrow from the largesse of the spring a scarlet smock of flowers, lest in the dishonour of her old clouts she might not decently be seen before the virgin.

GLOSSARY

GLOSSARY

All forms of all words are recorded. All forms (except obviously related inflected forms) appear as head-words with cross-references where necessary. All occurrences are marked by line references to the text, except where the word occurs frequently in the same sense and form, in which case only three references are given, followed by etc. The head-word in each case where more than one grammatical form occurs is the first form in the standard order of grammatical descent which occurs in the text. A word emended in text is indicated by †.

The following points of arrangement should be noted. Variation between *i* and *y* is disregarded, and *y* occupies the same alphabetical place as *i* (it should also be noted that initial *i* sometimes has the value of modern initial *j*); past participles with the prefix *i-* are given under the word-letter and the prefix is disregarded; variation between *u* and *v* is disregarded, and *v* occupies the same alphabetical place as *u*; variation between þ (thorn) and *th* is disregarded, and þ takes the same alphabetical position as *th*; ȝ (yogh) has a separate alphabetical place following *g*.

a, an, *indef. art.* a, an, 19, 20, 223, etc.

a, *see* **haue**

abasht, *past part.* abashed, 447†

aboue, *prep.* above, 394†

aboute, *adv.* about, 247; around, 80, 194, 232

acceptyth, *pres. 3 sg.* accepts, 532†

Achilles, Achilles, 290

acloyith, *pres. 3 sg.* overburdens, 517

acord, *n.* harmony, 197; agreement, 371, 38ː, 668

acordaunt, *adj.* agreeing; **acordaunt to,** in harmony with, 203

acorde, *v.* agree, 608

adamauntis, *n. pl.* magnets, 148

adoun, *adv.* down; **brought adoun,** brought down, refuted, 537

Affrycan, (Scipio) Africanus the Elder, 41, 44, 52, etc.

Affrik, Africa, 37

aftyr, *adv.* after, afterwards, 55, 59, 658, etc.; *conj.* according as, 216; *prep.* after, 60, 400, 649; according to, 305, 401; **aftyr that,** after, 79

aftyrward, *adv.* afterwards, 263

ago, *past part.* gone, 465

agon, *adv.* ago, 18

agre, *pres. subj. 3 sg.* agree, 409

agref, *adv.* amiss, 543

aȝen, *adv.* again, 100, 295; *prep.* facing, 443

aȝens, *prep.* against; at the approach of, 342

ay, *adv.* always, 74, 143, 173, etc.

al, *adj.* all, 4, 17, 23, etc.; **alle,** 525, 527, 665, etc.

al, *adv.* entirely, quite, 133, 139, 419, etc.; **al aboute,** all around, 194; **al be (that),** although, 8, 436; **al thus,** exactly like this, 30

al, *n.* all, everything, 69, 71, 199, etc.

aldirnex, *adv.* nearest of all, 244

Aleyn, Alan (Alanus de Insulis), 316

allas, *interj.* alas, 494

allone, *adj.* alone, 455†

almyghty, *adj.* almighty, 379, 647

alofte, *adv.* above, 203; olofte, 683

also, *adv.* also, 498

althow, *conj.* although, 651; althav, 475; althow that, 162

alwey, *adv.* always, 3, 80, 232, etc.

am, *see* be

amyddis, *adv.* in the middle, 277

amys, *adv.* faultily, 446

among, *prep.* among, 374

and, &, *conj.* and, 11, 20, 24, etc.

anoyeth, *pres. 3 sg.* annoys, 518

anon, *adv.* directly, straight away, 100, 120, 169, etc.

anonryght, *adv.* immediately, 218

anothir, *adj.* another, 51, 449; *pron.* 567

answerde, *pret. 3 sg.* answered, 446, 463, 580, etc.

apere, *v.* appear, 42

aray, *n.* state, condition, 255; dress, 96, 317, 318; (*personified*) Adornment, 219

argumentis, *n. pl.* arguments, 538

armys, *n. pl.* arms, 38

armonye, *n.* harmony, 63, 191

aros, *pret. 3 sg.* arose, 575

Art, *n.* (*personified*) Cunning, 245

arwis, *n. pl.* arrows, 212

as, *adv.* as, 34; (*pleonastic*) 26, 653; *conj.* as, 16, 22, 161, etc.; according as, 389; as þat, as, 95, 393

asaye, *v.* attempt, 257

asp, *n.* aspen tree, 180

aspye, *see* espie

assay, *n.* assault, 2

asse, *n.* ass, 255

assemblede, *past part.* assembled, 367

assent, *n.* assent, agreement, 557

assentid, *past part.* agreed, 526

assh, *n.* ash tree, 176

assure, *pres. 1 sg.* guarantee, protect, 448

astonyith, *pres. 3 sg.* bewilders, 5†; astonyd, *past part.* 142

at, *prep.* at, 92, 98, 154, etc.; in, 481; at regard of, with regard to, 58

Athalante, Atalanta, 286

atyr, *n.* attire, clothing, 225

attempre, *adj.* mild, 204

avayle, *pres. 3 pl.* avail, are of use, 538

auante, *pres. 1 sg.* (*refl.*) boast, 470

auauntour, *n.* boaster, 430

audyence, *n.* hearing, 308

auenture, *n.* fortune, 131

avise, *v.* (*refl.*) consider, 648

auysement, *n.* consultation, 555

auncestre, *n.* ancestor, 41

aungel, *n.* angel, 191; aungelis, *gen. sg.*, 356

avouterye, *n.* adultery, 361

auter, *n.* altar, 249

autorite, *n.* authority, 506

awey(e), *adv.* away, 656, 694; away, 682, 692

axe, *pres. 1 sg.* ask, 648; axede, *pret. 3 sg.* 50; axsede, *pret. 3 pl.* 579

Bacus, Bacchus, 275

bad, *pret. 3 sg.* commanded, told, 64, 320

batayle, *n.* battle, 539

be, *see* be(e)(n), by

be(e)(n), *v.* be, 12, 465, 537, etc.; am, *pres. 1 sg.* 133, 479, 512, etc.; ert, *pres. 2 sg.* 683; is, *pres. 3 sg.* 49, 57, 70, etc.; nys, is not, 501; are, *pres. 1 pl.* 611, be, 619; ben, *pres. 3 pl.* 79,

been, 13, 50, 101, etc.; **be,** *imper. sg.* 116, 132, 616, *pl.* **beth,** 660; **be,** *pres. subj. 1 sg.* 428, 432; *pres. subj. 2 sg.* 162; *pres. subj. 3 sg.* 81, 159, 431, etc.; **be,** *past part.* 455, **ben,** 472. Cf. **was**

bed, *n.* bed, 88†, 99, 265; **bedis,** *gen. sg.* 98

befalle, *pres. subj. 3 sg.* may happen, 664

beforn, byfore, byforn, *adv.* before, 97; earlier, 107†; in advance, 45; *prep.* before, 486; in front of, 239, 368

begynne, *v.* begin, 392; **begynyth,** *pres. 3 sg.* heading; **began,** *pret. 1 sg.* 118; *pret. 3 sg.* 382†, 561

begoon, *past part.* contented, 171

behette, *pret. 3 sg.* promised, 436†

behynde, *adv.* behind, 520†

beholde, *v.* look, 18, 142

bek, *n.* beak, 378

benygne, *adj.* gracious, 375

benygnely, *adv.* gently, with kindness, 370n

berafte, *pret. 3 sg.* deprived of, 87

bere, *v.* bear, 137; *pres. subj. 1 sg. (refl.)* behave, 459; **born,** *past part.* behaved, 109; **born,** 484

besekynge, *pres. part.* beseeching, 421

beset, *past part.* employed, 598

besy, busy, *adj.* busy, active, 369; painful, vexatious, 89

besyde, *prep.* beside, 211, 275

besyede, *pret. 3 sg. impers.* busied, 192

besily, *adv.* busily, 74; eagerly, 257

besynesse, *n.* activity, 86

best, *adv.* best, 116, 397, 535, etc.

bestis, *n. pl.* animals, 86, 196

bet, *adv.* better, 166, 451, 474, etc.; **me was bet,** it was better for me, 152

bethynke, *v.* think of, imagine, 483

betyde, *v.* happen, befall, 654

betyr, *adj. (as n.),* better, 200

betwix(syn), *prep.* between, 40†, 148

Beute, *n. (personified)* Beauty, 225

bewrye, *v.* conceal, 348†n

bi, by, be, *prep.* by, 221, 223, 241, etc.; at, during, 256, 357; in, 400; in accordance with, 387; on, 328; with, 371, 557; with regard to, 4, 158, 159, etc.; **be no manere weye,** in no kind of way, 653

Biblis, Byblis, 289

byfore, byforn, *see* **beforn**

Byheste, *n. (personified)* Promise, 245

byldere, *n. as adj.* builder; used for building, 176

bittere, *adj.* bitter, 252

byttyrnesse, *n.* bitterness, 161

blak, *adj.* black, 141 *(as n.)*; **blake,** *pl.* 682, 692

blent, *pres. 3 sg.* blinds, 600

blewe, *adj. pl.* blue, 186

blysful, *adj.* full of happiness, 48, 83, 127; joyous, happy, 113, 413; *pl.* **blisseful,** 689

blysse, *n.* joy, 39, 72†, 77, etc.

blythe, *adj.* glad, 504, 622

blyue, *adv.* quickly, 604†

blod, *n.* blood; race, lineage, 550

blosmy, *adj.* blossomy, covered with blossom, 183†n

bode, *n.* omen, 343

bok, *n.* book, 19, 29, 87, etc.; **bokis,** *pl.* 10, 16, 24, etc.

bolde, *v.* become bold, 144

bond, *n.* bond, 438

bone, *n.* boon, request, 643

boote, *n.* remedy; **doth of hungir boote,** gives the remedy for hunger, 276

bordit, *past part.* jested, 589

born, *see* bere

bothe, *adv.* both, 90

i-bounden, *past part.* bound, 268

bouris, *n. pl.* private rooms, 304

bow, *n.* bough, 190; bowys, *pl.* 183

bowe, *n.* bow, 213, 282

boxtre, *n.* boxtree, 178

bras, *n.* bronze, 231

braunche, *n.* branch, 612; braun-chis, *pl.* 304

brekeris, *n. pl.* breakers, 78†

brenne, *v.* burn, 249

brest, *n.* breast, 269

bryd, *n.* bird, 310; bryddis, *pl.* 190, 192, 336, etc.

bryghte, *adj. pl.* bright, 356

brynge, *v.* bring, produce, 564; forth to brynge, to give birth to, hatch, 192; bryngyth, *pres. 3 sg.* brings, 343; brouȝte, *pret. 3 sg.* 121 ; broughte . . . forth, brought forth, hatched, 613; brought, *past part.* 666; brought adoun, brought down, refuted, 537

i-broke, *past part.* broken, 282

brothir, *n.* brother, 566

buk, *n.* buck, 195

busy, *see* besy

but, *conj.* but, 14, 17, 26, etc.; unless, 159, 459, 469, etc.

Calyxte, Callisto, 286†

calle, *v.* call, 405, 524, 577

cam, *see* come, comyn

can, *pres. 1 sg.* can, am able to, 34, 106, 438, etc.; canst, *pres. 2 sg.* 163, 598, 602; can, *pres. 3 sg.* 209, 220, 348, etc.; cunne, *pres. 3 pl.* 333

Candace, Candace, 288

carayne, *n.* carrion, 177

care, *n.* anxiety, 363

Cartage, Carthage, 44

carte, *n.* cart, 102n

cartere, *n.* carter, 102

cast, *n.* design, 305

caste, *pret. 1 sg.* cast, 172

cause, *n.* cause, 63, 106, 251, etc.

causeles, *adv.* without cause, 590

centence, sentence, *n.* meaning, 35, 126; decision, judgment, 383; opinion, 530

Ceres, Ceres, 276†

certeyn, *adj.* certain, 20; *pl.* 67

certis, *adv.* certainly, 424.

chapiteris, *n. pl.* chapters, 32

charge, *n.* responsibility, 507†n, 545†

charite, *n.* charity, 508

chaste, *adj.* chaste, 281

chaunge, *v.* change, 582

cheere, cher, *n.* look, expression, 414, 488

cherl, *n.* churl, 596

che(e)se, schese, *v.* choose, 146, 388, 399, etc.; chese, *pres. 1 sg.* 417, shes, 417; chesith, *pres. 3 sg.* 623n; chosyn, *past part.* 528, 576, 673

choys, *n.* choice, 406, 408, 649

chosyn, *see* chese

choughe, *n.* chough, 345†

Cypyon, *see* Scipion

cipresse, *n.* cypress, 179

Cypride, Cypris, Venus, 277

Cytherea, Cytherea, Venus, 113

clad, *past part.* clad, 173

clepith, *pres. 3 sg.* calls, 352

cler, *adj.* bright, 210; cleere, *pl.* 77

clerkis, *pl.* learned men, 333

Cliopatre, Cleopatra, 291

cloth, *n.* cloth, 273

cofere, *n.* coffer, 177

cok, kok, *n.* cock, 350, 357

cokkow, kokkow(e), *n.* cuckoo, 358, 505, 603; (*as bird's cry*) 499

cold, *adj.* cold; *as n.* 205, 380; colde, *pl.* 187

colde, *v.* make cold, 145

colour, *n.* colour, 174

coloured, *past part.* coloured, 443

comaunde, *pres. 1 sg.* command, 617

come, comyn, *v.* come, 68, 72, 76; **comyth,** *pres. 3 sg.* 23, 25, 61, etc.; **come,** *pres. 2 pl.* 388; **cum of,** *imper. pl.* finish! 494; **cam,** *pret. 3 sg.* 252, 413, 597; come, *past part.* 36, 98, 295

com(o)un, *adj.* common; public, general, 47n, 75, 507

conclusioun, *n.* decision, judgment, 526, 620

condicioun, *n.* condition; **in this condicioun,** on this condition, 407n

confort, *n.* comfort, consolation, 170

conyes, *n. pl.* rabbits, 193

conquerynge, *n.* conquering, 2

conseyl, *n.* secret, 348; plan, 522

conseyl(e), *v.* advise, 633; *(as n.)* advising, 631

cormeraunt, *n.* cormorant, 362

corn, *n.* corn, 23

corner, *n.* corner, 260

corupcioun, *n.* corruption, 614

couercheif, *n.* kerchief, 272n

coward, *adj.* cowardly, 349

craft, *n.* art, skill, 1; *(personified)* 220n

crane, *n.* crane, 344

creature, *n.* created being, 301, 641

crewel, *adj.* cruel, 11

cri, *n.* cry, bray, 256

cryeth, *pres. 3 sg.* cries, shouts, 465; **cryede,** *pret. 3 pl.* called, 278; shouted, 494†, 499

crowe, *n.* crow, 363

cum, *see* come

cunne, *see* can

cunnyng(e), *n.* skill, 167, 487; knowledge, 513

Cupide, Cupid, 212, 652

cure, *n.* cure, remedy, 128; concern; **dede his besy cure,** was busily concerned, 369

cursede, *past part.* cursed, 495

Curteysie, *n.* *(personified)* Courtesy, 219

curtyn, *n.* curtain, 240

day, *n.* day, 21, 28, 93, etc.; **daylight,** 40, 85

dale, *n.* dale, valley, 327

dame, *n.* lady, 240, 242

dar, *pres. 1 sg.* dare, 13, 456, 479; **durste,** *pret. subj. 1 sg.* might venture, 541

Daunger, *n.* *(personified)* Power-to-Harm, 136

daunsith, *pres. 3 sg.* dances, 592; **daunsed,** *pret.* 3 *pl.* danced, 232n

dauntist, *pres. 2 sg.* tame, subdue, 114

ded, *adj.* dead, 585; **dede,** *pl.* 50, 79, 187

dede, *n.* deed, 8; *pl.* 82

dede, *see* do(n)

dedly, *adj.* mortal, 128

deere, *adj.* dear, 41, 427, 466; delightful, 76

defense, *n.* protection, 273

degre, *n.* rank, 394, 453, 662; manner, 646

deye, *v.* die, 423, 469, 471, etc.; **dye,** *pres. 3 pl.* 55†; **dyde,** *pret. 3 pl.* 294†; **deyede,** *pret. subj. 3 sg.* 587

delicasye, *n.* wantonness, 359

Delyt, *n.* *(personified)* Delight, 224

delite, *v.* delight, 27, 66

delyuere, *v.* set free, 508, 523; **delyuered,** *past part.* 491

demyn, *v.* judge, 166

departynge, *n.* departure, 675

derk(e), *adj.* dark, 85, 263

desyr, *n.* desire, 248; *(personified)* 227

desyrith, *pres. 3 sg.* wants, 559

desport, *n.* pleasure, 260

deth, *n.* death, 54, 179, 342, etc.

deuyne, *v.* divine; **to deuyne,** for divining, 182

deuyse, *v.* tell, 333; describe, 398; **deuyseth,** *pres. 3 sg.* 317

Dyane, Diana, 281

Dido, Dido, 289

dye, *see* **deye**

difference, *n.* difference, 125

diffyne, *v.* state clearly, 529

discheuele, *adj. pl.* with hair flowing loose, 235

discretly, *adv.* discreetly, 241

discussid, *past part.* discussed, 624

Disdayn, *n.* (*personified*) Disdain, 136

disfigurat, *adj.* disfigured, deformed, 222n

dishobeysaunt, *adj.* disobedient, 429

dispit, *n.* contempt; **in dispit of,** in defiance of, 281

disseyuable, *adj.* deceptive, 65

distraynyth, *pres. 3 sg.* clutches, 337

doinge, *n.* affair, 515

doke, *n.* duck, 498, 589, 594

dom, *n.* judgment, 308, 480, 546

do(n), *v.* do, make, 163, 221, 478, etc.; **doth,** *pres. 3 sg.* 335, 476, 517; **doth . . . boote,** gives the remedy for, 276; **don,** *pres. 2 pl.* 451, 542; *pres. 3 pl.* 599; **do,** *subj. 3 sg.* 166, 420; *subj. 2 pl.* 651; **do me hangyn,** *imper. pl.* cause me to be hanged, 458; **dede,** *pret. 3 sg.* 145, 369; **don,** *past part.* 70, 647†, **haue don!** finish! 492; **(i)-do,** 542, 693

donghil, *n.* dunghill, 597

dore, *n.* door, 239

doth, *see* **do(n)**

do(ɔ)ughtyr, *n.* daughter, 214, 448

dounward, *adv.* downward, 490

douue, *n.* dove, 341; **dowis,** *pl.* 237

drake, *n.* drake, 360

drede, *n.* doubt, 52, 81

dred(e), *imper.* fear; **dred(e) the not,** fear not, 157, 448

dredful, *adj.* full of fear, timid, 3, 195, 638

dreye, *see* **drye**

drem, *n.* dream, 31

dremyth, *pres. 3 sg.* dreams, 101, 102

dresse, *v.* prepare, 88; **dressid,** *past part.* 665

dreuyne, *past part.* driven, 682, 692

drye, dreye, *adj.* dry, 139, 380

drye, *pres. 3 pl.* suffer, 251

drynkyth, *pres. 3 sg.* drinks, 104

dronke, *past part.* drunken; causing drunkenness, 181

dulle, *adj.* lacking in feeling, 162†

dunne, *adj. pl.* dun, 334

dure, *v.* last, 616, 642

durste, *see* **dar**

dwelle, *pres. 3 pl.* dwell, 33

dwellynge, *n.* habitation, 51

ech(e), *pron.* each, 174, 607, 670, etc.

effect, *n.* effect; **in effect,** in fact, actually, 619n

egle, *n.* eagle, 330, 373, 393, etc.; **eglis,** *pl.* 332, 540

(e)ye, *n.* eye, 630†n; **eyen,** *pl.* 172, 341

eyr, *n.* air, 204†, 313

eythir, *adj.* either, 125, 496

ek(e), *adv.* also, 91, 119, 338, etc.

eleccioun, *n.* choice, 409, 621; election, 528

Eleyne, Helen, 291†

elis, *gen. sg.* eel's, 346

elm, *n.* elm, 177

emeroude, *n.* emerald, 175

emperesse, *n.* empress, 319

enclyne, *v.* incline, dispose, 325; **enclyned,** *past part.* bowed, 414

encresede, *pret. 3 sg.* increased, 143

ende, *n.* end, 49, 441, 495, etc.

endyte, *v.* compose, narrate with skill, 119, 167

endure, *v.* last, 130; endure, 661

engenderede, *past part.* produced; **engenderede with,** produced by, 248

engendrure, *n.* begetting, 306

entent(e), *n.* mind, 532; opinion, 580; desire, wish, 644

entyrmes, *n.* a delicacy served between the main courses of a banquet, or an entertainment between the courses; *hence* interval, 665

entirmetyn, *v.* (*refl.*) meddle (with), 515

entytlit, *past part.* entitled, 30†

entre, *v.* enter, 147, 153

entrikyth, *pres. 3 sg.* ensnares, 403

ere, *n.* ear, 519; **hadde an ere To,** had an ear for, was attentive to, 519–20; **erys,** *pl.*; **thourw myne erys . . . wente,** went through my ears, was quite deafening, 500

errour, *n.* doubt, perplexity, 146, 156

ert, *see* **be(e)(n)**

erthe, *n.* earth, 33, 57, 64, etc.

eschewyng, *n.* avoidance, 140

ese, *n.* ease; comfort, pleasure, 384, 480

esy, *adj.* gentle, 382

espie, aspye, *v.* look, observe, 194, 280; **espyede,** *pret. 1 sg.* 250

estat, *n.* rank, 550, 630

etith, *pres. 3 sg.* eats, 604; **etyn,** *pres. 3 pl.* 325

euene, *adj.* equal, 149, 381; exact, 668

euere, *adv.* always, 130, 358†, 419, etc.; ever, 374, 433

eueremore, *adv.* always, 185, 584

euery, *adj.* every, 68, 190, 206, etc.

euer(r)ich(e), *pron.* each, every one, 369, 401, 408, etc.; *adj.* 641†

ew, *n.* yew, 180

face, *n.* face, 155, 243, 317

facoun, *n.* falcon, 337, 529

facound, *adj.* eloquent, 521

facounde, *n.* eloquence, 558

faylyn, *v.* fail, 85†

fayneste, *adv.* most joyfully, 480

fayre, *adj. pl.* beautiful, 234, 237; **fayrere,** *comp.* 301

fayr(e), *adv.* clearly, loudly, 503, 594; well, 511

falle, *past part.* fallen; **is to ʒow falle,** is given to you, 406

fals(e), *adj.* false, 347, 456

fare, *v.* fare; **fare The bet,** get on the better, 698–9; **farst,** *pres. 2 sg.* behave, proceed, 599; **ferde,** *pret. 1 sg.* behaved, acted, 152

faste, *adv.* fast, quickly, 21, 133, 170, etc.; deeply, 94

fauour, *n.* favour, 626

federys, *n. pl.* feathers, 334, 356†, 366

fe(e)re, *n.* companion, mate, 410n, 416

fe(e)t, *n. pl.* feet, 213, 337

fey, *n.* faith, 24

feldefare, *n.* fieldfare, 364

feldys, *n. pl.* fields, 22

fele, *adj.* many, 329

felynge, *n.* feeling; understanding, 4

fer, *adv.* far, 440

ferbrond, *n.* flaming torch, 114

ferde, *see* **fare**

fere, *n.* fear, 143

ferforth, *adv.* far; **so ferforth,** to such an extent, 377

ferst(e), *see* **fyrst**

ferthere, *adv.* farther, further, 194, 280

fesaunt, *n.* pheasant, 357

fewe, *pron.* few, 286

fy, *interj.* fie, for shame, 596†

fyȝt, *pres. 3 sg.* fights, 103

fild, *past part.* filled, 610

file, *v.* file, 212

fynally, *adv.* finally, 92, 620

fynde, *v.* find, 318, 330, 367, etc.; *pres. subj. 3 sg.* 433, 456; **fond(e),** *pret. 1 sg.* 242, 261; *pret. 3 sg.* 374†, **founde,** *past part.* 428

fynnys, *n. pl.* fins, 189

fyr, *n.* fir, 179

fyrst, ferst(e), *adv.* first, 36, 69, 643, etc.

fisch, *n.* fish, 139; **fischis,** *pl.* 188

Flaterye, *n.* (*personified*) Flattery, 227

flaume, *n.* flame, 250

fle, *v.* fly; **fle ȝoure wey,** fly on your way, 388

flen, *v.* flee, 147

flete, *pres. 1 sg.* float, 7†

flye, *n.* fly, 501

flyght, *n.* flight, 694

flour(r)is, *n. pl.* flowers, 186, 259, 302, etc.

fol, *n.* fool, 505, 571, 574

folye, *n.* folly, foolishness, 221

folk, *n.* people, 9, 50, 55, etc.; followers, 245; sort, company, 524

fonde, *v.* try, 257

fond(e), founde, *see* **fynde**

fo(o), *n.* foe, enemy, 339, 346; **fon,** *pl.* 103

Fool-hardynesse, *n.* (*personified*) Foolhardiness, 227

for, *conj.* for, 8, 22, 90, etc.; because, 107; *prep.* for, 15, 38, 315, etc.; because of, 87, 146 (*first*), 336; (*pleonastic*) 18, 88, 146 (*second*), etc.; as to, 497; in return for, 454; **for me,** as far as I am concerned, for my part, 229; **for taryinge,** because of the delay, 468, to prevent delaying, 657

forbede, *pres. subj. 3 sg.* forbid, 582

force, *n.* force, 221†n; **fors,** consequence, importance, 615

forge, *n.* beat into shape, 212

forȝeuyn, *past part.* forgiven, 82

formel(e), *n.* formel (the female of the eagle or the hawk), 371, 373, 418, etc.

formyd, *past part.* formed, shaped, 396

fors, *see* **force**

forseyde, *adj.* aforesaid, 120

forsothe, *adv.* truly, 586, 653

forth, *adv.* forth, 192, 613; forward, 297, 603; on, 27; out, 352; **forth with,** along with, 121, 466

fortheryng, *n.* assisting, 384

forwery, *adj.* very tired, 93

foul, *n.* bird, 306, 320, 328; (*collective sg. for pl.*) 604; **foulis, foules,** *pl.* 323, 324, 684, etc.; *gen. pl.* 203†

foule, *adv.* foully, 517

i-founded, *past part.* founded; **i-founded stronge,** set on firm foundations, 231

Fraunce, France, 677

fre, *adj.* free, 649

freut, *n.* fruit, 137

fro, *prep.* from, 150, 664†

from, *prep.* from, 23, 43, 86, etc.

frosch(e), *adj.* fresh, 174n, 442; *pl.* 259, 354

frosty, *adj.* frosty; coming in the frosty winter, 364

fuyr, *n.* fire, 246

ful, *adj.* full, 65, 77, 183, etc.

ful, *adv.* very, 10, 21, 125, etc.

fulfyld, *past part.* filled, 89

gay, *adj.* finely dressed, 234n

Galaxye, Galaxy, Milky Way, 56†

game, *n.* playfulness, fun, 226

gan, *pret. 1 sg.* began, did, 88, 142, 194, etc.; *pret. 3 sg.* 27, 40, 42, etc.; **gan,** *pret. 3 pl.* 312, **gunne,** 193, 257, 283, etc.

gardyn, *n.* garden, 183

garlondis, *n. pl.* garlands, 259

gate, *n.* gate, 121, 123†; **gatis,** *pl.* 154

geaunt, *n.* giant, 344

gelous, *see* **ielous**

gent, *adj.* ' nice ' (*derisive*), 558n

gentil, *adj.* gentle, 196n; noble, 337, 485, 535, etc.; **gentilleste,** *superl.* most excellent, 373; noblest, of highest breeding, 550, 635

Gentillesse, *n.* (*personified*) Good Breeding, 224

gerdonynge, *n.* giving of reward, 455

ges(s)e, *v.* guess, 602; *pres. 1 sg.* suppose, imagine, 160, 200, 223

gete, *pres. 2 pl.* get, 651

gyde, *n.* guide, 136, 153

gilt, *n.* guilt, 434

gilte, *adj. pl.* gilt-coloured, 267

gyse, *n.* manner, 399

glad, *adj.* glad, 132, 171, 532

gladen, *v.* to be glad, rejoice, 687

glotenye, *n.* gluttony; **of glotenye,** gluttonous, 362

glotoun, *n.* glutton, 610, 613

God, God, 14, 84, 199, etc.

god, *n.* god, 253, 275

goddesse, *n.* goddess, 252, 303, 368, etc.

gold, *n.* gold, 103, 141, 265

goldene, *adj.* golden, 267

gole, *n.* mouthful, 556n

gon, *v.* go, 55, 544; **goth,** *pres. 3 sg.* 100; **gon,** *pres. 3 pl.* 127, 129, 134; **go,** *imper. sg.* 616; **gon,** *past part.* 102

good, *adj.* good, 131, 660; **in good fey,** in truth, 24

good, *n.* goods, possessions, 462

goodlieste, *adj.* goodliest, 375

goos, *n.* goose, 358, 498, 501, etc.; **gosis,** *gen. sg.* 586

goshauk, *n.* goshawk, 335

goth, *see* **gon**

gouernaunce, *n.* control, 387

grace, *n.* favour, grace, 84, 129, 319, etc.; **his grace,** favour for himself, 412: fortune, destiny; **harde grace,** ill-fortune, 65; **of al his grace,** of all his (future) destiny, 45

gras, *n.* herb, 206†

graunte, *pres. 1 sg.* grant, 645; *imper. sg.* 643†

gre(e)ne, *adj.* green, 122n, 130, 174, etc.; *pl.* 202, 352

greete, *n.* substance, essential part, 35

grey, *adj. pl.* grey, 335

grene, *n.* grassy ground, 328

gret, *adj.* great, 125, 508; **greete,** *pl.* 230

greuaunce, *n.* pain, discomfort, 205

gunne, *see* **gan**

ȝa, *see* **ȝe**

ȝaf, *see* **ȝeue**

ȝe, ȝa, *adv.* yea, yes, 52, 497, 594† etc.

ȝe, *pers. pron. 2nd pers. nom. pl.* you, 386, 388, 464, etc.; **ȝow, yow,** *acc. and dat.* 16, 35, 138, etc.; **ȝore, ȝoure, ȝure,** *poss. adj.* your, 384, 401, 495, etc.; **ȝoures,** *poss. pron.* yours, 642† ȝe(e)r(e), *n.* year, 23, 236, 321, etc.; ȝeris, *gen. pl.* 67

ȝelwe, *adj. pl.* yellow, 186

ȝerde, *n.* rod; rule, discipline, 640

ȝerne, *adv.* quickly, 3; eagerly, 21

ȝeue, *v.* give; ȝeue hire audyence, listen to her, 308 (cf. audyence); ȝif, *imper. sg.* give, 119; ȝaf, *pret. 3 sg.* 274, 667

ȝif, *see* ȝeue

ȝit, *conj.* yet, still, 10, 163, 208, etc.

ȝonge, *adj. pl.* young, 278

ȝoore, *adv.* long (of time) 17, 476

ȝ(o)(u)re(s), *see* ȝe, *pers. pron.*

Ȝouthe, *n.* (*personified*) Youth, 226

ȝow, *see* ȝe

hadde, haddist, hade, *see* haue

hale, *v.* draw, attract, 151

half(e), *n.* half, 468, 475; side, 125

hallis, *n. pl.* halls, 304

hals, *n.* neck, 458

han, *see* haue

hand, hond(e), *n.* hand, 169, 240, 256, etc.

hangyn, *v.* hang, 458; hyng, *pret. 3 pl.* 282

hap, *n.* fortune, 402

happyn, *v.* happen, 473; happith me, *pres. 3 sg.* it happens to me, 10; happede me, *pret. 3 sg.* happened to me, 18

hard(e), *adj.* hard, 2, 65, 534

hardy, *adj.* sturdy, 176; bold, 338

hat, *n.* hat, 589

haue, *v.* have, 412, 495†, 570, etc., han, 572, 621, 623, etc., a, 454; haue, *pres. 1 sg.* 396, 453, 462, etc.; hast, *pres. 2 sg.* 109, 160, 681, etc.; hath, *pres. 3 sg.* 38, 44, 105, etc., hathe, 688, han, 545; han, *pres. 3 pl.* 51, 528, 554, etc.; have, *subj. 3 sg.* 610; hadde, *pret. 1 sg.* 90, 91, 107, etc.; haddist, *pret. 2 sg.* 167; hadde, *pret. 3 sg.* 32, 377, 519,

etc.; hade, *pret. 3 pl.* 576; hadde, *pret. subj. 3 sg.* 455, 487, 493; haue, *imper. sg.* 427; hauynge, *pres. part.* 426

hautayn, *adj.* proud, stately, 262†

he, *pers. pron. 3 pers. nom. sg.* he, 9, 12, 37, etc.; hym, *acc. and dat.* 6, 38, 42, etc., himself, 603, 662†; his(e), *poss. adj.* his, 5, 11, 13, etc.; his, *poss. pron.* 169; hymself, 517

hed(e), *n.* head, 258, 269†, 414; heuedis, hedis, *pl.* 215, 554

hed, *n.* heed, attention, 383

he(e)re, *adv.* here, 50†, 57, 408, etc.

he(e)re, *v.* hear, 467, 658; herde, *pret. 1 sg.* 190, 198, 247; *pret. 3 sg.* 60, 200, 445, etc.; herd, *past part.* 618

heyest, *adj.* highest, 324

heysoge, *n.* hedge-sparrow, 612

held, *see* hold

hele, *n.* well-being, recovery, 128

helle, *n.* hell, 32

helpe, *n.* help, 116, 279

hem (self), *see* they

hente, *pret. 3 sg.* took hold of, 120, 154

Hercules, Hercules, 288

herde, *see* he(e)re

here, *see* he(e)re, she, they

heris, *n. pl.* hairs, 267

heris, *see* she

herkenyth, *imper.* listen to, 564

herof, *adv.* concerning this, 502

heroun, *n.* heron, 346

hert, *n.* hart, 195

herte, *n.* heart, 144, 355, 417, etc.; beloved one, 427; mind, 483; spirit, courage, 660; hertis, *gen. sg.* 128

hette, *pret. 3 sg.* heated, 145

heuedis, *see* hed(e)

heuene, *n.* heaven, 32, 56; *gen. sg.* of heaven, 72, heuenys, 58

heuge, *adj.* great, 312

heuy, *adj. as n.* heavy, 380

heuynesse, *n.* sadness, 89

hewe, *n.* colour, 258, 354†, 444

hye, *adj.* high, 683; *adv.* high; loudly, 499

hye, *v.* hurry, 193

hil, *n.* hill, 243, 302

hym(self), *see* **he**

hynde, *n.* hind, 195

hyng, *see* **hangyn**

hyre, *n.* reward, 9

hire, hires, hireself, *see* **she**

his, *see* **he, it**

hit, *see* **it**

hold, *imper. pl.* hold, 521; **held,** *pret. 3 sg.* 372; **holde,** *past part.*; **holde thyn pes,** kept silent, 572

holm, *n.* holm-oak, evergreen oak, 178

holsum, *adj.* wholesome, 206

ho(m), *see* **who**

hond(e), *see* **hand**

hony, *n.* honey, 354

honour, *n.* honour, 461, 676

hope, *pres. 1 sg.* hope, 522, 697

hote, *adj.* hot, 266, 362; **hot** (*as n.*) 205, 380; **hoote,** *pl.* 246

how, *adv.* how, 37, 41, 44, etc.; **how that,** how, 9, 548, 558; **how fer so,** however far, 440

humble, *adj.* humble, 414

hunderede, *adj.* hundred, 238

hungir, *n.* hunger, 276

huntere, *n.* hunter, 99

I, *pron.* I, 4, 6, 7, etc.; **me,** *acc. and dat.* 10, 18, 27, etc., (*refl.*) myself, 88, 147, 459; **myn(n)(e),** *poss. adj.* 4, 87, 88, etc.; *pl.* 172; **myn,** *poss. pron.* mine, 437; **mynseluyn,** myself, 297

iay, *n.* jay, 346

iangelere, *n.* chatterer, 457

iangelynge, *pres. part. as adj.* chattering, 345

iasper, *n.* jasper, 230

ye, *see* (**e**)**ye**

Ielosye, *n.* (*personified*) Jealousy, 252

ielous, gelous, *adj.* angry, irritable, 342, 458

if, *conj.* if, 50, 167, 456, etc.; **if that,** if, 106, 428, 541

ilke, *adj.* same, 433

in, *prep.* in, 8, 10, 24, etc.; into, 37; on, 407; *adv.* in, 133

inmortal, *adj.* immortal, 73

i-now, *adj.* plentiful, 185; **inowe,** *pl.* in great number, 233; *adv.* enough, 610

instreumentis, *n. pl.* musical instruments, 197

ioye, *n.* joy, 3, 38, 175†n, etc.

iolyte, *n.* merriment, 226

Ion, John, 451

yow, *see* **ʒe**

yre, *n.* anger, 11

yryn, *n.* iron, 149

is, *see* **be(e)(n)**

Isaude, Iseult, 290

it, hit, *pron.* it, 18, 32, 43, etc.; **his,** *poss. adj.* its, 68, 376

iuge, *n.* judge, 101, 496; **iugis,** *gen. sg.* 546

iuge, *pres. 1 sg.* decree, command, 524; decide, 629

iugement, *n.* judgment; punishment, 431

iwis, *adv.* certainly, indeed, 6, 697

iwrityn, *see* **write**

iwrought, iwrouʒt, iwrowhte, *see* **werche**

kakelynge, *n.* cackling, 562

kaughte, *pret. 1 sg.* drew, 170

kek, *interj.* kek (*represents the cackle of a goose*), 499

kep, *n.* attention; **tak kep,** pay attention, 563

kertelis, *n. pl.* gowns, 235

kerve, *v.* cut, 217; **korvyn,** *past part.* 425

keuered, *past part.* covered, 271

kynde, *n.* sort, kind, species, 174, 311, 360, etc.; nature, disposition, 196, 401; (*personified*) Nature, 316, 672

kyngis, *gen. sg.* king's, 338

kysse, *v.* kiss, 378

kyte, *n.* kite, 349

kneis, *n. pl.* knees, 278

knette, *v.* fasten, 438†; **knyt,** *past part.* joined, 381, **knet,** fixed, 628†.

knyght, *n.* knight, 103

knygthod, *n.* knighthood, 549

knowe, *v.* know, 553; *pres. 1 sg.* 8; *pres. 2 pl.* 386, 393; know, *imper. sg.* 73

kok, *see* cok

korven, *see* kerve

labour, *n.* hard work, 93, 112

lady, *n.* lady, 105, 113, 416, etc.

lay, *see* lye

lak, *n.* lack, 87, 615

lake, *n.* lake, 313

languyssynge, *pres. part.* languishing, suffering, 472

lapwynge, *n.* lapwing, 347

large, *adj.* large, 123; big, 556

larke, *n.* lark, 340

lasch, *n.* lash, 178

laste, *n.* last, 92

laste, *v.* last, continue, 173, 489; last, *pres. 3 sg.* 49

lat, *see* let

laughtere, *n.* laughter, 575

launde, *n.* grassy place, 302

laurer, *n.* laurel, 182

lawe, *n.* law, 78

ledith, *pres. 3 sg.* leads, 138

leid, *past part.* laid, 554

leyser, *n.* leisure, 464, 487

lengere, lengeste, *see* longe

lere, *pres. 3 pl.* learn, 25

lerne, *v.* learn, 1, 20; **lernyd,** *past part.* as *adj.* 46

lese, *v.* lose, 147, 402

lesse, *comp. adj.* less, 201, 264; **leste,** *superl.* least 452

lessoun, *n.* lesson, 609n

lest(e), *pres. impers. 3 sg.* (it) pleases, 114, 420, 441, etc.; **leste,** *pret. 3 sg.* 530, 551

leste, *see* lesse

let, *pres. 1 sg.* leave, 279; **let, lat,** *imper. pl.* let, 423, 492, 567, etc.

lete, *v.* hinder, obstruct, 391†; **lette,** *pres. 1 sg.* refrain; **lette To seruyn,** refrain from serving, 439–40; let, *pres. 3 sg.* prevents, 151

letteris, *n. pl.* letters, 19, 123

leue, *v.* believe, 496

leue, *v.* leave, 153

leue, *see* lyue

leuys, *n.* leaves, 137, 173, 202, etc.

lewed, lewid, *adj.* ignorant, 46, 616

lewedenesse, *n.* ill-bred behaviour, 520

lye, *v.* lie, 279; **lyth,** *pres. 3 sg.* lies, 573; **lay,** *pret. 1 sg.* 95; *pret. 3 sg.* 213, 265, 268, etc.

lye, *v.* lie, 222, 629

lyf, lyue, *n.* life, 1, 51, 607, etc.; **lyuys,** *gen. sg.* 53

lyght, *adj.* light (*as n., in weight*), 380; easy, 553

lyght, *n.* light, 87, 599; brightness, 299†

lightnesse, *n.* light, 263

liȝte, *adj. pl.* bright, 188†

lykyth, *pres. impers. 3 sg.* it pleases, 165, 397, 401

lykerous, *adj.* lecherous, 79

lyte, *adj.* little, 64; *pl.* 350

lyte, *n.* little, 28, 111, 264

lytil, *adj.* little, 57†, 464, 513; **litele**, *pl.* 193

lyue, leue, *v.* live, 420, 424; **lyuyth**, *pres. 3 sg.* 328; **leue**, *imper. sg.* 614

lo, *interj.* look, see, 568, 570

lok, *n.* look, sight, 331

loke, *v.* look, 378; *imper. sg.* see that, 74

lokynge, *n.* looking, 110

long(e), *adj.* long, 1, 21, 454, etc.; *pl.* 230, 682†, 692

longe, *adv.* long, 424, 606; **longere, lengere**, *comp.* 453, 657; **lengest**, *superl.* 549

loos, *adj.* loose, 570

lord, *n.* lord, 12, 14, 199, etc.; (*exclamation*) 171, 669

lore, *n.* learning, 15

lost, *past part.* lost, 160ʹ

loude, *adv.* loud, 492

ioue, *n.* love, 160, 294, 403, etc.; (*personified*) 4, 8; **Louys**, *gen. sg.* 159

loue, louyn, *v.* love, 567, 590; **loue**, *pres. 1 sg.* 430, 451, 452, etc.; **louyth**, *pres. 3 sg.* 435, 535, 625; **louede**, *pret. 3 sg.* 47; **louid**, *past part.* 454

louere, *n.* lover, 105, 582

loueste, *see* **low**

louynge, *n.* loving, 454

low, *adj.* low, base, 601; **lower(e)**, *comp.* of less worth, 332, 450; **loueste**, *superl.* lowest, 327

lust(e), *n.* pleasure, 15†; (*personified*) 219

lusty, *adj.* pleasant, 130

Macrobye, Macrobius, 111

made, madist, *see* **make**

May, *n.* (the month of) May, 130

may, *pres. 1 sg.* can, 385, 391, 424, etc.; **mayst**, *pres. 2 sg.* 116, 163; **may**, *pres. 3 sg.* can, 151, 164, 624, etc., may, 616; *pres. 2 pl.* 396, 509, 678; *pres. 3 pl.* 311, 608, **mowe**, 689; **myght, my3te, my3the**, *pret. 3 sg.* could, 201, 264, 270; **myghte**, *pret. 3 pl.* 318, **myghtyn**, 367

mayde, *n.* maiden, 287

maydenys, *n. pl.* maidens, 283

mak(e), *n.* mate, 310, 371, 466, etc.; **makis**, *pl.* 389

make, *pres. 1 sg.* make, 29; **make, makyn**, *pres. 3 pl.* 312, 354, 669; **madist**, *pret. 2 sg.* 115; **made**, *pret. 3 sg.* 94, 108, 202; **madyn**, *pret. 3 pl.* 249, 694; **makid**, *past part.* made, composed, 677†

makere, *n.* maker, 199

man, *n.* man, 161, 164, 207, etc.; vassal, 479n; **manys**, *gen. sg.* 210; **men**, *pl.* 22n, 25, 127, etc.

maner(e), *n.* kind of, sort of, 54, 653; manner, way, 533

manye, *adj.* many, 81, 164, 238, etc.

mankynde, *n.* mankind, 70

Massynisse, Massinissa, 37

mater(e), *n.* matter, 26, 168, 579

me, *see* **I**

mede, *n.* meadow, 184

Meede, *n.* (*personified*) Bribery, 228

meke, *adj. pl.* meek, 341

melodye, *n.* sweet sound, beautiful music, 60; tunefulness, 62

men, *see* **man**

mencioun, *n.* mention, 29

mene, *pres. 1 sg.* mean, 4, 335; **menyth**, *pres. 3 sg.* 54†; **mente**, *pret. 3 sg.* 581; **ment**, *past part.* 158

merci, *n.* mercy, 421, 437

merlioun, *n.* merlin, 339†, 611

Messagerye, *n.* (*personified*) Sending of Messages, 228

mesure, *n.* bound, limit; **ouer mesure**, beyond all bounds, immeasurably, 300; plan, 305†

mete, *v.* dream, 108, 115; **met,** *pres. 3 sg.* 104, 105; **mette,** *pret. 1 sg.* 95

mete, *v.* meet, find, 698; **metyth,** *pres. 3 sg.* 37†

meue, *v.* move, 150

myght, myȝt, *n.* strength, power, 119, 149, 150, etc.

myght, myȝ(h)te, myghtyn, *see* **may**

myn, mynseluyn, *see* **I**

mynde, *n.* mind, 100; memory, 69, 679

myraklis, *n. pl.* miracles, 11

myrtheles, *adj.* without joy, 592

mysse, *v.* miss; come to an end, 40; fail, 75

mo, *adj.* more (in number), 595

modyr, *n.* mother, 292

moyst, *adj. as n.* moist, wet, 380

more, *adj.* greater, 208; **most,** *superl.* 550

mo(o)re, *adv.* more, 474, 475; **most(e),** *superl.* 375, 392, 403, etc.

mo(o)re, *pron.* more, 14, 651, 655

mortal, *adj.* deadly, 135

mortherere, *n.* murderer, 353, 612

morwe, *n.* morning, 489

most(e), *see* **mo(o)re,** *adj. and adv.*

mot, *pres. 1 sg.* must, 469; *pres. 3 sg.* 408, may, 569; **motyn,** *pres. 2 pl.* must, 546

mowe, *see* **may**

murye, *adj.* merry, 592

murmur, *n.* murmuring, 520

musik, *n.* music, 62

muste, *pret. 1 sg. as pres.* must, 642†; *pres. 3 sg.* 539

na, *see* **no**

nay, *adv.* no, 497, 541, 582

nakyd, *adj.* naked, 269

name, *n.* name, 287; **namys,** *pl.* 229

nas, *see* **was**

nat, *see* **not**

natheles, *adv.* nevertheless, 162, 390, 407

nature, *n.* nature, disposition; race, species, 615; (*personified*) Nature, 303, 317†, 325, etc.

ne, *conj.* nor, 9, 137, 150 (*second*), etc.; *adv.* not (*preceding verb*), 66, 91n, 150 (*first*), etc.

necligent, *adj.* negligent, 429

nede, *n.* need; necessary business, 384; message we want to give, 559

nedith, *pres. 3 sg.* needs, is necessary, 398, 609

neythir, *adv.* neither, 446, 516

nekkis, *n. pl.* necks, 671

nele, *see* **wele**

nere, *adv.* nearer, 619

neuere, *adv.* never, 137, 200, 205, etc.

newe, *adj.* new, 23, 25, 250, etc.; *pl.* 259, 352; *pron.* new person, 430

next(e), *adj.* next, 679; *adv.* 276

nyght(e), nyȝt, *n.* night, 42, 256, 600†, etc.; **nyghtes,** *pl.* 682, 692

nyghte, *v.* become night, 209n

nyhtyngale, *n.* nightingale, 351

nyl, *see* **wele**

nyne, *adj.* nine, 59

nys, *see* **be**

nysete, *n.* foolishness, 572

nyste, *pret. 1 sg.* did not know, 152

no, na, *adj.* no, 14, 207, 326†

noble, nobil, *adj.* noble, 262, 303, 319, etc.

noht, nought, *adv.* not at all, 415, 448

noyse, *n.* noise, 202, 312, 491, etc.

nolde, *see* **wele**

i-nome, *past part.* taken, 38

non, *adj.* no, 489, 587, 630, etc.; *pron.* none, 159, 435, 537, etc.

north-nor-west, *adv.* north-north-west, 117n

not, nat, *adv.* not. 7, 8, 13, etc.

note, *n.* tune, 677

nothyng, *adv.* in no way, not at all, 158, 187, 470

nought, *see* **noht**

noumberis, *n. pl.* numbers, 381

nouþer, *adv.* neither, 602n

now(e), *adv. and interj.* 26, 126, 507†, etc.

o, *see* **of,** *prep.*

of, *adv.* off, away, 494

of, o, *prep.* of, 11, 24, 378, etc.; about, 31 (*first*), 32, 39, etc.; at, 110, 142; by, 70; for, 111, 421, 593; from, 22, 61, 93, etc.; in, 484; in respect of, 317†, 513; in, with reference to, 234 (*first*) 299, 549, etc.; to, 58; upon, as the result of, 555; with, 89, 250, 515; **of al his grace,** of all his (future) destiny, 45; **of care,** causing anxiety, 363; **of glotenye,** gluttonous, 362; **of vsage,** by custom, 15

ofcaste, *imper. sg.* cast off, 132

offys, *n.* occupation, 236; service, 518n

ofte, *adv.* often, 10, 16, 340, etc.

ok, *n.* oak, 176, 223

old(e), *adj.* old, 110, 207, 364; *pl.* 19, 22, 24

olyue, *n.* olive, 181

olofte, *see* **alofte**

on, *adj.* unanimous, 557; *pron.* one, 143, 145, 151, etc.

on, *prep.* on, 125, 190, 237, etc.; about, 6; at, 378; in, 16

onbyde, *v.* abide, wait, 509

onethe, *see* **vnnethe**

ony, *adj.* any, 210, 225, 301, etc.

onywyse, *adv.* in any way, 457

onkynde, *see* **vnkynde**

only, *adj.* only, 140; *adv.* 426

onto, *see* **vnto**

onworthieste, *adj.* unworthiest, 512

opyn, *adj.* open, 133n

opynyoun, *n.* opinion, 618

or, *conj.* or, 7, 147, 166, etc.; either, 147 (*second*)

ordenaunce, *n.* decree, 390n

ordere, *n.* order, succession, 400

orloge, *n.* clock, 350

oþer, *conj.* or, 46

othir, *adj.* other, 134, 438, 630n, etc.; **othere, oþer,** *pl.* 228, 332, 695

othir, *pron.* other, 144, 145, 151, etc.

othirwise, *adv.* otherwise, in an-other way, 654

oueral, *adv.* everywhere, 172, 284

ou(g)hte, *pret. 3 sg. as pres.* ought, 437, 637

ouyr, *adv.* above, 123; **ouer mesure,** immeasurably, 300

ovireshake, *past part.* shaken off, 681, 686, 691

oule, *n.* owl, 343; **oulys,** *pl.* 599

oure, ours, *see* **we**

out, *adv.* out, 22†, 24, 69, etc.; **out of drede,** without doubt, 81

outrageous, *adj.* excessive, 336

owene, *adj.* own, 320, 360, 506

Pacience, *n.* (*personified*) Patience, 242

pay, *n.* pleasure, 271; **more to pay,** so as to give greater satisfaction, 474

payne, peyne, *n.* pain, 80, 424

paynyth, *pres. 3 sg.* (*refl.*) endeav-ours, 339; **peyne,** *subj. 3 sg.* 662†

payre, peyre, *n.* pair, 238, 595

pale, *adj.* pale, 243

palm, *n.* palm-tree, 182

Paris, Paris, 290

park, *n.* park, 122

parlement, *n.* parliament, *heading*

part, *n.* part (of the body), 397

partie, *n.* party, side, 496

passith, *pres. 3 sg.* surpasses, 300; **passe,** *imper. sg.* pass, 133; **passid,** *past part.* passed away, 81

paunche, *n.* belly, 610

pece, *n.* piece, 149

peyne, *see* payne, paynyth

peynted, peyntid, *past part.* painted, 284†, 293

peyre, *see* payre

perde, *interj.* assuredly, 509, 571

perfit, *adj.* perfect, 568

persith, *pres. 3 sg.* pierces, 331

pes, *n.* peace, 181, 605; **holde thyn pes,** kept silent, 572; (*personified*) 240

pes, *imper. pl.* be silent!, 547n, 563, 617

pye, *n.* magpie, 345

pilere, *n.* pillar; *as adj.* for support, 177; **pileris,** *pl.* 230

pyne, *n.* pain, torment, 335

pipere, *n.* piper; (*as adj.*) for making musical pipes, 178

Piramus, Pyramus, 289

place, *n.* place, 43, 48, 51, etc.

playn, *adj.* open, honest, 528; **pleyne,** *pl.* smooth, 180

ple, *n.* pleading, 485; **pleis,** *pl.* lawsuits, 101

pley, *n.* play, 193

pleye, *v.* play, 198

pleyn, *adj.* full, 126

pleyne, *v.* lament; **to pleyne,** for lamenting, 179

pleyne, *see* playne

pleynly, *adv.* plainly, 580

pleynt, *n.* complaint, 316

plesaunce, *n.* pleasure, 389, 636, 676; (*personified*) 218

plese, *v.* please, 478

pletynge, *n.* pleading, 495

plyte, *n.* plight, 294†

poynt, *n.* point, 372; **From poynt in poynt,** at every point, on every occasion, 461†n

pokok, *n.* peacock, 356

popiniay, *n.* parrot, 359

port, *n.* bearing, 262

porter, *n.* door-keeper, 261

possible, *adj.* possible, 471

preye, *pres. 1 sg.* request, beseech, 383, 543; make supplication, 431; **preyede,** *pret. 3 sg.* asked earnestly, 71; *pret. 3 pl.* 560, **preyeden,** 578†

preyse, *v.* praise, 586

pres, *n.* crowd; **in pres,** in the crowd, 603

presence, *n.* presence, 307

present, *adj.* present, 53; being present, 423

presente, *v.* present, 531

prest, *adj.* ready, 307

preue, *n.* proof, 497

Priapus, Priapus, 253

prike, *pres. 1 sg.* spur, 389

prysoun, *n.* prison, 139

priue, *adj.* secret, 260

proces, *n.* process; **in proces,** in course of time, 430

profyt, *n.* advantage, good, 47n, 75

pronounce, *v.* make known, 559

proue, *v.* prove, 534

pulle, *n.* pull, 164†

purpos, *n.* purpose, 26

putte, *v.* put, 603

quaylis, *gen. sg.* quail's, 339

quantite, *n.* magnitude, size, 58

queen(e), *n.* queen, 298, 647

quek, *interj.* quack, 499, 594†

quyte, *adj.* clear, free, 663†

quyte, *v.* reward, 112; **quitith,** *pres. 3 sg.* pays, 9

quod, *pret. 3 sg.* said, 510, 540, 569, etc.

radde, *see* **rede**

rauen, *n.* raven, 363

rauyne, *n.* prey, 323, 527†; greediness, 336

rauyshyng, *adj.* enchanting, 198

rebel, *adj.* disobedient, 457

reche, *see* **rekke**

recheles, *adj.* careless; beyond care, 593

recorde, *v.* repeat, 609n

recouerede, *past part.* won, 688n

red, *n.* advice, 586, 608

red, redde, *see* **re(e)de**

red(e), *adj.* red, 442, 583; *pl.* 186, 189

rede, *pres. 1 sg.* advise, 566; **radde,** *pret. 3 sg.* 579†

redere, *n.* reader, 132

redy, *adj.* ready, 213, 540

re(e)de, *v.* read, 10, 27, 516, etc.; *pres. 1 sg.* 12, 16, 696; **redde,** *pret. 1 sg.* 21; **red,** *past part.* 107

regard, reward, *n.* regard, 58, 426

reherse, *v.* recount, 488

rekke, *v.* care, 593; **reche,** *pres. 1 sg.* 606; **roughte,** *pret. 3 sg.* 111

remedye, *n.* remedy, cure, 140, 502

remenaunt, *n.* remainder, 271

renne, *v.* run, move swiftly, 247

replicacioun, *n.* reply, 536

resoun, *n.* logical argument, 534n; reason, 564, 568, 591; (*personified*) 632n

respit, *n.* respite, 648

reste, *n.* rest, 94; **at his reste,** as at its home, 376

reste, *v.* rest; **to reste,** resting, 265; *pres. 3 subj.* be at rest, be still, 514

reuer, *n.* river-bank, 184

reufullest, *adv.* most pitiable, most dismal, 613†n

revith, *pres. 3 sg.* forces away, 86

reward, *see* **regard**

ryal, *adj.* royal, 330, 394, 415, etc.

riche, *adj. as n.* rich man, 103

Richesse, *n.* (*personified*) Wealth, 261

right, riȝt, *adv.* exactly, just, 96, 98, 300, etc.; right, 122 (*qualifying* **vnto** *in previous line*); very, 272† (*qualifying* **wel** *in previous line*), 644; **ful riȝt,** completely, 597; **right anon,** immediately, 645†

rightful, *adj.* righteous, just, 55, 390; rightful, 639

ryme, *v.* rhyme, 119

ro, *n.* roe, 195

rodok, *n.* robin redbreast, 349

Romulus, Romulus, 292

ronge, *pret. 3 sg.* rang, 492

rose, *n.* rose, 442

roughte, *see* **rekke**

roundele, *n.* roundel, 675n

route, *n.* company, 245

routhe, *n.* pity, 427

sadde, *adj.* serious; sober, 578

say, *see* **se(e)(n)(e), sey**

saylynge, *pres. part.* sailing; for sailing, 179

saynt, seynt, *adj.* saint, 309, 322, 683, etc.

sake, *n.* sake, 684

same, *adj.* same, 96

sat, *pret. 3 sg.* sat, 240, 275, 298, etc.

saue, *v.* save, 147; preserve, 461; *pres. subj. 3 sg.* save, 14

sauouris, *n. pl.* odours, 274

saw, *see* **se(e)(n)(e)**

schal, *see* **shal**

sche, *see* **she**

schese, *see* **che(e)se**

schewede, schewid, *see* **shew**

schul, *see* shal

science, *n.* knowledge, 25

Scipion, Cypyon, Scipio (Africanus) the younger, 31†, 36, 71, etc.

se(e)(n)(e), *v.* see, 163, 175, 270, etc.; seen, *pres. 2 pl.* 464; sen, *pres. 3 pl.* 600; seye, saw, say, *pret. 1 sg.* 117, 183, 211, etc.; say, *pret. 3 sg.* 97

secre, *adj.* discreet, able to keep a secret, 395n

sed, *n.* seed, 328

sed-f(o)ul, *n.* bird which lives on seed, 512; (*collective sg. for pl.*) 576

seyn(e), seye, say, *v.* say, 13, 78†, 270, etc.; sey(e), seyn, *pres. 1 sg.* 14, 477, 547; sey, *pres. 3 pl.* 22; seyd(e), seyide, *pret. 3 sg.* 46, 277, 556, etc.; seydyn, *pres. 3 pl.* 557; say, *imper. pl.* 441; seyd, *past part.* 574

seynt, *see* saynt

sek, *adj.* sick, ill, 161, 207; syke, (*as n.*) sick man, 104

seke, *v.* seek, 340

Semyramus, Semiramis, 288

semyth, *pres. 3 sg.* seems, 539

sentence, *see* centence

septure, *n.* sceptre, 256n

serys, *n. pl.* sirs, gentlemen, 464, 541, 543n

serve, seruyn, *v.* serve, 216, 419n, 440, etc.; seruyth, *imper. pl.* 660; seruyd, *past part.* 453, 476

seruyse, *n.* service, 284, 459, 470, etc.

serwaunt, *n.* servant, 159n

sese, *pres. subj. 3 sg.* seize, 481

sethe, *conj.* since, 688

sette, *v.* set, place, 258; set, *past part.* 149, 303, 324, etc.

seuene, *adj.* seven, 32

shaftys, *n. pl.* arrow shafts, 180

shal, schal, *pres. 1 sg.* shall, 30, 168, 285, etc.; shalt, *pres. 2 sg.*

75†; shal, *pres. 3 sg.* 130, 137, 392, etc.; shul, *pres. 2 pl.* 400, 402, 658; shal, s(c)hul, *pres. 3 pl.* 55, 83, 229, etc.; shulde, *pret. 1 sg.* should, 365; *pret. 3 sg.* would, 48, 68; schulde, 69 (*with elipse of following v. of motion*); ought to, 66, 454, 593; was to, 410; should, 496, 582; *pret. 3 pl.* were to, 216; should, 590†

shame, *n.* modesty, 444; shame, 583

shap, *n.* form, 373, 398

shappe, *v.* devise, 502

sharp(e), *adj.* bitter, 2; sharp, 331, 565

she, sche, *pron. fem. nom.* she, 216, 222, 265, etc.; hyre, *acc. and dat.* 270, 275, 378, etc.; hire, here, *poss. adj.* 215, 240, 304, etc.; heris, hires, *poss. pron.* 482, 588†; hireself, 377, 467, 552, etc.

shende, *v.* ruin, 494†; shente, *pret. 3 sg.* put to shame, 255

shene, *adj.* bright, 299

shes, *see* chese

shetere, *n.* shooter; (*as adj.*) for shooting, 180

shewe, *v.* show, 168, 581; s(c)hewede, *pret. 3 sg.* 56, 57, 59; schewid, shewed, *past part.* 44, 572†

shof, *pret. 3 sg.* pushed, 154

short(e), *adj.* short, 1, 555, 609; at shorte wordis, *pl.* in a few words, 481

shortly, *adv.* briefly, 34

shoutyng, *n.* shouting, 693

shulde, *see* shal

sich, *see* swich

syde, *n.* side, 98, 134, 241, etc.

syghte, *n.* sight, 210

syke, *see* sek

sykys, *n. pl.* sighs, 246, 248

sykyth, *pres. 3 sg.* sighs, 404

Silla, Scylla, 292

syluyr-briȝte, *adj. pl.* silver-bright, 189

syn, *conj.* since, 64, 608, 624, etc.; **syn that**, since, 435; *prep.* 484

synde, *pres. subj. 3 sg.* send; **God synde**, may God send, 84, 404

synge, *v.* sing, 190, 516†, 673, etc.; **syngith**, *pres. 3 sg.* 342; **syngen**, *pres. 3 pl.* 684

synke, *pres. 1 sg.* sink, 7

syre, *n.* master, 12

sittynge, *pres. part.* sitting, 238, 242

sittyngest, *adj.* most fitting, 551n

skalis, *n. pl.* scales, 189

skylfully, *adv.* reasonably, 634

skillis, *n. pl.* reasons, 537

skornere, *n.* scorner, 357

skornynge, *pres. part. as adj.* mocking, 346

sle, *v.* kill, 217

slep, *n.* sleep, 42, 95

slepe, *v.* sleep, 94; **slepynge**, *pres. part.* 99

slit, *pres. 3 sg.* slides, 3

smale, *adj. pl.* small, 188, 196, 324, etc.

so, *adv.* so, 1, 2, 3, etc.; **so I was glad**, how glad I was, 171; *conj.* provided that, 605

sobyrly, *adv.* quietly, 239

softe, *adj.* gentle, 202; mild, 680, 685, 690

solace, *v.* comfort, 297

soleyn, *adj.* solitary, 607, 614

some, *pron. pl.* some, 217, 233, 234

somer, somyr, somor, *n.* summer, 680, 685, 690; (*as adj.*) 299†, 443

sond, *n.* sand, 243

sone, *adv.* soon, 522, 644

sone, *n.* son, 351, 406

song, *n.* song, 203, 693

sonne, *see* **sunne**

sore, *adj. pl.* painful, 13

sore, *adv.* deeply, severely, 6, 447; **sorest**, *superl.* 404†

sorwe, *n.* sorrow, 132, 251, 469

sorweful, *adj.* sorrowful, 138

sote, *adj.* sweet-smelling, 274n, 296

soth, *adj.* true, 640; *adv.* truly, 78, 574

sothe, *n.* truth, 578

sothly, *adv.* truly, 270, 557, 581

souereyn(e), *adj.* highest, chief, 254; sovereign, supreme, 416, 422

soulis, *n. pl.* souls, 33, 77

soun, *n.* sound, 344

space, *n.* space (of time) 53, 67; room, 314

spak, *see* **speke**

spare, *v.* refrain from; **to rede I nele nat spare**, I shall not refrain from reading, 699

sparwe, *n.* sparrow, 351

speche, *n.* talk, speaking, 39†, 489

spede, *n.* advantage; **for comun spede**, for the good of all, 507†

speede, *v.* help, 385; **sped the**, *imper. sg.* prosper, 133; **spede**, *pres. subj. 3 sg.* prosper, help, 560; **sped**, *past part.* brought to an end, 101

speke, spekyn, *v.* speak, 382, 385, 399, etc.; **speke**, *pres. 1 sg.* 17, 469, 659; **spak**, *pret. 1 sg.* 296; *pret. 3 sg.* 134†, 415, 449, etc.

spekynge, *n.* speaking; what (they) said, 488

spere, *n.* spear, 135

sperhauk, *n.* sparrow-hawk, 338, 569

speris, *n. pl.* spheres, 59, 61

spice, *n.* spice-bearing plant. 206.

spirit, *n.* spirit, 92

squyrelis, *n. pl.* squirrels, 196

stant, *see* **stonde**

stare, *n.* starling, 348†

stature, *n.* form, size, 366n

statute, *n.* statute, 387n

stel, *adj.* steel, 395

sterre, *n.* star, 68, 300; **sterris**, *pl.* 595

sterry, *adj.* starry; among the stars, 43

sterve, *v.* die, 420

stylle, *adj.* quiet, 511, 574

stod, *see* stonde

ston, *n.* stone, 122

stonde, stondyn, *v.* stand, 254, 315, 322; withstand, 164; submit, 546; **stant**, *pres. 3 sg.* appears, 155; **stod**, *pret. 3 sg.* stood, 98, 108, 224

story, *n.* story, 285

stork, *n.* stork, 361

straunge, *adj.* unfriendly, 'distant', 584

strem, *n.* stream, 138

strengis, *n. pl.* strings, 197

stryve, *pres. 2 pl.* strive, contest, 606

stroyere, *n.* destroyer, 360

strokis, *n. pl.* blows, 13, 135

stronge, *adv.* strongly, securely, 231

subtyl, *adj.* of thin texture, 272

suche, *see* swich(e)

suffisaunce, *n.* sufficiency; **a suffisaunce**, enough, 637

suffyse, *v.* make able, 460

sum, *adj.* some, 427, 476, 697, etc.

sum, *n.* total, 650

sumdel, *pron.* some part, 112

sundery, *adj.* various, 258

sunne, sonne, *n.* sun, 266, 299†, 680, etc.

swalwe, *n.* swallow, 353

swan, *n.* swan, 342

swech, *see* swich(e)

swemyn, *pres. 3 pl.* swim, 188

swet(e), *adj.* sweet, gracious, 113n; (*as n.*) sweetness, 161

swetnesse, *n.* sweetness, 185, 198

sweuene, *n.* dream, 115, 118

swich, sich, suche, sweche, *adj.* such, 14, 515†, 570, 678, etc.; **swiche**, *pl.* 283

swiftly, *adv.* swiftly, 76

swythe, *adv.* quickly, 503; **as swithe**, immediately, 623†

swow, *n.* low noise, 247

tak(e), *v.* take, 320, 370, 507, etc.; receive, 308; **tak kep**, *imper. sg.* pay attention, 563; **tak hed of**, take heed of, 383; **takith not agref**, *imper. pl.* do not take it amiss, 543; **tak(e)**, *pres. subj. 2 sg.* 462, *pres. subj. 3 sg.* 588; **tok me to**, *pret. 1 sg.* betook myself to, went to, 695; **tok**, *pret. 3 sg.* 94, 169

tale, *n.* talk; **I telle no tale**, I say nothing, 326; speech, 441, 542; **telle our tale**, speak for us, 560

tame, *adj.* tame, 349

tariede, *pret. 3 sg.* delayed, 415

taryinge, *n.* delaying, 468, 565, 657

tast, *n.* taste, 160†

telle, *v.* tell, 30, 71, 209, etc.; *pres. 1 sg.* 326; **tellith**, *pres. 3 sg.* 36, 39, 43; **telle**, *subj. 2 sg.* 156; **tolde**, *pret. 1 sg.* 16; *pret. 3 sg.* 67; **told**, *past part.* 229

temperede, *pret. 3 sg.* tempered, 214

temple, *n.* temple, 231, 232, 237, etc.; *as adj.* 239

termyne, *v.* decide, 530

tersel, tercel, *n.* tercel (male of any kind of hawk), 393†, 405, 463, etc.; **tersels**, *pl.* 540†

terselet, terslet, *n.* tercelet (= tercel) 529, 533, 625†, etc.; **tersletis**, *pl.* 659

than, *conj.* than, 209, 476, 515, etc.

thankynge, *pres. part.* thanking, 672

than(ne), thenne, *adv.* then, 39, 82†, 250, etc.

that, *conj.* that, 6, 28, 43, etc.; when, 312 (*repeating* When, 310). *For pleonastic use with* al, how, *etc., see those words*

that, *demonstr. adj.* that, 28, 42, 72, etc.

that, *demonstr. adv.* to such an extent, 329 (*first*)

that, *pron.* that, 60, 163, 169, etc.

that, þat, *rel. pron.* that, 3, 4, 25, etc.

the, th', þ', *def. art.* the, 1, 2, 80, etc.

the, *v.* prosper, 569

the, *see* thow

thef, *n.* thief, 345

they, þey, *pron. pl. nom.* they, 55, 79, 83, etc.; hem, *acc. and dat.* 40, 216, 234, etc.; here, hir, *poss. pron.* 9, 39, 82†, etc.; hemself, themselves, 223, 234

thenne, *see* than(ne)

the(e)r(e), *adv.* there, 12†, 108, 235, etc.; where, 69, 130, 137†; there as, where, 49, 139, 185

there-ynne, *adv.* in there, 33†

therfore, *adv.* therefore, 547, 643

thervpon, *adv.* upon it, 20

therwith, *adv.* with that, 201

therwithal, *adv.* thereupon; having said that, 405

thes(e), *see* this

i-thewid, *past part.* provided with qualities; wel i-thewid, provided with good qualities, 47

thikkere, *adj.* thicker, 273

thil, *see* tyl

thilke, *adj.* those same, 61

thing, *n.* thing, 20, 90, 91, etc.

thynke, *v.* think of, 311; seem; me wolde thynke, it would seem to me, 548; *pres. 1 sg.* think, 6; thouȝte, *pret. 3 sg.* seemed, 28†; *impers.* 124

thynself, *see* thow

this, thes, *dem. adj.* this, 23, 25, 681, etc.; these, thise, *pl.* 141, 540†, 552, etc.

this, *pron.* this, 4, 17, 116, etc.; this, this is, 650; these, *pl.* 293

Thisbe, Thisbe, 289

tho, *adv.* then, 218, 297, 298, etc.

tho(u)r(w), *prep.* through, 127, 129, 134, etc.; as a result of, 387; out of, 437

thorpis, *n. pl.* villages, 350

though, thow, *conj.* though, 156, 566, 587; thow that, though, 584

thought, thouȝt, *n.* full consideration, 417; care, 89

thouȝte, *see* thynke

thousent, *adj.* thousand, 274

thousent-fold, *adv.* a thousand times, 208

thow, *pron.* thou, you, 74, 75, 113, etc.; the, *acc. and dat.* 114†, 117, 157, etc.; (*refl.*) 109, 157, 448; thy(n), *poss. adj.* thine, your, 112, 132, 680†, etc.; thynself, (*refl.*) 73

thow, *see* though

thre, *adj.* three, 61, 228; *pron.* 552, 660

thredde, *adj.* third, 463

threde, *n.* thread, 267†

thryes, *adj.* three times, 61

thurstil, *n.* thrush, 364

thus, *adv.* thus, so, like this, 30, 109, 279, etc.

tyde, *n.* time, 97

tyl, thil, *conj.* until, 81, 490; t(h)il that, until, 40, 266, 447, etc.

tyme, *n.* time; at this tyme, on this occasion, 412; in blisful tyme, in a happy hour, 413; tymys, *pl.* 283

tiraunt, *n.* tyrant (kind of hawk), 334

to(o), *prep. and mark of inf.* to, 1, 18, 20, etc.; for, 75, 178, 179, etc.; **too ne fro,** one way nor the other, 150

today, *n.* today, 471

togedere, *adv.* together, 555

tok, *see* **tak(e)**

told(e), *see* **tellen**

to-rent, *past part.* torn to pieces, 432

to-shyuered, *past part.* been broken to pieces, 493†

to-torn, *past part.* very much torn, 110†

touche, *v.* touch; touch on, briefly mention, 285; **touchede,** *pret. 3 sg.* gave finishing touches to, 216†n

trace, *pres. 1 pl.* go, 54

tre, *n.* tree, 137†, 211, 313; **treis,** *pl.* 173

trecherye, *n.* treachery, 347

trete, *v.* treat, deal with, 34

trewe, *adj.* true, 355, 395, 483, etc.; **treweste,** *superl.* 479

Tristram, Tristram, 290

Troylus, Troilus, 291†

trompis, *gen. sg.* trumpet's, 344

trouthe, *n.* truth, 426

trowe, *pres. 1 sg.* believe, 552, 677†

Tullyus, M. Tullius Cicero, 31

tunge, *n.* tongue, 514, 570; **tungis,** *pl.* 521

tunne, *n.* barrel, 104

turtil, *n.* turtle dove, 355, 510, 577†, 583†

twenty, *adj.* twenty, 473

two, *adj.* two, 148, 278

valence, *n.* cloth made at Valence (near Lyons), 272

Valentyne, Valentine, 683†; **Valentynys,** *gen.* 309†, 322†, 386†

veyne, *n.* vein, 425

Venus, Venus, 261†, 652; *gen.* 351

verdit, *n.* verdict, 503, 525

vers, wers, *n. pl.* lines, verses, 124, 141, 679

vertu, *n.* virtue, 376

vicayre, *n.* deputy, 379†

victor, *n.* victor; (*as adj.*) of victory, 182

vyne, *n.* vine, 181

vnbynde, *v.* unbind, 523

vncommytted, *past part.* not entrusted to one, 518†

vndyr, *prep.* under, 211, 223, 640

vnkynde, onkynde, *adj.* unnatural, 358; cruel, 434, 457

vnnethe, onethe, *adv.* scarcely, hardly, 201, 264, 314

vnto, onto, *adv.* to, 121, 129, 135, etc.; for, 177; until, 647

vntressede, *past part.* undressed, 268†

vntrewe, *adj.* unfaithful, 428, 434†

voys, *n.* voice, 191, 363, 382, etc.; right to decide, 545n

vp, *prep.* up, 269

vpon, *prep.* upon, 19, 184, 230, etc.; in, 696

vs, *see* **we**

vsage, *n.* custom, habit, 15, 411

vsance, *n.* custom, 674

vsed, *past part.* practised, 549

wake, *pres. 1 sg.* am awake, 482; *pres. 3 pl.* awake, 689; **wok,** *pret. 1 sg.* 695

wakyr, *adj.* watchful, 358

wal, *n.* wall, 282

wallid, *past part.* walled, 122

wan, *see* **when**

wante, *pres. 1 sg.* lack, 287

war, *adj.* aware; **was I war of,** I noticed, 218, 298

warnede, *pret. 3 sg.* gave previous information to; **warnede hym beforn,** gave him information about the future, 45

was, *pret. 1 sg.* was, 171, 218, 295, etc.; *pret. 3 sg.* 19, 30, 36, etc.;

we(e)re, *pret. 3 pl.* 124, 141, 233, etc.; *subj. 3 sg.* 106, 475, 511, etc.; *subj. 3 pl.* 656

waste, *v.* waste, 283

watyr-foul, *n.* waterfowl (*collective sg.*), 327, 504; **watyrfoulis**, *pl.* 554, 561

waxe, wexen, *v.* grow, 207; become, 444; **wex**, *pret. 3 sg.* 206, 583

we, *pron. pl. nom.* we, 54, 611, 619; **vs**, *acc.* 492, 494, 508; **oure**, *poss. adj.* 53, 212, 411, etc.; *poss. pron.* 545

wedded, *past part.* married, 355

wedres, *n. pl.* storms, 681, 686, 691

wey(e), *n.* way, 54, 72, 388, etc.

weked, *adj.* wicked, 82

wel(e), *adj. pl.* well, ' all right ', 611; *adv.* well, 7, 47, 109, etc.; certainly, 12, 493; clearly, 250

welcome, *interj.* welcome, 680, 685, 690

wele, *pres. 1 sg.* will, 35, 385, 419, etc., **nele** (=ne wele), 699, **nyl** (=ne wyl), 222; **wele**, *pres. 3 sg.* intends to, 12; wishes, 467; will, 567; *pres. 2 pl.* 494; **wolde**, *pret. 1 sg.* desired, 91; wish to, 112, 468; desire, 480, 656; would, 632; **nolde** (=ne wolde), did not want, 90; *pret. 3 sg.* would become, 209; wished to, 325; would, 548, 581; *pret. 2 pl.* desire, 544; *subj. 1 sg.* would desire, 587

welk, *pret. 1 sg.* walked, 297

welle, *n.* spring, 129, 211, 215; source, 62

welle-stremys, *n. pl.* streams fresh from the spring, 187

wemen, *n. pl.* women, 233

wende, *pret. 3 sg.* expected, 493

wende, *v.* go, 48, 492; *pres. 3 pl.* 668; *subj. 3 sg.* 440; **wente**, *pret. 1 sg.* 170†, 253; *pret. 3 sg.* 500, went, 490; **wente**, *pret. 3 pl.* 235

werche, *pres. subj. 2 sg.* work, 74; **i-wrowhte**, *past part.* made, 123†,

i-wrought, 305†, **i-wrouȝt**, 418, **wrought**, 636

were, *n.* weir, 138n

were, *see* **was**

wery, *adj.* weary, 99

werk, *n.* work, business, 666; **werkis**, *pl.* 374

werkynge, *n.* working, 5

werm, *n.* worm, 326, 604; **wermis**, *gen. pl.* 614†

werm-foul, *n.* (*collective sg.*) birds which live on worms, 505

wers, *see* **vers**

weste, *v.* draw near to the west, 266

wex(en), *see* **waxe**

wham, *see* **(w)ho**

whan, *see* **when**

what, *adj.* what, 294; whatever, 54, 420, 441; what man . . . That, whoever, 46–7; *adv.* what . . . what, partly . . . partly, 15; what that, as much as, 151; *interrog. pron.* 365, 579, 581; what . . . so, whatever, 664

when, w(h)an, *adv.* when, 6, 36, 255, etc.

wher(e), *adv.* where; **where that**, where, 172, 298

wher(e), whethir, *conj.* whether, 152, 166, 482†; **wher(e) that**, whether, 7, 172

wherfore, *adv.* for what purpose, why, 17

which(e), *rel. pron.* which, 29, 34, 126, etc.; whom, 287; what, 564; *pl.* 233, 248; **which(e) that**, 90†, which, 333; who, 519, 553

whil, *conj.* while, 616, 642

whyle, *n.* time, 214; while, 509

whippis, *gen. sg.* whip's, 178

whirle, *v.* whirl, 80

white, *adj. pl.* white, 186, 237

(w)ho, *rel. pron.* who, 487, 535, 625†, etc.; *interrog. pron.* 593†; **(w)ho so**, whoever, 410†, 412,

504, etc.; (w)hom, wham, *acc. and dat.* 114, 278, 622, etc.; whos, *gen. sg.* 419

wide, *adj.* wide, 154

wi(g)ht, *n.* person, 221, 511†; wyhtis, *gen. sg.* 514

wil(le), *n.* desire, 573n; (*personified*) 214†n; wish, 510; full intent, 417

wile, *n.* file, 215n

wilful, *adj. as adv.* purposely, 429

wyn, *n.* wine, 275

wynd, *n.* wind, 201

wynde, *v.* wind; embrace, 671

wyngis, *n. pl.* wings, 670

wynke, *pres. 1 sg.* am asleep, 482

wynne, *v.* obtain, win, 391, 402; wonne, *past part.* 105

winter, *n.* winter (*sg. for pl.*), 473†; wintres, *gen. sg.* 681, 686, 691

wys(e), *adj.* wise, 363, 395

wisely, *adv.* surely, 117

wysse, *pres. subj. 2 sg.* guide, direct, 74

wit, *n.* understanding, 146, 460, 573†n; mind, 547; intelligence, 565; good sense, 591

wit(h), *prep.* with, 5, 143†, 363, etc.; against, 103; by, 248, 432

withinne, *adv.* inside, 244; *prep.* 246, 254

withoute, *adv.* outside, 244

withoutyn, *prep.* without, 49, 52, 225, etc.

wo, *n.* misery, 427, 439, 472

wode, *n.* wood, 493; to wode, to the wood, 100

wok, *see* wake

wolde, *see* wele

wondyr, *adj.* wonderful, 329; *adv.* very, 241, 490

wondyrful, *adj.* wonderful, 5

wonyd, *adj.* accustomed to, wont, 321

wonne, *see* wynne

word, *n.* word; speech, 597; wordis, *pl.* words, 481, 678

world, *n.* world, 63, 66, 70, etc.; age, 81; present worldis lyuis space, *gen. sg.* space of life in the present world, 53†

worth, *adj.* worth, 501

worthi, *adj.* excellent, honourable, 392, 395, 635; worthieste, *superl.* 548

wot, *pres. 1 sg.* know, 7, 9, 513; *pres. 3 sg.* 552, 595, 663

wounde, *v.* wound, 217

woundis, *gen. sg.* wound's, 128

wrastelyng, *n.* wrestling, 165

wrechednese, *n.* wretchedness; vileness, 601

wrekere, *n.* avenger, 361

write, *v.* write, 118, 168; wrete, *past part.* 19, iwreten, 124†, iwretyn, 141†, iwrityn, 155†

writyng, *n.* writing, 158

wrong, *n.* wrong, 542

wroth, *adj.* angry, 504, 622

wrought, iwrowhte, *see* werche